FINANCIAL INSTITUTIONS AND SERVICES

MOBILE FINANCIAL SERVICES FOR ECONOMICALLY VULNERABLE AND UNDERSERVED CONSUMERS

AN EXAMINATION

FINANCIAL INSTITUTIONS AND SERVICES

Additional books in this series can be found on Nova's website under the Series tab.

Additional e-books in this series can be found on Nova's website under the e-book tab.

FINANCIAL INSTITUTIONS AND SERVICES

MOBILE FINANCIAL SERVICES FOR ECONOMICALLY VULNERABLE AND UNDERSERVED CONSUMERS

AN EXAMINATION

OSCAR CORTEZ
EDITOR

nova publishers
New York

Library of Congress Cataloging-in-Publication Data

ISBN: 978-1-63484-551-9

Published by Nova Science Publishers, Inc. † New York

CONTENTS

PREFACE

The consumer financial services market has seen the increasing use and proliferation of mobile technology to access financial services and manage personal finances. The Consumer Financial Protection Bureau's Office of Financial Empowerment issued a Request for Information (RFI) to find out more about mobile financial services and how low-income and economically vulnerable consumers are using them. This book provides a description of mobile financial services, a discussion of the opportunities and risks, and key takeaways from the comments. Furthermore, this book considers the ability of mobile financial services to increase financial inclusion among the underserved by providing them access to the banking system, retaining them in safe and sustainable account relationships, and fostering financial empowerment to improve financial stability and fulfill financial goals.

In: Mobile Financial Services ...
Editor: Oscar Cortez
ISBN: 978-1-63484-551-9

Chapter 1

MOBILE FINANCIAL SERVICES: A SUMMARY OF COMMENTS FROM THE PUBLIC ON OPPORTUNITIES, CHALLENGES, AND RISKS FOR THE UNDERSERVED*

Consumer Financial Protection Bureau

EXECUTIVE SUMMARY

The Consumer Financial Protection Bureau (Bureau or CFPB), established under the Dodd- Frank Wall Street Reform and Consumer Protection Act of 2010 (Dodd-Frank Act), has as part of its mission to empower consumers to take more control over their economic lives. Part of the Bureau's charge is to promote financial education, research developments in markets for consumer financial services and products, and provide information, guidance, and technical assistance regarding the offering and provision of consumer financial products or services to traditionally underserved consumers and communities.

A major development in the consumer financial services market over the past few years has been the increasing use and proliferation of mobile technology to access financial services and manage personal finances. Consumers are using mobile financial services (MFS) – financial services and products accessed through mobile phones and other devices – more and more to access accounts, pay bills, deposit funds and manage their financial lives. The increasing use is not surprising given that 87-90 percent of the adult population in the United States has a mobile phone and approximately 62-64 percent of consumers own smartphones.[1] For example, for those with bank accounts, the rate of mobile banking use went from 22 percent in 2011 to 39 percent in 2014; 52 percent of those with smartphones reported using mobile banking in 2014.[2]

The Bureau's Office of Financial Empowerment issued a Request for Information in June of 2014[3] to help the Bureau understand better the potential for mobile financial services to help underserved consumers – including low-income, unbanked, underbanked and economically vulnerable consumers – access products and services that help them achieve

* This is an edited, reformatted and augmented version of a report issued by the Consumer Financial Protection Bureau, November 2015.

their financial goals. The focus of the RFI was not mobile proximity (or "point of sale") payments except in so far as those products may be marketed to or used by underserved consumers. In response to the Request for Information, we received comments from individuals, financial services providers, financial institutions, regulators, trade associations, research and consulting firms, academics, nonprofits, and consumer advocacy organizations. While several trade associations submitted comments, we received few comments directly from financial institutions and providers themselves.

The following are some of the key takeaways from the comments related to mobile financial services and the underserved. This report is not intended to identify areas in which the Bureau may or will take regulatory, supervisory, or enforcement action. Some of the commenters' views on these topics are included where relevant to the particular topic of the discussion.

Increasing Smartphone Use Presents Opportunities for Expanded Use of MFS for the Underserved

The rate of growth in smartphone use among underserved households and individuals is growing and significant. For example, 44 percent of unbanked individuals[4] and 50 percent of adults living in households earning less than $30,000 per year have smartphones.[5] For many, their smartphones or devices are the primary way they access the internet.[6] Increased smartphone use appears to be correlated with increasing use of MFS among the banked as well as the un- and underbanked.[7] For certain demographic groups and subpopulations, however, there is considerable variation. For example, commenters provided evidence that Hispanic adults have a higher rate of smartphone ownership and mobile banking and mobile payments usage than the general population.[8] Rural residents on the other hand, appear to have lower rates of smartphone ownership and mobile financial services activity.[9]

Focus on Products First, Channel Second

Comments indicated while mobile may be a useful channel through which to access products for underserved consumers, it is critical that financial services providers focus first on ensuring the underlying products and services meet consumer demand in ways that advance consumer goals.

Faster Payments Could Help Industry and Consumers

Some of the commenters said that faster payments would help accelerate use of Remote Deposit Capture (depositing checks remotely with the camera on the phone) and other mobile financial services that were identified by commenters as potentially helping consumers save time and money, which could make higher priced alternative financial services such as high fee check cashing services less attractive to underserved consumers. Commenters stated that underserved consumers tend to use alternative financial services over bank services because they want immediate access to funds or they may not qualify for bank accounts.[10] Though industry comments supported faster payments, many acknowledged that delays are often not caused by the speed of the various payment systems, but caused by the need to address potential fraud issues (such as double deposits – discussed more fully at pages 22-25), and that technological or other solutions to fraud risks would be welcomed.

Mobile Financial Services Need to Be Paired with In-Person Services

There was general consensus among the commenters that for mobile financial services to effectively reach underserved consumers, the mobile channel must be paired with consultative or assistance services, at least in the short-term. Some commenters expressed concerns that the void left by branch closures in low-income neighborhoods could not be filled by mobile financial services alone. The value of MFS to underserved consumers, comments suggest, can be realized with the assistance of one-on-one or other in-person facilitation. One commenter gave as an example hybrid services, such as small kiosks with personnel, where personal assistance is linked to mobile. However, comments indicated that these options are not yet widely available or familiar to the underserved population.

Mobile Financial Services Can Save Consumers Money and Time

For consumers, the ability to access financial services anytime, anywhere can save time and money. Comments suggest that some underserved consumers are saving more as they use mobile financial services frequently to check balances, deposit checks remotely and use tools to manage their money. Accessing financial information and managing finances in real time is valuable to these consumers. Comments suggested more research is needed on the impact of using mobile financial services on consumers' financial lives.

Two capabilities that commenters identified as holding much potential for reaching the underserved in ways that could produce savings for both providers and consumers were mobile/online account opening and mRDC (mobile Remote Deposit Capture). Since customers typically continue conducting their financial services using the channel they initially used to acquire an account, comments suggested that enhanced lower-cost mobile/online account opening capabilities could incentivize more financial providers to target underserved consumers. Commenters agreed that if fraud risks could be mitigated in the context of mRDC, the potential to lower the cost for the providers and help underserved consumers access lower cost ways to cash checks could be significant.

Two specific types of products were also highlighted by commenters – virtual prepaid products and those that facilitate cash-based electronic transactions – as potentially serving some of the financial services needs of underserved consumers. Prepaid products in general are used disproportionately more by unbanked and lower-income households than banked, higher income households; comments indicated a significant increase in use of virtual prepaid products – that is, prepaid products accessed via computer or on a mobile device (without a physical plastic card). Comments also suggested that underserved consumers can benefit from products designed to help consumers using cash access digital platforms. An example is services that enable consumers to initiate a transaction online and complete it with cash at a retail establishment.

Industry Comments Were Split Over Whether and How Much the Mobile Channel Can Reduce Their Costs

Banks and some credit unions pointed to the "additive" nature of mobile financial services and the additional costs to develop and maintain the channel, including significant technical and other customer service support. Several comments related that this is especially true for smaller financial institutions that may find it very difficult to support new technology and systems to support the technology. Some nonbank providers who commented seemed to lean more in the direction of mobile being a cost savings channel. Some comments reported that using the mobile channel has helped providers reduce costs for products targeting the underserved.

Privacy and Security Concerns – Real or Perceived – Pose Barriers and Risk

Comments indicated that real and perceived privacy and security concerns remain a significant barrier to adoption of MFS. Commenters cited concerns about access to and security of financial account and personal information, security of transaction-specific information, online/mobile fraud and scams, and security related to the devices used for MFS, including loss or theft. Consumers managing limited resources are also less able to absorb financial losses or interruptions that may result from security-related problems.

More Transparency, Protections and Consumer Control May Be Needed Around Use of Consumer Data

Comments across the stakeholder spectrum highlighted as unique to mobile financial services the amount and type of data collected, used and shared. Consumers are often required to provide this data, commenters pointed out, in exchange for accessing the services, products or information. Several commenters discussed the benefits of data for linking consumers to products and services at lower cost and reducing fraud. Some of these commenters pointed to the risks associated with personal, location, financial and other data all connected to the consumer through the device. The potential risks identified in comments include disparate impacts in marketing, underwriting and other decision-making processes; and the potential for "virtual segregated neighborhoods" that would continue to limit access to affordable and safe products for underserved consumers.

Several comments pointed to the numerous entities involved in the opaque mobile financial services ecosystem. Some suggested a need to clarify, or develop new, protections to ensure transparency, and oversight and accountability of those entities that provide information that is used to market to or make decisions about consumers. Some commenters urged clearer privacy policies and opt-in processes for consumers as well as accountability by all entities in the mobile payment chain.

Digital Access and Digital Financial Literacy Need to Be Improved for Mobile to Be an Effective Channel for Underserved Consumers

Commenters discussed challenges related to accessing digital channels as well as the need for digital financial literacy. Comments pointed out that while many think smartphones and devices are a growing necessity, the cost of devices and data plans, as well as lack of service in some geographic areas, can leave many behind. Many commenters highlighted the need for efforts to enhance digital financial literacy in addition to broader digital and technological literacy. Comments identified key challenges for underserved consumers including those with disabilities and older adults, around language access, screen size and adaptability, and lack of comfort with using mobile technology.

Comments noted that mobile financial services will not help underserved consumers who don't know about them or don't know how to use them safely and effectively. Education, outreach and marketing are always needed to attract underserved consumers but it appears even more critical with mobile, where the most difficult link for industry to make with consumers may be the link to the technology itself. Comments identified efforts focused on 1) enhancing affordable access to the technology and 2) educating consumers and intermediaries about the safe and effective use of the technology for accessing financial services, products and personal financial management tools as key to making MFS a way to reach more underserved consumers and help those consumers achieve their financial goals.

Policymaking Should Be Widely Informed

Comments varied as to whether and to what extent additional consumer protections are needed in the area of mobile financial services. There was general consensus, however, that there are a wide array of stakeholders, including the CFPB, other financial regulatory agencies, the Federal Communications Commission (FCC), the Federal Trade Commission (FTC), state regulatory bodies, other regulatory organizations and others. Comments suggested that any regulator acting in this area should act with certainty but should not choose technological winners and losers as the mobile financial services landscape is continuing to evolve.

Some commenters encouraged the CFPB and other agencies to continue to work to better understand both the risks, including those associated with data collection and use, and the entities involved in the mobile financial services ecosystem.

1. About This Report

A major development in the consumer financial services market over the past few years has been the increasing use and proliferation of mobile technology to access financial services and manage personal finances. For example, in 2013, 74,000 new customers a day began using mobile banking services.[11] Using a mobile device to access accounts and pay bills can reduce cost and increase convenience for consumers. By enabling consumers to track spending and manage personal finances on their devices through mobile applications or text messages, mobile technology may help consumers achieve their financial goals. For economically vulnerable consumers, mobile financial services accompanied by appropriate consumer protections can enhance access to safer, more affordable products and services in ways that can improve their economic lives.

In order to learn more about opportunities, challenges and risks associated with the mobile financial services market, especially for underserved consumers (i.e. unbanked and low-income consumers) and other economically vulnerable consumers[12] – the Bureau's Office of Financial Empowerment issued a Request for Information on June 11, 2014. The RFI used the term "mobile financial services" (MFS) to cover mobile banking services and mobile financial management services. The RFI was not intended to address mobile point-of-sale ("POS") payments, except with respect to mobile payment products that are targeted specifically at underserved consumers.

The purpose of the RFI was to inform the Bureau's consumer financial education and empowerment strategies related to developments in these areas. We received more than 50 comments from individuals, financial services providers, financial institutions, regulators, trade associations, research and consulting firms, academics, nonprofits, and consumer advocacy organizations. While several trade associations submitted comments, we received few comments from individual financial institutions and providers.

The purpose of this report is to describe the responses by the commenters to help inform the discussion around 1) identifying the scope and types of mobile financial services available with a focus on the underserved; 2) opportunities mobile technology provides for enhancing access to financial services and improving financial lives of underserved consumers; 3) challenges, barriers and risks to accessing financial products and services via mobile technology; and 4) recommendations for how the CFPB might educate and empower consumers in using mobile technology for financial services.

Nothing in this report is intended to identify areas in which the Bureau may or will take regulatory, supervisory, or enforcement action. Some of the commenters' views on these topics are included where relevant to the particular topic of the discussion.

2. Scope of Mobile Financial Services for the Underserved

The market for and scope of mobile financial services (MFS) is expanding as the use of mobile phones, smartphones, and other digital devices increases and the services and products designed for mobile evolve rapidly. The use of mobile financial services has risen significantly throughout the general population but, with some exceptions, has yet to see the same adoption by underserved consumers, despite the fact that many rely on smartphones as their primary or only access to the internet. However, according to several commenters, once connected, many underserved consumers are more likely than others to use mobile to access those services.

2.1. Mobile and the Underserved

There are many efforts, including by financial providers and community organizations, to reach underserved populations to help either bring them into the traditional banking system or enhance their access to safe and affordable financial services from nonbank providers. Mobile financial services are one potential way to help to achieve these goals.

Mobile phone use among underserved populations is significant, and for many in this population is the primary way to access the internet. The MFS survey by the Federal Reserve Board, Consumers and Mobile Financial Services 2015 [hereinafter FRB 2015 Mobile Survey], conducted in 2014, shows 90 percent of underbanked consumers had access to mobile phones and 68 percent had access to smartphones. [13] Unbanked consumers' access to mobile phones (67 percent) and smartphones (44 percent) was also significant.[14] The percentage of unbanked consumers with access to smartphones rose from 35 to 44 percent between 2013 and 2014.[15]

Other estimates provided in the comments suggest even higher levels of smartphone use among the unbanked individuals. According to Javelin Research and Strategy's (Javelin) research, 55 percent of unbanked consumers own smartphones.[16]

Among the lower income population generally, mobile phone use is high – Pew Research Center (Pew) 84 percent of adults living in households earning less than $30,000 per year have a cell phone;[17] and 50 percent have a smartphone (compared to 64 percent ownership of a smartphone for all American adults).[18]

With regard to minorities, Pew found 71 percent of Hispanic adults and 70 percent of non- Hispanic black adults had a smartphone, compared to 61 percent of non-Hispanic white adults.[19] The Federal Reserve Board's recent survey on mobile financial services also found adoption of smartphone use higher among Hispanic consumers (82 percent are mobile phone users) than among non-Hispanic white consumers (68 percent) but found a lower percentage of smartphone use among non-Hispanic black consumers (66 percent).[20]

Pew found that 52 percent of adults in rural areas own smartphones.[21] Not surprisingly, young adults have a high rate of smartphone adoption – 85 percent of individuals between the ages of 18-29 have smartphones.[22]

Reliance on smartphones to access the internet is significant among younger adults, low-income households and people of color. The Pew Research Center found 19 percent of Americans rely to some extent on smartphones for internet access[23] but identified consumers in three categories as "smartphone-dependent", meaning they had neither broadband access at home nor an easily available alternative way to access the internet except through their phone:

- *Younger adults — 15% of Americans ages 18-29 are heavily dependent on a smartphone for online access.*
- *Those with low household incomes and levels of educational attainment — Some 13% of Americans with an annual household income of less than $30,000 per year are smartphone-dependent. Just 1% of Americans from households earning more than $75,000 per year rely on their smartphones to a similar degree for online access.*

- *Non-whites — 12% of African Americans and 13% of Latinos are smartphone-dependent, compared with 4% of whites.*

Pew Research Center, *Smartphone Use in 2015*[24]

Netspend, a prepaid card program manager that identified its customer base as low- to moderate-income consumers, reported in its comments that almost 85 percent of its cardholders reported owning a smartphone.[25] Netspend stated that in focus groups its customers said that they "maximize their limited incomes by consolidating their phone and Internet service to a single source - typically by relying on mobile phone and data plan in lieu of home phone and home Internet. With cell phone upgrade plans, such consumers can frequently be early adopters of new technology."[26] This is not surprising given that less than half of consumers (43 percent) with annual household incomes below $25,000 have access to broadband internet at home.[27]

Though not specific to mobile, Javelin found that 17 percent of underserved consumers switched financial institutions, compared with 10 percent of all consumers, in the 12 months preceding the date of submission of their comments in September 2014.[28] Javelin suggested that these consumers "are open to transferring to new financial service providers."[29] Another commenter reported that 65 percent of banked customers surveyed indicated mobile banking services played an important or extremely important role in their choice to switch financial institutions.[30] As financial institutions and providers want to build a loyal customer base, how and whether mobile maintains that loyalty will affect the way in which companies provide financial services. One banking trade association commenter stated that "[t]he prevalence of mobile phones among such persons [unbanked and underbanked] suggests a particularly egalitarian vehicle for bringing access to mainstream bank products and services."[31] In its comments, Javelin also suggested, "[u]nderserved Americans are fueling demand for new, improved methods to monitor and manage their finances – and they won't necessarily turn to or be satisfied with traditional banking products, services, or providers."[32]

2.2. Defining MFS and Its Use

Several of the comments raised the need to define and clarify the meaning of "mobile financial services" to avoid confusion and to ensure that public policy discussions take place in the context of commonly understood terms and scope.

For example, the U.S. Chamber of Commerce (Chamber) pointed out potential confusion around whether the term depends on the device, the size of the screen, the network connection used, the location of the user or some other factor.[33] As a result, the Chamber noted, the following questions remain unanswered in the context of defining MFS:

- *Whether the term "mobile financial services" exclusively covers financial services accessed through cell phones and smart phones, or whether it covers accessing financial services with other devices, such as tablets, phablets, wearables, devices embedded in cars, laptops, or laptop/tablet hybrids;*
- *Whether accessing financial services through any device that connects through a mobile network meets the definition of the term "mobile financial services," whereas*

accessing those same financial services with the same device, but on a WiFi network would not meet the definition; or

- *Whether the mobile nature of the user defines the term "mobile financial services," irrespective of the type of device or the nature of the network.*

U.S. Chamber of Commerce, #42, at 5-6.

These questions point out the complex nature of the discussion around mobile financial services and the need for clarity when engaged in these issues.[34] This may be relevant for future disclosure or other requirements that may be designed to address a particular channel.

A related but different perspective of the broader market was provided by U.S. Public Interest Research Group and the Center for Digital Democracy, which pointed out that the "online industry views the mobile platform as an integral part of a holistic 'marketing and media ecosystem' " where the "provision and marketing of financial services on mobile devices are integrated into a broader set of industry practices on all digital media."[35] These commenters urged the inclusion of issues related to marketing and data of mobile financial services in a broader discussion.

The comments included references to myriad products and technology that pertain to mobile financial services. The number and technical nature of the terms suggest a potential value in developing common nomenclature around products, technology, channels, and type of use to help guide consumers, regulators and industry.

2.2.1. Mobile Banking

Mobile banking refers to a system or a channel that allows customers of a financial institution to conduct financial transactions through a mobile device such as a mobile phone or tablet. Some mobile banking can be done via SMS (short message service), or texting, through the mobile phone. Other types of mobile banking require access to internet through the financial institution's website or an app provided through the financial institution or others, e.g., links to accounts through money management or account aggregation applications or services.

Mobile banking is on the rise and in demand - it has steadily gained momentum and is preferred, according to a study conducted for American Banker Association in 2014, by 10 percent of bank customers, up from 8 percent in 2013.[36] The FRB 2015 Mobile Survey found that 39 percent of those with bank accounts had used mobile banking in the previous 12 months, compared to 22 percent in 2011; for those with bank accounts who use smartphones, the rate is 52 percent.[37] Deloitte Services LP reported in its comment letter that according to a January 2014 survey by Deloitte Center for Financial Services, nearly 40 percent of surveyed bank customers would bypass branches and interact directly via mobile if offered additional types of mobile banking services.[38]

The Credit Union National Association (CUNA), in its comments, reported that 23 percent of members from the largest credit unions have enrolled in mobile services.[39] One credit union reported that an average of 52 percent of its membership accessed their account via mobile device monthly.[40] In its comments, CUNA said generally larger credit unions are more likely to offer a broader range of mobile financial services, while smaller credit unions continue to evaluate whether it is cost effective to provide or expand their mobile services.[41]

Both the FRB 2015 Mobile Survey of individuals and the Federal Deposit Insurance Corporation's (FDIC) 2013 FDIC National Survey of Unbanked and Underbanked

Households [hereinafter FDIC 2013 Survey] found that underbanked consumers had a higher use of mobile banking as their primary means to access accounts than the overall population with a deposit account.[42] For lower income customers, a 2014 survey done by the Deloitte Center for Financial Services found that use of mobile is significant - 56 percent of surveyed customers with incomes between $25,000 and $49,000 use smartphones to interact with a financial institution, which is not that different from higher income users (61 percent for customers with incomes above $100,000).[43]

The potential for managing one's money via mobile is great. The FDIC 2013 Survey indicated two of the three most common mobile banking activities reported for consumers in underbanked and fully banked households are monitoring of account balances or recent transactions (underbanked - 88.5 percent and fully banked - 85.7 percent) and bill payment (60 percent for both underbanked and fully banked consumers).[44] According to the FRB 2015 Mobile Survey, 63 percent of mobile banking users reported that they had checked their account balance before making a large purchase in the 12 months preceding the survey, and 53 percent of them decided not to purchase an item as a result of their account balance or credit limit.[45]

Javelin also found underserved[46] consumers had higher rates of mobile banking (53 percent vs. 42 percent in 90 days previous to comment submission) and mobile bill pay than among all consumers (33 percent v. 22 percent).[47] On the other hand, the Alliance for Stabilizing our Communities (ASOC) reported that its Banking in Color: New Findings on Financial Access for low- and Moderate-Income Communities survey found though 59 percent of the respondents had internet access via phone, only 17 percent used it for mobile banking and only 11 percent of respondents reported they were comfortable with conducting financial transactions online or on their mobile phone, citing security most often as the concern when banking via the use of the smartphone.[48] This contrasts with comments from the Consumer Bankers Association, which reported a study by Alix Partners that showed non-Caucasian *banked* customers were more likely to use mobile banking than their Caucasian counterparts (52 percent for Hispanic customers, 41 percent for African American customers, and 38 percent for Asian customers, versus 28 percent for non-Hispanic Caucasian customers).[49]

As suggested in comments, this use is significant but there is still untapped potential.[50] MFY Legal Services, which provides legal services to low-income and other vulnerable consumers in New York City, commented that mobile access, which would allow clients to check their account balances anywhere, could be a benefit as "they are more likely to avoid purchases that overdraw their accounts and lead to overdraft fees."[51] MFY Legal noted, however, that "simply because people have technology does not mean they know how to use it, or use it safely."[52]

According to financial industry members, because the acquisition channel is so important to developing an ongoing customer relationship, successful account opening strategies are very important for financial institutions. The Center for Financial Services Innovation (CFSI) commented that it identified two services that allow consumers to open an account directly from their mobile device.[53] A credit union reported that members can open accounts via mobile device.[54] Some comments raised the issue of KYC (know-your-customer) and AML (anti-money laundering) rules as barriers to mobile and online account opening. Comments noted that although innovative products may be designed to assist with account opening, it remains difficult to comply with the rules through an online channel, e.g., gathering the information to validate a customer's identity.[55] But one comment noted that "innovations including photo recognition of common forms of identification should improve this situation in the next several years."[56]

Many respondents highlighted the potential of mobile Remote Deposit Capture (mRDC) to help underserved bank customers and attract unbanked consumers to the banking system.[57] Mobile Remote Deposit Capture (mRDC) allows consumers to take a photo of and deposit a check remotely via their mobile device. As one commenter noted: "To date, this has perhaps been the most transformational mobile development for the underserved because it overcomes the limitations of branch hours and locations."[58] It has the potential to save time and reduce costs for the 38 percent of the unbanked households that use nonbank check cashing services,[59] which the Center for American Progress (CAP) noted may charge as much as 2 to 5 percent of the check value.[60] According to the FRB 2015 Mobile Survey, 51 percent of mobile banking users surveyed said that they had deposited a check electronically using their phone camera.[61]

Though the benefits may be significant, a number of comments raised issues that might make banks wary of offering mRDC to all customers, and might make mRDC not as appealing for all consumers. These included:

- Fraud: The ABA, in its comments, stated that "quick access to funds via RDC deposits presents fraud risks."[62] The ABA cited the risk that a check could be deposited more than once or might be forged or fake as one of the reasons for the lag between deposit and access.
- Delay in access to funds: The report, Assessing the Economic Inclusion Potential of Mobile Financial Services [hereinafter FDIC Staff paper], issued by staff of the FDIC in June 2014, noted that banks typically require consumers to wait a period of time before their remotely deposited funds become available for withdrawal.[63] Commenters stated that they think institutions hold checks deposited remotely because it is not clear to them whether Regulation CC funds availability rules apply, and because of the fraud risk inherent in RDC (described in the previous paragraph).[64] Research by Consumers Union confirmed reports from consumers about delay of funds issues with mRDC, finding that checks deposited via mRDC into accounts at one bank took 10 days to become available.[65] Consumers Union noted that the potential to attract customers away from higher priced check cashing services may be limited as "RDC may not satisfy the need/want of many of the unbanked – and underbanked – to have immediate access to funds or cash."[66] In contrast, the ABA suggested that "[e]fforts to improve the payment system to make it faster and more efficient will further reduce and perhaps eliminate the need for holds."[67]
- Different regulations apply: At least one comment noted that checks deposited via mRDC may be subject to different laws and regulations than checks deposited by traditional means.[68]
- Errors from the quality of the image itself: One commenter noted that errors from the quality of the image captured by consumers may affect low-income consumers more than others because they may have cheaper, inferior phones and cameras.[69] If there is a blurred image, the amount of the check may be erroneously recorded. Comments

noted that this could cause serious consequences such as overdraft and other fees that may result from such errors.[70]

- Problems when the original check is not destroyed: If the original check is not destroyed, comments suggested, there is risk that it may be deposited again. If a check is deposited more than once there may be a double debit to the account of the customer who wrote the check and a payee who accidentally deposits a check more than once may think he has more money available than he does.[71] This too might lead to insufficient funds or other types of fees.[72]

Comments reported that financial institutions often offer fee-based options to get faster access.[73] For example, according to comments from the Consumer Bankers Association, one bank charges its customers who deposit checks through mRDC - 50 cents for funds availability within two business days, $3 for funds availability the same night, and 1 percent to 3 percent of the check amount for immediate funds access, with a $5 minimum fee.[74] One comment suggested that if institutions develop mobile systems that enable consumers to deposit checks without paying a fee before the check has cleared, that may help move consumers away from higher priced check cashing services.[75]

2.2.2. Personal Financial Management Tools

Personal financial management (PFM) tools are available online not only via websites, but also via mobile applications. Some "alerts" and other tools use text messaging that can be received on a smartphone or other cell phone. (See Texting discussion below)

These tools provide a variety of services, such as aggregating account information, sending alerts and reminders about balances and bill payments, and tracking and reporting on spending habits. CFSI noted that of the 900 mobile applications it reviewed for personal financial management capabilities "there are relatively few apps that focus on savings goals or debt reduction."[76] Intuit, however, claimed that users of its product, Mint.com, a money management software system that aggregates accounts and helps consumers establish individualized savings goals and set up alerts, are saving over $1 billion per month towards their goals.[77]

Commenters noted that when consumers can access more than one type of account via mobile they can make an informed decision about when and whether to switch from a debit to a credit method for their purchase.[78] Such features help in managing accounts and possibly avoiding fees. However, commenters raised issues about privacy and security in these situations as discussed later in Section 4.

Evidence suggests that underserved consumers use and value alerts as a key function of their mobile financial service. According to the FRB 2015 Mobile Survey, 57 percent of mobile banking users received an alert in the previous 12 months.[79] Javelin found that while 86 percent of all mobile bankers receive email alerts, 93 percent of underserved mobile bankers received alerts.[80] CFSI reported that consumers who use one MFS app that also offers users transaction accounts issued by a bank check their account three to five times per day.[81]

Netspend, which noted that it has 3.4 million active prepaid cards, commented that between 55-65 percent of its GPR cardholders and 40-45 percent of its payroll cardholders are enrolled in its alerts program, and 150,000 unique users use Netspend's smartphone apps per month.[82] The company stated that its customers, many of whom maintain low average balances – typically less than $100 on any given day - "closely and actively manage their accounts."[83]

CFED (Corporation for Enterprise Development) stated that while MFS has many potential benefits for low-income consumers, more product development and innovation is needed to meet some of their unique needs. For example, financial management software may not be able to accurately capture payments such as government benefits and tax credits, which "limits their ability to help users review their finances to make decisions in real time and plan ahead with an understanding of what their resources will be in the future."[84]

One use of personal financial management tools is in the area of credit scores. Knowledge and understanding of credit scores can be very useful for consumers because improved credit scores are associated with greater access to a variety of credit products and lower cost credit. One commenter discussed a credit score/credit report card mobile app it provides to its customers and reported that its members in "very poor," "poor," and "fair" (according to the credit score it uses) who check the credit scores on its app on a regular basis showed higher credit scores than members with the same credit score ratings who check their credit scores less frequently.[85] As the market moves in the direction of providing free credit scores on credit card and other types of account statements provided by lenders to consumers, credit score mobile apps may have a broader positive impact for consumers with lower scores.

2.2.3. Text Messaging

Commenters highlighted the importance of text messaging to low-income bank customers. They noted that many low-income consumers do not have smartphones; text messaging is one of the only ways for them to benefit from alerts and push notifications from financial services providers.[86] Texting was viewed as an important yet untapped function to enable consumers to set up alerts and track their accounts. One commenter suggested that providers could use texts to "nudge their more at-risk consumers … into better financial behavior"[87] but noted that any tradeoffs with regard to fees charged would need to be explored.[88]

One commenter noted that "text-based mobile financial services may also offer greater opportunities in serving the unbanked."[89] According to comments from One Financial Holdings Group (One Financial), some providers noted measurable changes in consumer spending habits, "based purely on post-transaction, real-time text-messaging to increase awareness of spend and spend patterns."[90]

One commenter reported examples of nonprofits successfully using SMS as their primary engagement platform with their customers, adopting the target audience's preferences to better reach them.[91] ASOC reported that its local affiliates have begun to utilize texting to reinforce personal financial goals and action plans developed by the client through their financial coaching process and to provide ongoing encouragement as part of their financial capability program.[92]

While many comments acknowledged the use of texting and its benefits,[93] some industry commenters objected that the Telephone Consumer Protection Act (TCPA) requires consumer permission before text messages are sent to a consumer.[94] The American Financial Services Association (AFSA) cited litigation risk and disclosure requirements (perceived as difficult to meet because texts have character limits) as two challenges their members face when providing texting services.[95]

Some industry commenters stated that the cost of TCPA compliance, uncertainty regarding whether certain activity complies with the TCPA, and the risk of liability are all factors that discourage banks from investing more in text messaging, "especially as text is viewed as an interim system as people move to smart phones."[96] Deloitte Services LP, in its comments, also stated that the prospects for texting are limited "given the dramatic rate of change in technology and reduction in price, it may not make sense to invest heavily in text banking."[97] The National Consumer Law Center (NCLC) shared its viewpoint that many providers may not be complying with Electronic Signatures in Global and National Commerce (ESIGN) Act,[98] which requires consumer consent in order to deliver certain communications electronically.[99]

2.2.4. Mobile Applications

Many financial products and services, including financial management services, are accessed through applications on mobile devices.

In its review of nearly 900 financial apps, a substantial proportion of which were personal financial management (PFM) apps, CFSI found most are available free of charge.[100] According to CFSI, some apps had been downloaded more than 10 million times, while others were downloaded fewer than 10,000 times.[101] But CFSI remarked that there is virtually no data on use patterns, length of engagement and retention, or on consumer financial outcomes as a result of using the apps.[102] It is also not known how downloads correlate with actual use.

Some commenters cited problems with some money management and other apps that include a failure to disclose whether a fee applies to a particular transaction, a failure to provide required disclosures before the app is downloaded or alerts are activated, requiring consumers to visit the website to find out the terms and conditions, and a lack of uniform terminology among providers.[103] One commenter stated that consumers should have access to disclosures before they enroll in a service or download an app and suggested that consumers should see a simple box display with any fees before being asked to provide any personal information or download an app.[104]

One commenter raised concerns about the impact of cell phone service providers moving away from providing unlimited data in mobile phone plans, suggesting that such a change may limit the ability of low-income consumers to comparison shop via mobile because such activity uses a lot of data.[105] Another commenter, however, suggested an increasing availability of prepaid phone plans and unlimited data plans at reduced prices as a positive trend.[106] In addition, for mobile users mobile apps are increasingly becoming the way some consumers access their deposit accounts.[107] Commenters noted concerns about the privacy and security of data shared with apps, one stating that account access apps are not all the same in functionality or in level of security or privacy protections.[108]

2.2.5. Prepaid Products

Prepaid products are typically loaded with funds by a consumer or by a third party, such as an employer. Consumers can use these products to make payments, store funds, get cash at ATMs, receive direct deposits and tax returns, and send funds to other consumers, among other things. Prepaid products are often purchased by consumers at retail stores or online. Prepaid products are amongst the fastest growing types of consumer financial payment products in the United States.[109] For example, according to one estimate the amount of money consumers loaded onto "general purpose reloadable" prepaid cards grew from less than $1 billion in 2003 to nearly $65 billion in 2012.[110]

One commenter noted that the increasing use of prepaid products, including via mobile devices, among unbanked and underbanked consumers demonstrates a willingness to use alternative products.[111] CFSI's market size report for 2013 found a 30 percent increase in growth in volume between 2012 and 2013 (to $84.3 billion) in GPR prepaid cards.[112] The FDIC 2013 Survey found that in 2013, the use of GPR cards was more common among lower income, unbanked and underbanked households.[113] Specifically, it found that more than a quarter (27.1 percent) of unbanked households had used a prepaid account, compared with 19.6 percent of underbanked households and 8.8 percent of fully banked households.[114] More than a quarter (28.3 percent) of unbanked consumers in households with incomes between $30,000 and $50,000 reported using prepaid cards whereas only 13.7 percent of those earning $75,000 or over reported using them.[115] The increased use of prepaid cards by unbanked and underbanked consumers was noted by Javelin in its comment letter, which reported that in the 12 months preceding its comment submission, 43 percent of underserved consumers had used prepaid cards for purchases, versus 28 percent of all consumers.[116]

Some prepaid products that target the lower-income market provide consumers with the ability to access a savings account or set-aside account, and some provide check writing services.[117] Also, comments noted that some consumers who cannot get bank accounts because of blemished reports with specialty consumer reporting agencies that provide checking account screening services may find providers of prepaid, often accessed via mobile device, more willing to take them as customers.[118]

The Network Branded Prepaid Card Association (NBPCA) stated in its comment that its members had a "significant increase in the issuance of virtual prepaid card products which can be accessed through a mobile device."[119] They noted that the physical prepaid card had served as a replacement for the check and today "disbursement is increasingly being handled through mobile applications and virtual prepaid products."[120] One industry commenter reported that while it sees a mobile app usage rate of only 10 percent among active consumers of GPR prepaid cards, an increasing number of prepaid card program managers are providing customers with the ability to access and manage their finances via mobile application and there is a steady growth in usage by prepaid cardholders.[121] The commenter noted that several card providers tend to market to lower-income consumers.[122]

The ABA stated that "[m]obile banking features, when coupled with prepaid cards, show promise to attract the unbanked to bank products."[123] It highlighted the prepaid product it has endorsed, which it said allows users to access their account via a mobile application, in discussing the potential benefits for potential unbanked customers of using prepaid and mobile together.[124]

A consumer group noted that some prepaid cards are marketed more like an application than a card, with the expectation that consumers will manage their account via mobile or online.[125] It also suggested that protections may vary among debit and credit cards, which can be confusing for consumers when they are accessing those cards through one device.[126] The commenter suggested that there should be more uniformity and clarification of consumer financial protections as they apply to prepaid and other products that are accessed via mobile device.[127]

2.2.6. Mobile Payments

In this report, the term "mobile payments" refers to mobile point-of-sale (mPOS) payments made through a mobile device. Using mobile payment (m-payment), a consumer with a mobile device can pay for purchases in a retail store or restaurant through a point-of-sale terminal. Bank accounts, credit cards, debit cards, and prepaid cards can be accessed through the consumer's device, often through a "digital wallet." The most common models of retail contactless payments terminals require consumers to "tap-and-pay" by waving the mobile device across the terminal or to use a Quick Response (QR) or other readable code at the POS. If a terminal accepts near-field communication (NFC)-based payments,[128] communication allows for information to travel across to the terminal without the devices having to touch each other. Loyalty cards, insurance member cards, coupons, boarding passes, tickets and many other types of information can also be added to the associated mobile wallet. Digital wallets offer varying levels of security. For example, some require biometrics for authentication purposes.[129] Some examples of digital wallets that facilitate m-payments include Android Pay and Apple Pay.[130]

Appleseed, which works with immigrant communities, commented that "[i]nnovations in mobile payment services, the development of mobile wallets, and the introduction of personal money management tools and applications have effectively transformed how some individuals manage their money and may have ramifications for broad scale use by underserved communities, including immigrants."[131] Another commenter noted that experience in other countries suggests that mobile payments could facilitate financial access in this country as well.[132]

The Federal Reserve Board's 2014 survey found, conditional on owning a mobile phone, minorities are more likely to adopt mobile payments (the Federal Reserve Board's definition of which includes bill payments).[133] The Federal Reserve Board found Hispanic consumers accounted for 32 percent of all mobile payment users relative to 22 percent of all mobile phone users.[134] For non-Hispanic black consumers, the rate was higher – 34 percent of those with mobile phones made mobile payments.[135]

2.2.7. Mobile Carrier Billing

Mobile carrier billing enables consumers to charge goods or services directly to a mobile phone account. The consumer is billed through her mobile carrier and charges show up on her statement from the mobile carrier or telecommunications firm. The FTC commented that it is a payment method that "may be useful for consumers who do not have credit cards, or do not want to use them, especially for small transactions. In this way, carrier billing may be especially beneficial for unbanked and underbanked consumers."[136] However, commenters identified important potential problems with mobile carrier billing for the underserved.[137] Reasons cited by commenters for caution include fraud, the potential lack of adequate error resolution procedures, and impact on credit reports and scores from unpaid bills in dispute.[138] The FTC estimates that consumers have lost millions due to mobile cramming – the unlawful practice of placing unauthorized third-party charges on mobile phone accounts.[139]

2.2.8. Mobile P2P

One area of fairly rapid adoption is mobile person-to-person money transfers (such transfers are sometimes included in "mobile payments").[140] Consumers can send money directly to others through email or texts or mobile applications. This service is provided by banks, credit unions and through other product providers (e.g., PayPal, Square). Some comments discussed the potential benefits of person-to-person for providing a less expensive and more convenient option for consumers.[141] Javelin stated that underserved consumers are highly open to mobile P2P payments as a replacement for cash transactions.[142] According to its research, Javelin reported that in the 30 days preceding the submission of its comments, 28 percent of mobile underserved consumers conducted a mobile P2P transfer, twice the percentage of consumers overall.[143]

2.2.9. Accessing Digital Channels with Cash

There are products that enable consumers who use cash to access digital channels through various means, including using in-person retail to accept cash and confirm transactions initiated through a digital channel. Low-income consumers carry out a significant portion of transactions with cash. According to a report published by the Cash Product Office of the Federal Reserve System, 55 percent of consumers with household incomes less than $25,000 per year prefer cash over non-cash payment instruments. [144] The total value of low-income consumers' cash spending, at $558 average per consumer per month, is much higher than any other income group's cash spending and this group uses cash much more frequently for bill payments than other groups of consumers.[145] Javelin reported that it found the underserved are more likely to use cash through online payment services (22 percent v 10 percent of all consumers).[146]

Commenters noted that access to mobile bill-payment channels could present a safe, convenient and possibly cheaper alternative to cash for unbanked, low-income consumers who may use cash for transactions such as bill payments.[147] One provider, for example, commented that its service enables consumers to go online to initiate an electronic bill payment that is completed in cash at a nearby retail outlet.[148] A person who wanted to pay his or her rent the day before it is due, for example, could go online and submit the transaction, complete the transaction at a nearby retail partner of the provider, and have a receipt to show payment.[149] A consumer group acknowledged the potential benefits of the such services but stated it had concerns that certain recourse and other protections may not available to customers of those services.[150]

One industry commenter discussed cash reload networks that allow users of prepaid cards to load cash for a fee onto their prepaid cards, which can then be used to initiate card-not-present transactions with merchants over the phone, via internet, or through electronic bill pay of utilities.[151] Its comments highlighted services such as self-serve kiosk-based solutions that allow users to directly transform cash into a variety of electronic payments, including remittances and bill payments.[152]

2.3. MFS Is a Channel, Not a Separate Product

While various mobile financial services may be described as "products," many commenters pointed out that "mobile financial services" is not a discrete set of products and services but rather a channel through which consumers can access financial services and products through many devices. The ABA stated that the FDIC has defined it as such.[153] The ABA noted that "[mobile banking] is a channel, not a product, and does not address the primary reasons people do not use bank products."[154] Both consumer and some industry groups cautioned that using the mobile channel should not be viewed as a replacement for accessing products and services via other, more traditional channels.

2.3.1. Channels Are Secondary to Ensuring Access to Appropriate Products and Services

Pointing to consumer benefits associated with having a bank account, several commenters suggested that mobile is secondary to the need for safe, affordable accounts. One commenter stated: "People with mainstream bank accounts tend to keep more of their earnings, fare better against financial shocks, and save more for the future. Conversely, lack of a bank account is directly related to poverty. Yet, traditional banking accounts remain out of reach for many people."[155]

In discussing whether mobile will facilitate access to financial products, the ABA stated that "the primary reasons people use nonbank credit products such as payday loans rather than a bank loan or credit card are that they do not think that they qualify for a bank loan or credit card product or find alternative loans quicker and more convenient to obtain."[156] The ABA further commented that some consumers do not know or believe that banks make small loans, which may indicate a need for outreach and marketing to the underserved, through mobile or other means.[157] Though the ABA acknowledged that "mobile banking may assist some people in moving from alternative credit products to bank products," it stated that mobile banking will not address the primary reasons people use alternative credit products.[158]

Consumer and community advocates stressed the need to focus on an overarching goal of ensuring access to products that meet the needs of low-income consumers and communities. As one community group remarked:

> *However services are delivered, regulators must also look at the products banks offer and their impact on the community, including the availability of low-cost bank accounts without high and hidden fees, equal access for immigrants, outreach and flexibility to truly reach unbanked and under-banked people, and finally how those products are marketed and utilized. Basic banking products must be accessible, affordable, and appropriate to the needs of the communities in which they operate. Mobile banking has the potential to be one such product to increase access to banking.*

ANHD, #12, at 2.

3. Opportunities

There was a general consensus among the commenters that mobile provides opportunities to enhance access to financial services and products. But not all commenters agreed that increasing mobile opportunities for customers will reduce provider costs associated with providing financial services and products. Some commenters suggested that the time and money savings have the potential to help low-income consumers achieve their financial goals.[159] To achieve such improvements, however, commenters acknowledged that consumers need to know how to use them and in ways that provide an overall net benefit to them.[160]

3.1. Industry: Costly but Scalable Options

Some commenters identified as significant the cost to industry of developing the necessary infrastructure to support mobile financial services. In addition, commenters highlighted the resources needed to provide ongoing technical support for the mobile channel, including support for customers new to or unfamiliar with how to use mobile technology to access financial services and products.[161] Some providers described mobile as an "additive" channel. As a result, some industry comments asserted that mobile does not necessarily reduce costs for financial services providers.[162] In its comments, the ABA provided an estimate of the "additive" costs banks are charged monthly by vendors for various add-on account features:

- Mobile: $1.86;
- Debit card: $1.08;
- Internet banking: $2.06;
- Bill pay: $5.56;
- IP and statement rendering $3.43; and
- Mailing costs $.16[163]

CUNA stated in its comments that credit unions incur significant costs to implement and integrate rapidly evolving different mobile services with their systems and "secure the mobile, online, and other channels. Additional costs could include fees for software licensing, third party providers, and legal review."[164] CUNA acknowledged that as consumers continue to make greater use of mobile financial services, there is potential for cost savings on a per-transaction basis over time.[165]

The ABA and CBA both took issue with the example in the RFI comparing the costs of an in- branch transaction to a mobile transaction.[166] ABA suggested that "[i]t is misleading to compare mobile banking transaction costs with branch transactions."[167] It noted that "the ease of use often increases the volume of transactions, offsetting cost-savings from the lower-cost channel. For example, customers use ATMs more frequently and withdraw less per transaction ($118 on average) than they do with branches ($715 on average)."[168]

The CBA noted various benefits of mobile banking for unbanked and underbanked consumers but stated that "mobile banking imposes great expense on our members through research and development, innovation, vendor management, system maintenance, and cybersecurity mearsure [sic]."[169]

One Financial expressed the view that MFS presents an opportunity to "realize significant reductions in customer acquisition and customer services costs," which it described as historical barriers that prevent traditional or non-predatory financial institutions from servicing low- income consumers.[170] It noted that data from some prepaid providers "suggest cost-to-serve a low-income consumer through a prepaid channel with MFS is approximately 20 percent of the cost of using a traditional checking account and branch infrastructure."[171]

In its comments, CFSI stated that one provider expects average customer acquisition costs to be one-third to one-tenth that of a traditional brick and mortar bank (citing typical checking account customer acquisition costs of $200 to$300).[172] CFSI went on to state that this model "translates into direct benefits for the consumer: the provider is able to offer a free app and debit card with no monthly minimum balance or transaction fees while offsetting operating expenses entirely from interchange revenue."[173]

By allowing consumers to open an account directly on their phones, CFSI reported that one provider has also been able to save on customer acquisition costs.[174] Since consumers generally have their mobile phones with them at all times, CFSI opined, they can act on the advertising and messaging they receive to immediately open an account, rather than waiting to return home to their computers or having to visit a brick and mortar location.[175] As a consequence, according to CFSI, mobile account opening results in a higher revenue rate for each marketing dollar spent.[176]

Sending customer notifications through mobile channels has also been an important cost-saving feature for the provider mentioned, according to CFSI.[177] Mobile push notifications are free and are efficient; unlike email, CFSI noted, push notifications have a nearly 100 percent open rate since they appear at the top of a user's screen even when the program itself is not open.[178]

Intuit, owner of Mint.com, stated that it assumes that savings from lower transaction costs for providing financial products and services through mobile channels "will inevitably be passed through to consumers."[179] Deloitte said that "once the core infrastructure is in place, scaling is relatively inexpensive—the same trait that makes software startups able to reach millions."[180] One commenter noted that it is not surprising that informational services, deposits and transfers, and inquiries hold the most potential for reducing costs.[181]

Electronic Payments Core of Knowledge (EPCOR), a trade association focused on payments education and support to its member financial institutions, reported that its members were "split on whether there is cost savings to financial institutions in offering mobile services, especially when factoring in higher amounts of fraud often present in this environment."[182] Some members reported savings related to fewer in-branch transactions, but others said it creates more work in the back office.[183] Also, members identified as expensive the implementation of remote deposit capture and mobile bill pay, as well as the existence of ongoing expenses such as upgrades to technology and security.[184]

One Financial also stated that the ability of "innovators" to offer a "nationwide distribution channel at almost no cost" through MFS is limited by state Money Services Business (MSB) regulations.[185] One Financial said that bank partners were harder for it to find and suggested that may mean more costs and delay for third-party entities wanting to issue products to vulnerable population through bank partners.[186]

3.1.1. Costs to Maintain

Commenters noted that the move to mobile may mean fewer visits to the teller or calls about transactions. This does not alleviate customer service needs, commenters stated, but merely changes the nature of the calls to more technological inquiries. The National Association of Federal Credit Unions (NAFCU), for example, stated that once credit unions have mobile applications designed or their websites are optimized for mobile use, "the overhead increases to provide those services and the technical support to troubleshoot those features for members."[187] According to one credit union, "[m]obile financial services are effective at reducing the need for call center representatives to provide basic teller functions, but have increased the need for call center representatives who understand technical issues, are familiar with various mobile devices, and can help diagnose technical problems."[188]

Comments also included concerns about trying to support a large percentage of account holders and field increased call volume of questions or issues with applications given the various number of issues that could be causing the problem, such as the operating system itself.[189]

EPCOR noted that most of its members report that it would prove cost-prohibitive to offer enhanced customer service times beyond normal business hours, and that a small institution is not likely to have staff available to address technical questions since the services are generally contracted through a third-party.[190] EPCOR said that this could prove a major impediment to the adoption of mobile services.[191] The NBPCA suggested that over time, as MFS and applications are able to serve consumers more efficiently, there may be less need for customer service by telephone.[192]

3.2. Consumers: Saving Money and Time

Although commenters disagreed about whether adoption of mobile technology would raise industry costs, which might be passed on to consumers, most commenters agreed that in other respects MFS has great potential to lower costs for consumers. Commenters noted that mobile can provide access via a less expensive, "anytime, anywhere" means, for example, minimizing wait times and transportation costs.[193] They said that mobile can also help consumers avoid higher cost products by using a product such as mRDC rather than a check casher.[194] Commenters said that it can also help consumers avoid fees associated with lack of real-time information such as overdrafts on accounts that could have been avoided by checking balances or alerts.[195] Commenters also noted that the extent of savings for consumers also depends on whether provider cost savings are passed along by the financial services provider.[196]

Comments varied about the charges and costs for MFS currently incurred by the consumer. For example, EPCOR reported that its members generally do not charge account holders for mobile services; a few indicated they charge for Remote Deposit Capture (RDC) services due to the reported expense of this service.[197] At least one consumer group stated that providers should be encouraged or required to offer multiple free ways to find out balances, such as by text message, so that consumers can find a convenient method that works for them.[198] The groups reasoned that because consumers so frequently access account information via mobile and such access enhances their money management and other goals, free access will enhance consumers' ability to achieve their financial goals.

In terms of accessing financial services, one commenter pointed out that many higher fee, alternative financial services providers gain market share from lower-cost banks and credit unions due to their slightly extended hours of operation.[199] Commenters noted that prepaid provider NetSpend reports that 40 percent of prepaid account loads, or deposits, take place outside of traditional banking hours.[200] Comments suggested that the mobile channel could enhance the ability of lower-cost providers to provide access to their services and products 24/7, potentially enhancing access to lower cost services for underserved consumers.[201] At least one commenter suggested, however, that low cost benefits of mobile products may be undermined by "fees, certain credit features, and other add-ons to the baseline cost" of the mobile products.[202]

The "real time" nature of mobile was discussed as a benefit in several ways. Several comments highlighted the ability to pay bills and access other services in real time via mobile, decreasing time and costs and possibly late fees.[203] NetSpend reported that its customers, many of whom it reports are low to moderate income, like the ability to control and decide spending, and pay bills in real time.[204] It noted that while online automatic withdrawals or bill pays may be attractive to people with regular and consistent paychecks, if income volatility is an issue then the ability to control transaction by transaction in real time may be an even more important feature of mobile.[205]

Commenters said that access to mobile financial services may encourage consumers to comparison shop. One commenter identified a product feature that provides notification of alternative products that may benefit individual users, such as cheaper financial products.[206] Another comment highlighted that MFS enables "consumers who otherwise lack internet access to shop and pay for a wider array of goods and services, often with higher quality and better prices than are available locally." [207] Related to this point, one commenter noted that those consumers who may move from using cash to using MFS may also start to use mobile more to access other kinds of products and services.[208]

Real time and location services also can help people detect fraud by helping them monitor accounts and receive alerts from their providers.[209] Location services can also help consumers identify services available nearby. For example, Deloitte suggested that, during tax season, an application could show a consumer the closest free or low-cost tax preparation centers or Volunteer Income Tax Assistance (VITA) sites.[210] Applications could also use geolocation to direct citizens to government resources on public benefits and explain the process or information required for processing.[211]

3.3. Outreach Efforts to Connect Underserved Consumers to Mobile

Commenters suggested that, based on the FDIC 2013 Survey findings and other information low-income and vulnerable consumers often seek the in-person experience of bank tellers, telephone customer service, storefront alternatives and working with trusted partners.[212]

According to FDIC's 2013 survey on unbanked and underbanked, about one-third of customers primarily used bank tellers to access their accounts (nearly 80% had used a bank teller in the previous 12 months) and another third primarily used online as their means to access their accounts.[213] Underbanked people were less likely to use the online channel but were more likely to use mobile devices as the primary method.[214] Roughly half (54.7 percent) of households age 65 or older and 47.5 percent of households with annual income under $15,000 primarily used bank tellers to access their accounts.[215]

Several comments cited a concern over the potential loss of bank branches and the impact on various segments of the underserved population who, for a variety of reasons, may need or want in-person guidance.[216] One commenter stated that "mobile services should be used to make branches more efficient and expand outreach to underserved areas, not shrink financial inclusion."[217] Some commenters suggested that mobile and human assistance and other hybrid approaches may be very beneficial or needed to enhance access for this population.[218]

Deloitte recommended that financial firms could improve outreach to underserved consumers by applying the strategy of adapting the audience's preferred mode of communication to the design and marketing of mobile financial services.[219] It also suggested that gaining a better understanding of the targeted population could help identify effective partnership or marketing campaign opportunities. [220] It gave as examples partnering with a utility company or partnering with a trusted government agency to leverage infrastructure and reach large numbers of consumers.[221]

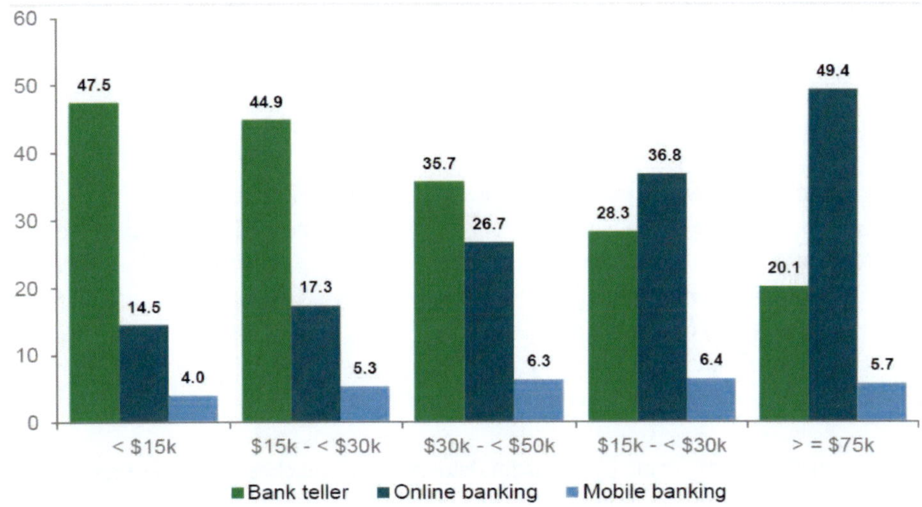

2013 FDIC Survey of Unbanked and Underbanked Households, p. 56

Figure 1. Use of Bank Tellers, Online Banking, and Mobile Banking as Primary Methods by Income.

EPCOR reported that its members use a variety of methods to market mobile financial services to underserved populations: radio and television ads; billboards; social media; online banking websites; training of all consumer-facing institution staff to discuss mobile options with consumer account holders; digital signs outside of branches; lobby displays; community events; and statement stuffers were the highest used methods.[222] They did not report the extent to which each of these efforts was successful.

Several commenters pointed out that for mobile to reach the underserved in a meaningful way, it must be coupled with appropriate products and marketing. For example, a few commenters suggested ideas such as that "the current banking industry should be incentivized, if not required, to offer free or low cost checking accounts to the income eligible underbanked."[223] One of the requirements suggested was that "the account must be advertised and promoted, available online, and understood and marketed by all branch staff so that any customer will have it readily available to them."[224]

Some comments highlighted the need for increased education and outreach.[225] Appleseed noted that its "Immigrant-Friendly Financial Services" characteristics as applied to mobile would include efforts to increase financial education and ensure mobile financial services are used appropriately by consumers.[226] The ABA stated that, "[m]obile banking does not make people smarter or supply individual financial acumen. Improving financial literacy remains a priority even in a mobile world."[227]

In their comments, the Federation of Community Development Credit Unions (CDCUs) and CUNA highlighted a proposal to invest in the expansion of these mobile technologies in trusted community development financial institutions to help ensure that MFS is used to empower and address the financial needs of consumers in affordable and safe ways.[228] Specifically, they proposed a national strategy to:

- Increase the delivery and reach of electronic services in trusted financial institutions, such as credit unions; and
- Support the training and education of the most economically vulnerable consumers to take advantage of online banking and mobile applications.[229]

4. Challenges and Risks

Most commenters agreed that mobile provides opportunities for greater access to safe, low-cost and appropriate financial services for lower income and underserved consumers. Many commenters also stated that there are challenges and risks that prevent more widespread adoption of mobile.[230] Not all agreed, however, about what those barriers and risks are and how best to overcome them.

The most significant barriers and risks mobile poses for low-income and economically vulnerable consumers identified by commenters are:

- perceived risk of financial loss from data security breaches and loss of devices;
- lack of digital financial literacy;
- lack of digital access due to cost or technological issues;
- interconnectedness of digital media, e.g., social media, with financial services;
- eliminating in-person support services;
- ubiquitous use of data for marketing and underwriting that may create "virtual segregated neighborhoods;" and
- potential for a multi-tiered system where non-mobile enabled consumers are left behind and nonbank customers are left with fewer protections.

4.1. Security

Data security is not an issue that is particular or limited to mobile devices but many comments discussed security issues in the context of mobile financial services. There was widespread consensus among commenters that concern over security – real or perceived – is one of the most significant barriers to MFS adoption for consumers.[231]

4.1.1. Data and Transaction Security

Data Breaches and Hacking

Many commenters discussed the risk and the increasing frequency of data breaches in general.[232] The Massachusetts Attorney General's office stated in its comment letter, "the storage and transmittal of financial information on and through mobile devices presents unique security risks."[233] Comments discussed the risks the mobile channel presents including the amount of personal and financial information provided and accessed through the channel;

the wide range and variability of operating systems and reliance on the customer to implement updates; and that more advanced security measures are not yet widely offered on more affordable smartphones.[234] One commenter cautioned that "even if the number of attacks on mobile financial services is much lower than on online services, we must understand this will not last forever."[235]

Identity Theft

Several commenters identified identity theft as a risk, particularly because consumers are more likely to be in a public place when they access accounts through a mobile phone and they may not be aware of the risks when they transmit data using WiFi that is not their own.[236] The impact of identity theft is more significant for low-income consumers, a commenter pointed out, because they have "few funds to absorb any economic loss that results."[237]

Transaction Security Issues

Commenters noted that while there may be risks generally of personally sensitive data being transmitted electronically, risks also arise on a per transaction basis. Making sure that a transaction is both secure (from the consumer's perspective) and not fraudulent (from the provider's perspective) is important to maintain trust in the e-commerce environment. Biometrics, innovative authentication measures, and tokenization were all raised by commenters as potential ways to help ensure that financial transactions remain safe.[238]

4.1.2. Security Associated with the Device

Theft of Devices

Commenters noted that mobile devices can be easily lost, stolen, or damaged, and consumers may not be able to access information if it was deleted or if they changed phones or providers.[239] A commenter noted that consumers may become crime targets when they use mobile devices.[240] Consumers Union reported that based upon a nationally representative survey of adult Internet users, Consumer Reports® projected that 1.6 million American were victims of smartphone theft in 2012.[241] Consumers in cities appear especially vulnerable.[242]

Consumers Union reported that 36 percent of consumers surveyed do not have a passcode on their phone.[243] In addition, few consumers understand that when they retire a phone, they have to overwrite the information or the phone has to be destroyed to get rid of the data – merely deleting it doesn't remove it permanently.[244] EPCOR also noted that lost devices that are not passcode-protected and mobile malware represent significant threats to all mobile services.[245]

In its comments, Appleseed raised the concerns of both personal and financial security for immigrants and posed the question of how the shift to mobile may affect those concerns.[246] Appleseed commented that vulnerable populations, such as immigrants, are more often the victims of street crimes and theft than other population subgroups.[247]

Difference in Operating System Security

Though all operating systems can experience security breaches, a few commenters pointed out the different levels of risk associated with iOS (Apple phones) versus Android systems. According to comments, the Android's open platform enables a greater number of users to access the platform, making it harder to monitor.[248] Though Android and iPhone use across the general population is fairly equal, there is a contrast at the lower-income levels. According to Pew, in households with incomes under $30,000, 13 percent have iPhones, and 28 percent have Android (compared with 40 percent iPhone ownership rate in households with incomes above $75,000).[249] According to Javelin, 24 percent of the unbanked who own a smartphone are on the iOS system and 57 percent are on the Android system.[250] In contrast, 44 percent of the phones owned by underbanked and fully banked consumers run on the iOS system.[251]

Applications

The Privacy Rights Clearinghouse stated that the major app stores such as the Google Play store and Apple iTunes store may be "more likely to catch bad actors than other third-party app stores" but, it noted, an app doesn't have to be malicious to contain security vulnerabilities.[252]

Denial of Service Attack

One commenter described the risk that consumers will not be able to access their institution because of a "distributed denial of service" attack.[253] When these attacks occur, the commenter stated, consumers are not able to conduct timely financial transactions, which may result in late fee charges, or other consequences of late payment.[254] The commenter suggested that current laws do not directly address protection for consumers harmed by these attacks.[255]

4.1.3. Enhancing Security

Many pointed to the flip side of security concerns – positive characteristics such as the ability to track and manage accounts and to detect fraud. Comments pointed to real-time alerts of suspicious transactions and the ability to block or manage account access instantaneously from the phone as "a powerful new kind of defense against fraud and theft" for consumers.[256] In addition, the ability to detect when phones and payment instruments are not co-located and to track the location of a device, commenters explained, can help deter fraud and theft.[257] As some commented, however, consumers need to be comfortable with using their mobile devices safely for this to be effective.[258] For example, Appleseed cautioned that recent innovations in mobile payments may require an even "higher level of comfort with technology and many consumers may find it easier to pay with another method."[259]

4.2. Privacy

Many commenters pointed to a lack of privacy of consumers' data as a risk of MFS. Comments reported that this risk often arises because consumers may not be aware of the extent and type of data collection practices and their consequences.[260] Even if they are aware, one commenter pointed out, they may "have no opportunity or mechanism to avoid or mitigate them."[261]

Some commenters asserted that consumers have control over their privacy because they can choose to not turn on location-based services or choose to exchange data for real-time information or services they may want.[262] Others pointed out that the business model for MFS and mobile commerce in general has become service in exchange for data, with little to no choice for consumers.[263] There is evidence that consumers are growing more concerned about their online information sharing. According to the Pew Mobile Technology Fact Sheet:

- *54% of app users have decided to not install a cell phone app once they discovered how much personal information they would need to share in order to use it*
- *30% of app users have uninstalled an app that was already on their cell phone because they learned it was collecting personal information that they didn't wish to share....*
- *19% of all cell owners have turned off the location tracking feature on their cell phone because they were concerned that other individuals or companies could access that information.*

Pew Research Center, *Privacy and Data Management on Mobile Devices* (2012)[264]

More recently, in a survey conducted by Pew on Americans' views on data collection and security, 90% of respondents said that controlling *what* information is collected about them is important– 65% think it is "very important" and 25% say it is "somewhat important."[265] Only 9 percent of respondents, however, believed that they had "a lot" of control over how much information is collected about them and how it is used.[266] Though the survey was not limited to mobile services, the survey indicates "Americans hold a range of strong views about the importance of control over their personal information the importance of control over their personal information..."[267]

The FTC pointed out the risks to privacy (and security) due to the high number of companies involved in the mobile payments system and the large volume of data collected.[268] AgeCheq and PrivacyCheq, both companies that provide mechanisms designed to help consumers control access to their identification, suggested a streamlined disclosure design.[269] Suggesting that consumers may be more comfortable with MFS if devices gave them more control over their identification, AgeCheq suggested that "[a] logical way to provide that ability would be for ... vendors of mobile devices to create a new pseudo identifier for "privacy" that would give the consumer full control over the identification of their device for privacy purposes."[270] The Privacy Rights Clearinghouse suggested that privacy protection must be built into products from the beginning, as the creation of detailed personal profiles, which it said may result in discriminatory practices, grows more pervasive.[271]

Commenters noted that providing disclosures that are clear and sufficient for consumers to make informed decisions is difficult in the MFS environment. The Privacy Rights Clearinghouse offered that "it is completely unrealistic to expect a consumer who only has access to a mobile device with a small screen to read the privacy policies."[272] Industry comments identified the small screen size as limiting providers' ability to comply with disclosure requirements.[273] Comments suggested that required disclosures should be adapted to mobile technology in ways that enhance understanding about the product such as its costs and fees.[274]

Data Brokers and Lead Generators

Another issue related to data raised by comments involves data brokers and lead generators. According to one set of comments, credit card and other financial companies, auto dealers, for-profit schools, and many other businesses pay online "lead generators" or data brokers to gain access to and information about "qualified potential customers."[275] The FTC stated that when data is sold to data brokers and other entities, "often outside the protections of specific privacy laws, questions arise regarding how this data may be used to either benefit or disadvantage low-income and underserved communities."[276]

Some respondents perceived regulatory gaps related to these practices.[277] One consumer group stated that a recent report from the World Privacy Forum "highlighted the fact that new types of predictive consumer scoring, fueled by thousands of pieces of information about consumers, are largely unregulated [by] either the FCRA or the Equal Credit Opportunity Act."[278] The group also referred to a survey it conducted on data brokers that it reported revealed "serious inaccuracies in some uses of big data."[279] Along with other recommendations, it suggested that "[A]t a minimum, providers must comply with the FCRA for any data that is assembled or evaluated by third parties and might be used for credit, insurance, employment or other FCRA purposes. In particular, data should be provided to and used by mobile providers and others only if they have a permissible purpose under the FCRA."[280]

Industry comments suggested that existing laws such as FCRA and the Gramm-Leach-Bliley Act (GLBA) protect consumer information.[281] But some consumer groups opined that the GLBA prohibitions on sharing information only apply to financial institutions and their accounts, not to sharing by or accounts of other types of providers.[282] One commenter also noted that GLBA only prohibits sharing of account numbers for purposes of marketing, and some inappropriate sharing may fall outside that restriction.[283] The commenter noted that there are other laws designed to restrict sensitive information from being shared, but mobile transactions may not be covered by these protections or they may not be sufficient to protect consumers.[284]

One consumer group called on the Bureau to "go beyond GLBA and FCRA data sharing provisions, and adopt additional protections for consumers."[285] Groups recommended that consumers should have to affirmatively opt in to data sharing or entities should not be permitted to share certain types of sensitive personal and financial information at all.[286] US Public Interest Research Group (PIRG) and the Center for Digital Democracy (CDD) urged the Bureau to take more action to protect privacy, including building on a proposal for a Consumer Privacy Bill of Rights developed by President Obama's Administration in 2012 and work already done by the FTC, and to develop rules that place consumers' financial data more under their control.[287]

4.2.1. Data for Marketing and other Purposes

Consumer advocates cited a significant risk of MFS data being used to segment the market with potentially negative consequences for low-income consumers, people of color, and other traditionally underserved populations.[288] These commenters noted various ways such segmentation could be done.[289] Whether referred to as "digital dossiers" or "personal profiles," commenters discussed concerns over the extent of locational-based data collection and targeting technologies, and other geo-technologies that permit highly granular geographic focused marketing practices.[290] The commenters raised concerns that geographic-based targeting, combined with data profiling predictive analytics, can lead to potentially discriminatory practices, e.g., denial of credit to certain segments, which further sub-divide a neighborhood based on race, ethnicity, income, buying behaviors, and other factors.[291]

One commenter noted that as the digital marketing ecosystem grows larger and more integrated, "the provision and marketing of financial services on mobile devices are integrated into a broader set of industry practices on all digital media. Increasingly, consumers are identified and tracked across all "screens," which, due to our often-simultaneous use of multiple devices, enables far more effective commercial targeting."[292]

Others expressed concerns related to data being used to track where consumers reside, their movements and purchasing patterns, and also to determine with whom a person associates.[293] Commenters also noted that a significant finding of a report on big data from the Executive Office of the President, in a letter to the President from the agencies submitting the report, was that "big data analytics have the potential to eclipse longstanding civil rights protections in how personal information is used in housing, credit, employment, health, education, and the marketplace."[294]

Some groups warned that mobile financial services without strong consumer protections related to data collection and use could lead to "virtual segregated neighborhoods."[295] Others warned about the use of cultural differences in behavior to market products. An example provided by a commenter involves situations in which some in a "group" are ranked financially lower based on social media or other information.[296]

Some commenters spoke positively about the use of big data for validating identity or for fraud detection purposes,[297] as well as its use to help financial institutions identify and reach potential new customers, including the underserved.[298] Recognizing that "big data is here to stay," one commenter suggested that the focus should be on how the data is "operationalized."[299] This commenter expressed concerns that the use of big data may bring about both "general privacy problems" as well as "thousands of new possible methods for disparate and adverse impacts upon protected classes."[300] It suggested that the "proper unit for regulatory analysis is the creator of the analytics [that use big data.]"[301]

4.3. Digital Financial Literacy and Access

4.3.1. Digital Financial Literacy

The existing challenges and barriers to underserved consumers accessing financial services and products may be exacerbated by a lack of "digital financial literacy." Digital financial literacy includes knowing how to use devices to safely access financial products and services via digital channels in ways that help consumers achieve their financial goals, protect against financial harm and enhance ability to know where to get help. There seems to be consensus in the comments that along with investments in mobile technology to bridge access, there is a need for "major investments in digital literacy to ensure that consumers are able to navigate the technology necessary to conduct their financial services online."[302] Commenters noted a need for more understanding for both consumers and those intermediaries and front-line staff working with consumers who may benefit from knowing more about MFS options and how to engage in digital finance in ways that help clients achieve their goals.

A recent study conducted by the Federation of Community Development Credit Unions and the Aspen Institute revealed that very low-income members with annual incomes below $20,000, do not use financial services offered via the internet because "they do not understand the terms and costs associated with services and are afraid of being scammed."[303]

This is not surprising given the level of complexity involved in many MFS. As one commenter noted, in pointing out the need for technological literacy: "MFS applications require users to understand how to download MFS applications, navigate websites using a mobile browser, upload photos for remote deposit capture, etc. Recent innovations in mobile payment services, such as Near Field Communications (NFC) technologies and mobile wallets, require an even higher level of comfort with technology and many consumers may find it easier to pay with another method."[304]

4.3.2. Access to Financial Services

"Access" to financial services has long meant having physical access to branches and personnel that help low-income consumers achieve their financial goals. Commenters noted that mobile, as a channel, raises other issues of "access."

Cost

Comments raised concerns about the increasing costs of data plans, and fewer unlimited plans, as a challenge for underserved and immigrant consumers.[305] One commenter noted that various nonfinancial service providers such as social media sites are competing for scarce data allotments.[306] Pew's research found 44 percent of smartphone owners with household incomes less than $30,000 reported cancelling or having their service cut off for a period of time because maintaining their service was a financial burden.[307]

In the FRB 2013 Mobile Survey, 11 percent of all mobile phone owners noted that data costs prevented them from using mobile banking and payment services.[308] In the FRB 2015 Mobile Survey, 6 percent of respondents chose "my bank charges a fee for using mobile banking" as one of the reasons they did not use mobile banking.[309]

In addition, commenters expressed concern that the inability to obtain or afford the latest technology could leave low-income and economically vulnerable people behind and may create another means of being "underserved." One commenter noted that the greater reliance on pay-as-you-go or prepaid phones may mean that consumers do not have 24/7 access if phones run out of minutes or data or service is not good.[310] This could affect the ability of the consumer to access his or her prepaid products, potentially locking the consumer out of access to financial services, at least in a convenient and timely manner.[311] One commenter suggested that prepaid phones are helping to make smartphones more accessible to the population at large by reducing prices.[312]

Some groups pointed to the Lifeline Assistance and other programs where the government provides access to and discounts on cell phone service. Though this may be a way to help low- income consumers access mobile technology, groups pointed out that many low-income consumers still have no access to smartphones through these programs.[313] AARP suggested many still view smartphones as a luxury even as more and more financial and other services are moving to online and mobile channels.[314]

Language

According to comments, many if not most mobile applications do not provide multilingual options, limiting the ability of non-English speaking consumers to use MFS or understand the terms and fees.[315] Some services, one commenter noted, may be marketed in the consumer's primary language, but many of the details in the fine print may only be in English.[316] One commenter suggested that mobile applications should have a default language feature, which would allow access to the user's native language.[317] Others suggested that providers should make services available in the different languages used in the bank or credit union's customer service and marketing areas and have service personnel available to explain how to use the system.[318] Appleseed also pointed to the need to "ensure to the greatest extent possible that the terms of the services being marketed to non-English speaking customers are the same as those marketed to English-speaking mobile money users."[319]

Technology

Though technology can enhance access, commenters pointed out that it can also present barriers to access if the technology is turned off, the device is lost or the phone service is terminated.[320] Lower-cost devices may not have the latest technology such as high resolution cameras, larger screens, near-field-communication (NFC), and other features.[321] Commenters noted that mobile apps that require the latest features would not be accessible to consumers that do not have or cannot afford the latest technology.[322]

Commenters noted that small screens may not be conducive to reading text-heavy disclosures, particularly for consumers who may be visually impaired. While the small screen may make it difficult to provide detailed or complex information, NCLC noted that "[s]mart design can use that small screen as an advantage, to provide clear information in manageable bites, enhancing understanding."[323] One industry commenter listed the following reasons that user experience (UX) design for MFS for underserved consumers is particularly difficult:

a. High proportion of customers with limited technological aptitude or experience
b. Low income consumers' use of a large variety of different smartphones, including those with varying operating systems, screen sizes, hardware, and other key features
c. Difficulties designing MFS that provide access to consumers in multiple languages
d. Health problems with higher incidence among low-income consumers (e.g. diabetic retinopathy or arthritis) and which may affect their ability to use the device
e. Limited affordances for consumers who are uncomfortable reading small text or large bodies of text
f. Mandated or standard disclosures that make it difficult for service providers to provide plain English or translated explanations of terms and conditions
g. Trust issues around remote account opening and surveillance

One Financial, #33, at 6-7.

In addition, another set of access barriers was noted by the ABA, stating that "opening an account through a mobile app (or online) may be more difficult for the unbanked because they may lack commonly used identification verifiers, such as information contained in credit reports, that banks use to verify identities for purposes of compliance with identity theft and customer identification requirements."[324]

4.4. Financial Loss

Many comments noted that many underserved or economically vulnerable consumers are living within tight margins and can benefit from MFS because of its real-time tracking and other features.[325] But, they cautioned, the risk of loss also exists as more products may not have safety of funds (FDIC insurance), clear dispute resolution consumer rights and procedures or understandable fee disclosures.[326]

It may also be unclear which entity in the mobile payment chain is liable for loss. In "Paper, Plastic ... or Mobile? An FTC Workshop on Mobile Payments," the FTC pointed out that when compared to a more traditional payment system, a mobile payment system involves numerous, unrelated parties that comprise the mobile payment chain, including:

- The developer of the application ("app") that enables the transaction or activity;
- The developer of the operating system of the mobile device;
- The manufacturer of the mobile device;
- The carrier of cellular and data service for the mobile device;
- Payment processors that facilitate the transfer and authorization of payments;
- Advertisers, marketers, data aggregators, billing aggregators, and other third parties who may collect, aggregate, analyze, and/or sell information about the user for marketing, advertising, and other business purposes;
- The financial entity providing funds; and
- The recipient of the funds.[327]

One commenter identified risks when third party agents are involved as including that the fund transfers may not occur as directed by the consumer or may not occur at all, or the payment may be late, for an incorrect amount, or sent to the wrong person.[328] The commenter suggested that the problem may be due to an error caused by the financial institution or a third party agent; or it may instead be due to one of the parties facilitating the transfer.[329] The commenter questioned whether current law is sufficient to protect against these risks of loss given the various parties that may be involved in mobile transactions.[330]

Though many commenters spoke to the convenience and benefits of providing access to multiple forms of payment via a mobile device, commenters raised issues arising from the fact that there are multiple parties to the transaction and the protections that apply may depend on the payment method used for the transaction.[331] The presence of multiple parties can cause confusion for consumers, which, in turn, may cause financial loss if it is not clear from which entity they must seek redress.

The varying levels of protection can also cause confusion and loss, commenters noted. From one device, a consumer may use a credit card, a debit card or mobile carrier billing to pay for a transaction. Depending on which payment method is used, varying rules apply. If there is an unauthorized charge on a credit card, for example, one commenter said, there is no liability if the charge is reported, and payment is not due during the time the charge is being investigated.[332] The commenter further noted that unauthorized debits are subject to varying caps on liability depending on whether the access device was lost or stolen and when the unauthorized transfer is reported. In that instance, with debits, funds must be restored in the account unless an investigation shows the transaction was authorized.[333] But, commenters noted concerns that payments charged directly to a mobile carrier may be treated differently.[334]

4.5. Loss of other Channels – Person-to- Person Contact and Customer Service

Several comments pointed out the benefits of branches while other comments focused on the impact of more branch closures, which have disproportionately affected low-income communities.[335] One industry commenter expressed the view that "MFS provides an opportunity to replace and supplement the 'vanishing branch network' in low income neighborhoods.[336] It viewed MFS as a 'mitigating factor' that could help maintain access to mainstream financial services.[337] But consumer groups and others made clear that they believe there is an ongoing need for some physical, in-person presence.[338]

In its comment, One Financial noted that its customers typically access accounts at financial institutions through the marketing channel by which they were acquired. But One Financial reported that "customers return again and again to their neighborhood locations for service"[339] for both insured banks and nonbank AFS providers.

While ASOC reported that its Banking in Color survey of low- and moderate-income communities of color showed that "bank branches remain a vital part of how some communities access financial products and services," [340] they noted interesting differences across different communities, as follows:

> *The proximity to home or work was a priority for nearly half (48%) of all survey respondents when choosing where to conduct financial transactions. Forty percent of all survey respondents deposit checks or cash inside a bank branch. While more than one-third of African American and Latino respondents deposited checks within a branch, fifty-two percent of AAPI [Asian Americans and Pacific Islanders] respondents deposit checks inside a bank or credit union branch, 45% deposits [sic] cash inside the branch, and 39% cash checks inside bank branches. By comparison, only 25% of AAPI respondents use online banking services for managing payments and accounts.*
>
> *The reliance on bank branches was especially high for Chinese and Taiwanese respondents, who deposit checks in bank branches at 57% and 64%, respectively. Chinese language respondents also indicated distance from home (70%) and ability to communicate in their native language (56%) as a top consideration for determining where to bank.... Taken together, survey results reflect both a high level of comfort and reliance on bank branches as well as high prevalence of bank branches with culturally and linguistically relevant services in neighborhoods and communities with high concentrations of the Chinese community.*

ASOC, #40, at 6.

A related concern raised by commenters about the move to mobile is loss of customer service. In a survey of low-income Hispanic consumers across California conducted by National Council of La Raza (NCLR) in 2013, 85 percent of account holders and 71 percent of those without a transaction account rated customer service as very important in choosing financial services.[341] In the Banking in Color survey, LMI consumers, regardless of banking status, identified customer service as a significant factor in what they were looking for in a bank.[342] As the FDIC Staff Paper noted (citing a Javelin survey from July 2013) "25 percent of consumers who do not use mobile banking stated that one of the top three reasons they do not use mobile banking was that they preferred to deal with people."[343]

Commenters cited problems related to obtaining service from some mobile service providers, including prepaid products often accessed via mobile channel, that fail to provide a phone number, clearly display the phone number, make phone access difficult to navigate, or charge customers who wish to speak with a customer service representative.[344] Commenters pointed to the ongoing need for free customer service via phone, for those using the mobile channel as well as those who cannot easily access internet or who do not transact via mobile.[345] As CAP commented: "[t]his is particularly important for mobile products that have either a limited physical retail presence where customers may ask questions and get help, or no physical presence at all."[346]

Comments suggested an ongoing need for paper statements or account agreements.[347] NCLC also added that "[p]aper copies of account agreements or statements may be unnecessary for mobile transactions that are used only once or for small dollar amounts. But for larger transactions and more significant, ongoing relationships, paper options can ensure that consumers can carefully read or reference account terms and can see ongoing charges."[348]

NCLC also pointed out that the person who opens or views an account on a mobile device may not be the account holder. In that circumstance, NCLC noted, it would be inappropriate to have as a consequence taking away the account holder's access to paper statements or other communications.[349] Other comments noted the cost savings from moving to mobile and online statements, including saving paper.[350]

5. Education and Empowerment – Ideas for the Future

Consumer and industry commenters discussed the potential for mobile financial services to help the underserved access financial products and services, and manage financial resources to achieve their goals.[351] The comments also noted the increasing use of smartphones among the underserved has not led to widespread adoption of mobile financial services, with some exceptions.[352] For those who use MFS, the use appears to be significant, especially as it relates to managing money through checking balances and alerts.[353]

Though there are many reasons for the rate of adoption, comments suggest that there is a need to enhance digital financial literacy to help bridge the divide. But there are impediments to digital financial literacy. As identified in the comments, these include 1) the cost of the technology and data plans; 2) the lack of comfort with the technology and digital literacy; 3) the lack of transparency with regard to data; 4) the concern about security; 5) the language access issues; and 6) the number of entities in the payment chain. Commenters agreed about the need for more efforts specifically targeting low-income and economically vulnerable populations and the groups that serve them about how to engage through mobile devices safely and effectively.

Many conveyed the same opinion expressed by Javelin that "[a] winning combo" for underserved consumers is "[c]ommunity outreach, personalized support, in their own language."[354] As previously discussed, they noted that underserved consumers show an interest in using both digital and in-person channels. The preference often for in-person transactions was partly attributed to the underserved consumer's frequent use of cash, or needing guidance when opening accounts or language barriers. Targeted, sensitive, face-to-face education can help underserved consumers move to more sophisticated products and services.

5.1. Suggested Areas for Further Information and Research

Personal Financial Management Apps

Several commenters suggested more research on how underserved consumers (and specific subpopulations) might use mobile tools and the impact of such use in areas such as reducing debt and increasing savings.[355]

Impact Analysis of Digital Analytics

Commenters suggested a need for research to analyze the impact that the real-time and location-aware financial mobile services marketplace will have on economically vulnerable consumers. These commenters pointed out that there will be legitimate advantages for consumers using mobile financial services to obtain product information, pricing options, and discounts.[356] But commenters also cited potential risks and suggested that policymakers could do more research on how and what types of information are being shared and how to help inform efforts to prevent discrimination and virtual segregated neighborhoods.[357]

Security

Several commenters suggested that there is a need to promote greater consumer awareness regarding important security issues.[358] Also, commenters noted that more information is needed around the extent to which consumers understand the differences in security among operating systems they use or among mobile applications. One commenter also suggested research and analysis on how personal and financial security are advanced or imperiled by a shift to mobile technologies.[359]

One commenter, who provides digital security services, outlined various security risks and some of the ways technology can be used to provide more security.[360] Along with specific examples of some actions consumers can take, the commenter also suggested the need for providers to give "simple and to the point" messages about mobile security, such as reminders about using a pin code and activating the remote location and phone wipeout feature to help if the phone is lost or stolen.[361]

Specific Population Needs

Several comments pointed to the need for more research on specific populations and how they use mobile and access financial services, including issues around language and culture, to help identify ways to remove barriers to access, for both mobile and physical channels. Commenters pointed out that communities of color and underserved consumers are often lumped together but they often have different needs, challenges and use patterns. For example, Appleseed commented that there is little information on how non- Hispanic immigrants use technology for financial services.[362] Those groups for which comments suggested more information should be sought include:

- Unbanked and underbanked;
- Rural consumers;
- People with disabilities;
- Consumers with limited English proficiency;
- Recent immigrants;
- Underserved youth or "opportunity youth" (i.e., youth between the ages of 16 and 24 who are neither enrolled in school nor participating in the labor market); and
- People residing in traditionally underserved communities.

Use of Text Messaging

Commenters highlighted the importance of text messaging, pointing out that many underserved consumers do not have smartphones and their only way to benefit from alerts, etc. would be via text.[363] To facilitate effective texting and mobile banking, particularly for communities of color, ASOC proposed partnerships with government entities to work to better understand the problems and test out the solutions to bring more consumers and communities of color into the mobile banking space.[364]

5.1.1. Moving Forward

Commenters provided various suggestions to help make MFS a more viable option for helping to empower and improve the financial lives of low-income and economically vulnerable consumers, including:

Consumer Security Toolkit

One suggestion was for financial service providers to develop "a simple customer security toolkit, showing consumers how to protect their mobile devices and payments data by creating passwords for login and access; using antivirus software to ensure the applications downloaded are safe from viruses and malware; loading software that enables the phone to be remotely wiped, locked, or deactivated if lost or stolen; and encouraging more consumers to set up fraud alerts."[365]

Tokenization

To help mitigate the loss associated with data breaches, several commenters suggested and highlighted the benefits of tokenization. Tokenization works by substituting a sensitive data element with a non-sensitive equivalent "token" that has no extrinsic or exploitable meaning or value.[366] Using tokens for transactions, known only to the parties to the transaction, reduces the digital footprint that enables others to track or steal information.

Privacy

Many commenters suggested the need for consumers to be able to control their privacy and access to their data. Some stated a need for additional regulatory mechanisms. Other comments from products providers pointed to technology to give consumers the ability to control their privacy when data is used in transactions.[367] A commenter suggested a box display with fees that comes up before any personal information is submitted to help prevent entities not involved in a transaction from obtaining personal information.[368]

Public Service Campaigns

One commenter suggested that any campaign encouraging use of mobile device software have as a component a Public Service Advertisement campaign targeted toward low-income and limited-English proficient communities to help educate about the risks of mobile banking to consumers who are new to it.[369]

Training

Several comments suggested the need for education and training programs, though not as a replacement for consumer protections, that help teach technological literacy (generally or focused on specific topics), and recommended training workers who already interact with low-income populations to address some of the vulnerabilities as well as the benefits.[370] One comment identified municipally run financial empowerment centers as examples of appropriate places in which to locate such trainings.[371]

Mobile-Enabled Websites

One commenter noted that mobile-enabled websites are able to detect the size of the user's screen and provide full website-level services regardless of the access device.[372] This can help consumers who primarily use smartphones access a broader range of financial services features and functions available on the website.

CONCLUSION

The increasing access to and use of mobile technology available to conduct financial transactions and manage personal finances presents opportunities and risks for the underserved. Commenters suggested that mobile financial services can drive access to products and services that meet the needs of the underserved and enhance opportunities for saving time and real time money management.[373] But several industry and consumer commenters expressed the viewpoint that mobile financial services is not a panacea or a silver bullet and "will not undo fundamental financial issues that cause some consumers to be underserved."[374] Commenters suggested that while MFS may help people access financial services and products and achieve cost savings, the reasons underlying consumers' use of higher-cost products and the need for "in-person consultation" (e.g., brick and mortar) will continue for some time.[375] Many noted that unless MFS is coupled with strategies to address the underlying issues related to lack of access to safe and affordable products, the full potential benefits for low-income and underserved consumers will remain elusive.[376] In order for MFS to achieve those benefits, comments suggest, there needs to be broader digital financial literacy, more confidence that appropriate consumer protections are in place and greater comfort with the technology, including around security and other potential risks associated with this data driven ecosystem.

End Notes

[1] FEDERAL RESERVE SYSTEM, CONSUMERS AND MOBILE FINANCIAL SERVICES 2015 1-2 (MARCH 2015) [hereinafter FRB 2015 MOBILE SURVEY]; Pew Research Center, *Mobile Technology Fact Sheet* (2014)

available at http://www.pewinternet.org/fact-sheets/mobile-technology-fact-sheet/ (last visited May 25, 2015)[hereinafter *Pew Mobile Technology Fact Sheet 2014*]; Pew Research Center, *U.S. Smartphone Use in 2015* 13 (April 2015)[hereinafter *Pew Smartphone Use 2015*].

[2] FRB 2015 MOBILE SURVEY, *supra* note 1, at 6, 10.

[3] http://www.gpo.gov/fdsys/pkg/FR-2014-06-12/pdf/2014-13552.pdf.

[4] FRB 2015 MOBILE SURVEY, *supra* note 1, at 1-2.

[5] *Pew Smartphone Use in 2015, supra* note 1, at 2, 13.

[6] According to Pew, 13 percent of those in households earning less than $30,000 annually are "smartphone-dependent," defined as having neither traditional broadband service at home, nor easily available alternatives for going online other than their cell phone. *Pew Smartphone Use in 2015, supra* note 1, at 2, 13.

[7] See discussion later in section 2.

[8] See discussion later in section 2. In this report, when describing or summarizing study results, the terms used to identify race, ethnicity or other demographic characteristics of populations are those used by the publishers of the reports or other information sources. These terms or demographic characterizations are not necessarily those used by or endorsed by the CFPB.

[9] See FRB 2015 MOBILE SURVEY, *supra* note 1, at 7-8.

[10] American Bankers Association (ABA) #45, at 6; Consumers Union, #30, at 6; Center for Financial Services Innovation (CFSI), #6, at 9 (overall desire of low-income consumers for immediate access to funds).

[11] Javelin Strategy and Research, *Mobile Banking, Tablet and Smartphone Forecast 2013-2018: Smart Device Adoption Drives Mobile Banking Boom in 2013*, March 2014 (95 million U.S. adults used mobile banking – a gain of 27 million mobile bankers over 2012, or 74,000 per day) *available at* https://www.javelinstrategy.com/brochure/318/

[12] The term "underserved" for purposes of this report includes low-income, underbanked, unbanked, economically vulnerable, and traditionally underserved consumers as well as consumers with thin or no credit file.

[13] FRB 2015 MOBILE SURVEY, *supra* note *1*, at 1-2.

[14] *Id.*

[15] *See* FEDERAL RESERVE SYSTEM, CONSUMERS AND MOBILE FINANCIAL SERVICES 2014 1-2 (MARCH 2014) [hereinafter FRB 2014 MOBILE SURVEY](The 2014 report of the survey conducted in 2013 found 69 percent of unbanked consumers had access to a mobile phone, approximately half of which were smartphones, so approximately 35 percent of those surveyed had smartphones).

[16] Javelin, #49, at 3.

[17] *Pew Mobile Technology Fact Sheet, supra* note 1.

[18] *Pew Smartphone Use in 2015, supra* note 1, at 13. The FRB 2015 MOBILE SURVEY found 74 percent of adults living in households with less than $25,000 have a mobile phone and 53 percent have a smartphone.

[19] *Id.*

[20] FRB 2015 MOBILE SURVEY, *supra* note 1, at 4-5.

[21] *Pew Smartphone Use in 2015, supra* note 1, at 13.

[22] *Id.*

[23] *Id.* at 2.

[24] *Id.* at 17.

[25] Netspend, #52, at 3.

[26] *Id.*

[27] National Consumer Law Center (NCLC), #35, at 16 *citing* White House Office of Science and Technology Policy, National Economic Council, Four Years of Broadband Growth at 8-9 (June 2013), *available at* http://www. whitehouse.gov/sites/default/files/broadband_report_final.pdf.

[28] Javelin #49, at 5.

[29] *Id.* According to a report in April published by Mercator, approximately 31 percent of young adults and 28 percent of other mobile banking users surveyed in 2014 reported a financial institution switch during the past two years, compared to 20 percent who reported doing so in 2013. Mercator Advisory Group, Mobile and Tablet Banking: P2P Is Driving Growth April 2015, Press Release, *available at* https://www. mercatoradvisorygroup.com/Press_Releases/Mobile_and_Tablet_Banking P2P_Is_Driving_Growth/.

[30] Consumer Bankers Ass'n (CBA), #10, at 4 (citing research by AlixPartners).

[31] American Bankers Ass'n (ABA), #45, at 1.

[32] Javelin #49, at 5.

[33] U.S. Chamber #42, at 3-8.

[34] For example, the ABA, #45, at 3 urged that "[i]n considering the potential for "mobile phones" to expand opportunities for the unbanked and underbanked it is important to look beyond just mobile phones and recognize in the discussion other easily and commonly transported devices that continue to evolve in terms of capabilities, features, ease of use, size and transportability."

[35] U.S. Public Interest Research Group (US PIRG) and Center for Digital Democracy (CDD), #19, at 3 [hereinafter PIRG and CDD].

[36] ABA, #45, at 2. The ABA stated that the study was conducted by Ipsos Public Affairs, an independent market research firm, for the ABA during August 7-12, 2014.

[37] FRB 2015 MOBILE SURVEY, *supra* note 1, at 9.

[38] Deloitte #44 at 2, n. 2, citing Mobile Financial Services Survey, Deloitte Center for Financial Services, January 2014. According to Deloitte, the online survey included 2,193 responses from a broad cross section of demographic groups. All respondents had a bank account and were at least 21 years old.

[39] Credit Union National Ass'n (CUNA), #24, at 1-2 (Nearly 60% of the more than 200 credit unions that responded to CUNA's 2014 Technology Spending survey currently offer mobile financial services).

[40] Randolph-Brooks Federal Credit Union (RBFCU), #27, at 2.

[41] CUNA, #24, at 3.

[42] FRB 2015 MOBILE SURVEY, *supra* note 1, at 5 found 48 percent of underbanked had used mobile banking in previous 12 months compared to 39 percent of all mobile phone owners with bank accounts; 32 percent of the underbanked reported making mobile payments in the previous 12 months; FDIC National Survey of Unbanked and Underbanked Households 10 (2013) found that among mobile banking users, underbanked households were considerably more likely (32.4 percent) than the fully banked (21.6 percent) to use mobile banking as their main banking method [hereinafter FDIC 2013 SURVEY].

[43] Deloitte, #44, at 5.

[44] FDIC 2013 SURVey, *supra* note 42, at 61.

[45] FRB 2015 MOBILE SURVEY, *supra* note 1, at 25.

[46] Javelin, #49, at 5 defines underserved as consumers who lack a checking account or have used alternative financial services in past 12 months, which is different from definitions used by the Federal Reserve Board in its survey: unbanked (not having a bank account) and underbanked (having a bank account but also using an alternative financial service such as a money order, check cashing service, pawn shop loan, auto title loan, paycheck advance/deposit advance, or a payday loan) FRB 2015 MOBILE SURVEY, *supra* note 1, at 5 or the FDIC in its survey: underbanked households (having an account, but have also obtained financial services and products from non-bank, alternative financial services (AFS) providers in the prior 12 months) FDIC 2013 Survey, *supra* note 42, at 4.

[47] Javelin, #49, at 6.

[48] Alliance for Stabilizing our Communities (ASOC) #40 at 5, 7. ASOC is a collaboration between National CAPACD (Coalition of Asian and Pacific Americans for Community Development), the National Council of La Raza, and the National Urban League.

[49] CBA, #10, at App. 2.

[50] *See, e.g.*, FRB 2015 MOBILE SURVEY, *supra* note 1, at 5 (gradual rise in mobile payments by smartphone users suggests smartphone adoption substantially contributed to the increased use of mobile payments).

[51] MFY Legal Services, #17, at 2.

[52] *Id.*

[53] CFSI, #6. at 4.

[54] RBFCU, #27 at 2.

[55] ABA, #45, at 17; One Financial, #33, at 6.

[56] One Financial, #33, at 6. *See also*, CFSI, #6, at 3 (There are software programs that enable financial institutions to use device features such as the camera, the GPS locator to execute know your customer protocols for account opening or loan applications).

[57] *See, e.g.*, ABA, #45, at 7-8; CBA, #10, at 5; CFED, #26, at 5. Susan Burhouse, Matthew Homer, Yazmin Osaki and Michael Bachman, FDIC, Assessing the Economic Inclusion Potential of Mobile Financial Services 24 (2014) [hereinafter FDIC Staff Paper] (as of 2013, 77 percent of the 25 largest banks offered mRDC, and about 25.7 percent of mobile banking users have used mRDC in the previous 12 months).

[58] Center for American Progress (CAP), #34, at 1-2.

[59] FDIC Staff Paper, *supra* note 57, at 25.

[60] CAP, #34, at 2.

[61] FRB 2015 MOBILE SURVEY, *supra* note 1, at 12.

[62] ABA, #45, at 14.

[63] FDIC Staff Paper, *supra* note 57, at 24.

[64] NCLC, #35, at 19; Consumers Union, #30, at 6.

[65] Consumers Union, #30, at 6. The comment refers to time "to clear," but in context, it appears to refer to the time when funds become available to the depositor.

[66] ABA, #45, at 8.

[67] *Id.* at 19.

[68] Mark Budnitz, Georgia State University School of Law (Budnitz) #48, at 1-3.

[69] *Id.*

[70] *Id.*

[71] *Id.*

[72] *Id.*

[73] CBA, #10, at 5; CFSI, #6, at 9.
[74] CBA, #10, at 5.
[75] NCLC, #35, at 23.
[76] CFSI, #6, at 2.
[77] Intuit, #21, at 12. According to a recent posting on Mint.com website, Mint has more than 20 million registered users. http://blog.mint.com/news/the-time-is-now-mint-available-on-apple-watch041515/ accessed online May 27, 2015. The number of active users, however, would presumably be lower.
[78] Appleseed, #41, at 8; PayPal, #29, at 2.
[79] FRB 2015 MOBILE SURVEY, *supra* note 1, at 12.
[80] Javelin, #49, at 7.
[81] CFSI, #6, at 3.
[82] Netspend, #52, at 1-2.
[83] *Id.* at 2.
[84] CFED, #26, at 3-4.
[85] Credit Karma, #32, at 4.
[86] Intuit, #21, at 19, recommended that CFPB consider the opportunities available to consumers through texting because it may "provide real-time information to consumers in a way that they are most likely to read."
[87] PIRG and CDD, #19, at 9-10.
[88] *Id.*
[89] Deloitte, #44, at 19.
[90] One Financial Holdings Group, (One Financial), #33, at 5 (One Financial Holdings Group is a "laboratory for innovation in financial services focusing on the underserved, funded by a consortium of the most prominent early- stage financial services investors in the United States." In its comments, it stated that one provider saw changes within one month of adoption).
[91] Deloitte, #44, at 19.
[92] ASOC, #40, at 7.
[93] *See, e.g.,* CUNA, #24, at 3 (reported that half their credit unions offered SMS/text messaging).
[94] ABA, #45, at 16; American Financial Services Association (AFSA), #18, at 4. On July 1oth, the Federal Communications Commission (FCC) issued a declaratory ruling reaffirming that the TCPA applies to text messages and that consumer consent therefore is generally required. FCC, TCPA Omnibus Declaratory Ruling and Order, FCC 15-72 (July 10, 2015)[hereinafter FCC Declaratory Ruling and Order].
[95] AFSA, #18, at 4.
[96] ABA, #45, at 17. Though smartphones also have texting capability, data plans on smartphones allow consumer and providers to communicate in additional ways.
[97] Deloitte, #44, at 19.
[98] The Electronic Signatures in Global and National Commerce (ESIGN) Act 15 U.S.C. §7001 *et seq* addresses requirements for electronic records and signatures.
[99] NCLC, #35, at 15-18.
[100] CFSI, #6, at 2 (these were "popular financial apps independent of those related to bank and GPR accounts").
[101] *Id.*
[102] *Id.*
[103] *See* Consumers Union, #30, at 2-4; Staff of the Bureau of Consumer Protection, Federal Trade Commission (FTC), #11, at 7-8. FTC cited staff recommendations from its report, FED. TRADE COMM'N, WHAT'S THE DEAL? A FTC STUDY ON MOBILE SHOPPING APP, (Aug. 2014), *available at* http://www ftc.gov/ system/ files/ documents/reports/whats- deal-federal-trade-commission-study-mobile-shoppingapps-august-2014/ 140801 mobileshoppingapps.pdf, including that companies clearly describe how they collect, use and share consumer data so that consumers can make informed choices about the apps they use.
[104] Consumers Union, #30, at 2-4.
[105] NCLC, #35, at 23.
[106] One Financial, #33, at 3, 9.
[107] *See, e.g.,* FRB 2015 MOBILE SURVEY, *supra* note 1, at 12 (Mobile banking users appear to be using mobile applications to conduct their banking transactions, as 71 percent of mobile banking users have installed their bank's application on their phones).
[108] ASOC, #40, at 5; FTC, #11, at 7-8; Privacy Rights Clearinghouse, #31, at 2.
[109] *See generally* Prepaid Accounts Under the Electronic Fund Transfer Act (Regulation E) and the Truth in Lending Act (Regulation Z), 79 Fed. Reg. 77101 (Dec. 23, 2014).
[110] *Id.* Citing to projections by the Mercator Advisory Group, which estimated that the amount loaded onto GPR cards grew from less than $1 billion in 2003 to nearly $65 billion in 2012.
[111] Javelin, #49, at 5. *See also* Association for Neighborhood and Housing Development, Inc. (ANHD), #12, at 3.
[112] Center for Financial Services Innovation (CFSI), 2013 Financially Underserved Market Size 6 (December 2013) available at http:// www.cfsinnovation.com/ CMSPages/ GetFile.aspx?guid=c032e4aa-039b-4723-8f2d-

4fbf7fc0eb19 (CFSI in the market size report defined a GPR card as "An open-loop card which serves as an account where consumers can load, store and spend funds electronically.").

[113] FDIC 2013 SURVEY, *supra* note 42, at 29.

[114] *Id.*

[115] *Id.* at 33.

[116] Javelin, #49, at 6.

[117] *See generally* ELISA TAVILLA, FEDERAL RESERVE BANK OF BOSTON, HOW MOBILE SOLUTIONS HELP BRIDGE THE GAP: MOVING THE UNDERSERVED TO MAINSTREAM FINANCIAL SERVICES (DECEMBER 2013).

[118] Consumers Union, #30, at 4-5.

[119] Network Branded Prepaid Card Association (NBPCA), #13, at 3.

[120] *Id.* Also, the ABA noted that a key feature of their prepaid card, which more than 170 member banks have issued over 200,000, was the ability of users to access account information online via a mobile app. (ABA, #45, at 20-21).

[121] One Financial, #33, at 3-4.

[122] *Id.* at 5.

[123] ABA, #45, at 8 (citing as support Elisa Tavilla, Federal Reserve Bank of Boston, How Mobile Solutions Help Bridge the Gap: Moving the Underserved to Mainstream Financial Services (December 2013)).

[124] *Id.* at 19-20 (More than 170 ABA member banks have issued over 200,000 of the ABA endorsed prepaid cards).

[125] Consumers Union, #30, at 4.

[126] *Id.* at 4-5.

[127] *Id.* at 6-8.

[128] Near field communication (NFC), according to NearFieldCommunication.org, is a technology that allows a device, known as a reader, interrogator, or active device, to create a radio frequency current that communicates with another NFC compatible device or a small NFC tag holding the information the reader wants. Passive devices, such as the NFC tag in smart posters, store information and communicate with the reader but do not actively read other devices. Peer-to-peer communication through two active devices is also a possibility with NFC. This allows both devices to send and receive information. http:// www.nearfieldcommunication.org/ about-nfc.html.

[129] *See* Deloitte, #44, at 15; Gemalto, #37, at 4; Netspend, #52, at 7.

[130] Android Pay and Apple Pay are payment systems provided by Google and Apple that allow users to store various credit and debit card payment and other information, and make payments via their devices.

[131] Appleseed, #41, at 2. (Appleseed is a nonprofit network of 17 public interest justice centers in the United States and Mexico).

[132] Deloitte, #44, at 20.

[133] FRB 2015 MOBILE SURVEY, *supra* note 1, at 14-18.

[134] *Id.* at 15.

[135] *Id.*

[136] FTC, #11, at 5; NCLC, #35, at 7; Consumers Union, #30, at 9-10.

[137] *Id.* at 1, 5-6; ABA, #45, at 22, NCLC, #35, at 7; Budnitz, #48, at 3-4.

[138] From its report from a workshop, FED. TRADE COMMISSION, MOBILE CRAMMING. AN FTC ROUNDTABLE (MAY 2013), the FTC recommended that: (1) mobile carriers give consumers the option to block all third-party charges on their phone accounts; (2) market participants take appropriate action so that advertisements for products or services charged to a mobile bill are not deceptive; (3) market participants obtain consumers' express, informed consent to charges before they are billed to a mobile account, and maintain reliable records of such authorizations; (4) mobile carriers disclose all charges for third-party services clearly and conspicuously to consumers in a non-deceptive manner; and (5) carriers implement an effective dispute resolution process. FTC, #11, at 6.

[139] FTC, #11, at 5. The CFPB, in coordination with state attorneys general and the FCC, filed orders in federal courts against Sprint and Verizon which provide $120 million in redress to wireless customers who were illegally billed hundreds of millions of dollars in unauthorized third-party charges. See http:// www. consumerfinance.gov/newsroom/cfpb-takes-action-to-obtain-120-million-in-redress-from-sprint-and- verizon-for-illegal-mobile-cramming/.

[140] See Business Insider, The Peer-to-Peer Payments Report: The Exploding Market For Smartphone Apps That Transfer Money (August 28, 2014) http://www.businessinsider.com/explosive-growth-in-peer-to-peer-payment- apps-2014-8.

[141] CBA, #10, at 6; Consumers Union, #30, at 10.

[142] Javelin, #49, at 5.

[143] *Id.*

[144] BARBARA BENNETT, DOUGLAS CONOVER, SHAUN OBRIEN, AND ROSS ADVINCULA, FEDERAL RESERVE SYSTEM, CASH PRODUCT OFFICE, CASH CONTINUES TO PLAY A KEY ROLE IN CONSUMER SPENDING: EVIDENCE FROM THE DIARY OF CONSUMER PAYMENT CHOICE 9 (APRIL 2014).

[145] *Id.* at 11.

[146] Javelin, #49, at 6.
[147] *See* Assets and Opportunity Network (AON), # 28, at 5; CFED, #26, at 4; NBPCA, #13, at 6-7; NCLC, #35, at 27; One Financial, #33, at 6.
[148] Intuit, #21, at 1, 12.
[149] *Id.*
[150] NCLC, #35, 27-28.
[151] One Financial, #33, at 6.
[152] *Id.*
[153] ABA, #45, at 4, 10.
[154] *Id.* at 1.
[155] ANHD, #12, at 5.
[156] ABA, #45, at 10 (citing FDIC Staff Paper, *supra* note 57 and FRB 2015 MOBILE FINANCIAL SERVICES, *supra* note 1).
[157] *Id.*
[158] *Id.* at 10.
[159] See discussion later in this section.
[160] See discussion later in this section.
[161] *See* ABA, #45, at 15-16; CBA, #10, at 10; CUNA, #24, at 1-3; Electronic Payments Core of Knowledge (EPCOR), #46, at 1.
[162] See ABA, #45, at 15-16; CBA, #10, at 10; CUNA, #24, at 1-3; EPCOR, #46, at 1.
[163] ABA, #45, at 15 (the comment did not specify whether these costs were per transaction, per account or other basis).
[164] CUNA, #24, at 2.
[165] *Id.*
[166] In the RFI, the Bureau provided an example from the FDIC Staff Paper, *supra* note 57, at 29-30:"One industry estimate cited in the White Paper calculated the average cost of an in-branch transaction was $4.25 whereas the average cost was $0.10 for a mobile transaction." RFI, at 5, *available at* http:// files.consumerfinance.gov/ f/ 201406_cfpb_request-for-information_mobile.pdf.
[167] ABA, #45, at 16.
[168] *Id.* (citing FEDERAL RESERVE SYSTEM, THE 2013 FEDERAL RESERVE PAYMENTS STUDY 19 (DECEMBER 2013)).
[169] CBA, #10, at 10.
[170] One Financial, #33, at 4.
[171] *Id.* As PayPal, #29, at 2 noted, by making MFS faster (citing a study that found that certain types of contactless mobile payments can increase transaction speed by up to 15-30 seconds) it enhances convenience and flexibility, which could be critical for certain types of services, especially in the aggregate.
[172] CFSI, #6, at 6. In its comments, the ABA, #45, at 15, cited an estimate by Celente, a unit of Marsh & McLennan Cos., of $250-$300 per year to maintain a bank account, as reported in the Wall Street Journal, Robin Sidel and Dan Fitzpatrick, "End is Seen to Free Checking" (June 16,2010).
[173] CFSI, #6, at 6.
[174] *Id.* at 6-7.
[175] *Id.*
[176] *Id.* at 6.
[177] *Id.* at 6-7.
[178] *Id.* at 6-7.
[179] *Id.* at 6.
[180] Deloitte, #44, at 8.
[181] *Id.*
[182] EPCOR, #46, at 1.
[183] Id.
[184] Id.
[185] One Financial, #33, at 7.
[186] *Id.*
[187] National Association of Federal Credit Unions (NAFCU), #14, at 4.
[188] RBFCU, #27, at 3.
[189] EPCOR, #46, at 3. *See also* CFSI, #6, at 9 ("The possible proliferation of multiple types of operating systems (beyond Android and iOS currently in use) could also place a burden on providers who will need to customize their apps for each system.").
[190] EPCOR, #46, at 3.
[191] *Id.*
[192] NBPCA, #13, at 9.
[193] Appleseed, #41, at 9; CFSI, #6, at 5, 6; Intuit, #21, at 6, 8, 10; NBPCA, #13, at 2, 9.
[194] CAP, #34, at 1-2. *See also* ABA, #45, at 7-8; CBA, #10, at 5; CFED, #26, at 5.

[195] CAP, #34, at 2; Consumers Union, #30, at 2.
[196] CUNA, #24, at 2; Deloitte, #44 , at 6; Intuit, #21, at 6; RBFCU, #27, at 2-3.
[197] EPCOR, #46, at 1.
[198] NCLC, #35, at 16.
[199] One Financial, #33, at 2.
[200] CAP, #34, at 2, n. 9 (citing Bailey Reutzel, *Prepaid Card Use Shows More Differences from Bank Habits*, AMERICAN BANKER, April 9, 2013, http://www.americanbanker.com/issues/178_68/prepaid-card-use-shows-more- differences-from-bank-habits-1058162-1.html); CBA, #10, at 4.
[201] CBA, #10, at 4; Intuit, #21, at 3-4; One Financial, #33, at 2.
[202] The Commonwealth of Massachusetts Office of the Attorney General (Mass AG), #20, at 6.
[203] CBA, #10, at 5-6; Intuit, #21, at 4; NBPCA, #13, at 2.
[204] Netspend, #52, at 2-3. In its comments, NetSpend stated that it is focused on providing the estimated 68 million underbanked U.S. consumers with innovative and affordable financial products tailored to their unique needs.
[205] *Id.* at 5-6.
[206] Intuit, #21, at 12 (citing a feature of Mint.com that provide information about alternative products).
[207] NCLC, #35, at 22.
[208] AON, #28, at 5.
[209] Intuit, #21, at 14; NBPCA, #13, at 2.
[210] Deloitte, #44, at 6.
[211] *Id.*
[212] ANHD, #12, at 4; Americans for Financial Reform (AFR), #23, at 3; NCLC, #35, at 13-18, 29.
[213] FDIC 2013 SURVEY, *supra* note 42, at 53.
[214] *Id.*
[215] *Id.* at 8.
[216] See discussion later in section 4.
[217] NCLC, #35, at 30.
[218] *Id.* at 28; ASOC, #40, at 8; Javelin, #49, at 6; Mass AG, #20, at 9; One Financial, #33, at 5.
[219] Deloitte, #44, at 21.
[220] *Id.* at 7.
[221] *Id.*
[222] EPCOR, #46, at 2.
[223] Mass AG, #20, at 10; Appleseed, #41, at 6.
[224] ANHD, #12, at 5.
[225] *Id.* at 2; CUNA, #24, at 4-5; ASOC, #40, at 9; Appleseed, #41, at 11.
[226] Appleseed, #41, at 11.
[227] ABA, #45, at 20.
[228] CDCUs, #38, at 2.
[229] *Id.*
[230] See discussion later in this section.
[231] ASOC, #40, at 3,5; Gemalto, #37, at 1; ABA, #45, at 14; EPCOR, #46, at 3 ("Mobile device authentication and consumer authentication measures need to advance to make mobile banking safe").
[232] Budnitz, #48, at 4; One Financial, #33, at 6 ("Consumers are legitimately concerned about identity theft and data breaches, as well as about broader spectrum surveillance").
[233] Mass AG, #20, at 2. The Office reported that from January 1, 2008 through December 31, 2013, it received notice of over 5,330 data breaches, affecting approximately 4.75 million Massachusetts consumers across a multitude of technologies.
[234] ABA, #45, at 14; EPCOR, #46, at 3; Mass AG, #20, at 1.
[235] Gemalto, #37, at 8.
[236] MFY, #17, at 3.
[237] Budnitz, #48, at 5.
[238] See, e.g., Gemalto, #37, at 4.
[239] *Id.*; CFSI, #6, at 8; CBA, #10, at 8: "As many of us can unfortunately attest, the portable nature of mobile phones makes potential loss or theft an unavoidable reality."
[240] Consumers Union, #30, at 13.
[241] *Id.*
[242] *Id.* at 13-14. (Over fifty percent of the robberies committed in San Francisco during a certain period, for example, were of mobile devices; Consumers Union also noted that N.Y. Attorney General has characterized smartphone theft as a "growing public safety problem," citing article Lisa Ward, "NY AG asks smartphone makers to fight theft," Silicon V. Bus. J (May 14, 2013) 2013 WLNR 11882324).
[243] *Id.* According to the FRB 2015 MOBILE SURVEY, the share of smartphone owners who password protect their phone increased to 69 percent in 2014 from 61 percent in 2013.
[244] Consumers Union, #30 at 13.

[245] EPCOR, #46, at 2.
[246] Appleseed, #41, at 7.
[247] *Id.*
[248] See NAFCU, #14, at 2; Gemalto, #37, at 9 (citing to 2013 figures that showed 97 percent of the malware attacks targeted android platforms at http://www.forbes.com/sites/gordonkelly/2014/03/24/report-97-of-mobile-malware-is-on-android-this-is-the-easy-way-you-stay-safe/).
[249] Pew Research Center, *Smartphone Ownership 2013,* http://www.pewinternet.org/2013/06/05/smartphone-ownership-2013/.
[250] Javelin, #49, at 3.
[251] *Id.*
[252] PRC, #31, at 2.
[253] Budnitz, #48, at 6.
[254] *Id.*
[255] *Id.*
[256] One Financial, #33, at 8. The FCC TCPA ruling discussed *supra* at n. 94 above exempted from the TCPA's consent requirements financial institutions sending free-to-end-user messages relating to identity theft, fraud, data security breaches, and arranging for the receipt of pending money transfers, if financial institutions meet various conditions. See FCC Declaratory Ruling and Order, paragraphs 125-139.
[257] *Id.*
[258] MFY Legal, # 17, at 2; NCLC, #35, at 16.
[259] Appleseed, #41, at 8. According to the FRB 2015 MOBILE SURVEY, *supra* note 1, at 18, among those surveyed who do not use mobile payments, 75 percent reported that is easier to pay with other methods.
[260] AFR, #23, at 2; Mass AG, #20 , at 3; Reinvestment Partners, #22, at 3.
[261] Mass AG, #20, at 3.
[262] *See, e.g.,* Intuit, #21, at 15.
[263] PIRG and CDD, #19, at 5, 7; PRC, #31, at 3.
[264] *Available at* http://www.pewinternet.org/2012/09/05/privacy-and-data-management-on-mobile-devices.
[265] Pew Research Center, Mary Madden and Lee Rainie, *Americans' Views About Data Collection and Security* (May 20, 2015) *available at* http://www.pewinternet.org/2015/05/20/americans-views-about-data-collection-and- security/.
[266] *Id.*
[267] *Id.*
[268] FTC, #11, at 7.
[269] AgeCheq, #9, at 1-2; PrivacyCheq, #8, at 1-2.
[270] AgeCheq, #9, at 2.
[271] PRC, #31, at 4.
[272] *Id.*
[273] ABA, # 45, at 16; AFSA, #18, at 2-3; NAFCU, #14, at 3.
[274] CAP, #34, at 3; NCLC, #35, at 5.
[275] PIRG and CDD, #19, at 10 (terms were in quotes in comments).
[276] FTC, #11, at 10. See also FED'L TRADE COMM'N, DATA BROKERS: A CALL FOR TRANSPARENCY AND ACCOUNTABILITY (MAY 2014), *available at* http://www.ftc.gov/system/files/documents/reports/data-brokers-call-transparency- accountability-report-federal-tradecommission- may-2014/140527databrokerreport.pdf cited by the FTC and other commenters, e.g., PRC, #31, at 3.
[277] NCLC, #35, at 11. *See also*, Appleseed, #41, at 16; FTC, #11, at 9-11; #PRC, #31, at 3-4.
[278] NCLC, #35, at 11.
[279] *Id.* n. 21 citing NCLC, "Big Data: A Big Disappointment for Scoring Consumer Credit Risk" (March 2014), available at http://www.nclc.org/issues/big-data.html.
[280] *Id.* at 12. *See also* Mass AG, #20, at 4.
[281] CBA, #10, at 10.
[282] See AFR, #23, at 2; NCLC, #35, at 3-4, 9-11.
[283] NCLC, #35, at 10.
[284] *Id.* For example, it cited the Telemarketing Sales Act (prohibits telemarketers from using pre-acquired account information to charge consumers' credit or debit cards without their express informed consent) and the Restore Online Shoppers Confidence Act (prohibits the initial merchant from disclosing a consumer's billing information to any "post-transaction third-party seller" for purposes of charging the consumer's account).
[285] AFR, #23, at 2.
[286] *Id.*; NCLC, #35, at 1.
[287] PIRG and CDD, #19, at 9.
[288] AFR, #23, at 3; NCLC, #35, at 25; PIRG and CDD, #19, at 6.
[289] PIRG and CDD, #19, at 8; PRC, #31, at 3-4.
[290] *Id.*; Reinvestment Partners, #22, at 2.

[291] See PIRG and CDD, #19, at 5; AFR, #23, at 2.

[292] PIRG and CDD, #19, at 3-4 went on to explain that "[k]ey features of this system include widespread data gathering and analysis; use of real-time location; specialized mobile ad-targeting services that reach a person in real time; formats for ads and commercial content specifically honed for the mobile platform; measurement services that identify how we interact with mobile applications; apps and other specialized applications that make ongoing targeting easier to accomplish; frameworks to utilize mobile and other digital "path-to-purchase" strategies; a focus on multicultural consumers' use of mobile services; and "Big Data"-driven technologies and practices that incorporate consumer mobile data into comprehensive and actionable user profiles."

[293] Reinvestment Partners, #22, at 2.

[294] *Id.* citing Executive Office of the President, Big Data: Seizing Opportunities, Preserving Values Introduction, 65 (May 2014).

[295] *See, e.g.,* AFR #23, at 3; PIRG and CDD, #19, at 8; Reinvestment Partners, #22, at 2-3.

[296] NCLC, #35, at 11-12.

[297] Intuit, #21, at 15.

[298] AFSA, #18, at 5.

[299] Reinvestment Partners, #22, at 2.

[300] Reinvestment Partners, #22, at 2.

[301] *Id.*

[302] ASOC, #40, at 6.

[303] CDCU, #38, at 2.

[304] Appleseed, #41, at 8.

[305] *Id.* at 9; NCLC, #35, at 23.

[306] NCLC, #35, at 23.

[307] *Pew Smartphone Use in 2015, supra* note 1, at 14.

[308] FEDERAL RESERVE BOARD, CONSUMERS AND MOBILE FINANCIAL SERVICES 2013 11 (MARCH 2013).

[309] FRB 2015 MOBILE SURVEY, *supra* note 1, at 13.

[310] ABA, #45, at 18.

[311] *See, e.g.,* ABA #45, at 18; NCLC #35, at 23; One Financial #33, at 9.

[312] One Financial, #33, at 9.

[313] AARP, #51, at 9; PIRG and CDD, #19 at 7.

[314] AARP, #51, at 9.

[315] AFR, #23, at 3; CUNA, #24, at 4; NCLC, #35, at 25-26.

[316] NCLC, #35, at 25-26.

[317] Deloitte, #11, at 13.

[318] Appleseed, #41, at 6-7 (Appleseed noted the remittance disclosure provisions added to the Electronic Funds Transfer Act (EFTA) in the Dodd-Frank financial reform legislation that require that the disclosures be made in English and in each of the foreign languages principally used by the remittance transfer provider, or any of its agents, to advertise, solicit, or market, either orally or in writing, at that office).

[319] *Id.*

[320] *See* ASOC, # 40, at 5; CFSI, #6, at 8; NCLC, #35, at 22.

[321] CUNA, #24, at 4.

[322] *See, e.g.,* CUNA, #24, at 4.

[323] NCLC, #35, at 5.

[324] ABA, #45, at 17.

[325] MFY Legal, #17, at 2; NCLC, #35, at 22; Netspend, #, 52, at 2.

[326] *See generally* NCLC, #35; Consumers Union, #30.

[327] FTC, #11, at, 7.

[328] Budnitz, #48, at 8.

[329] *Id.*

[330] *Id.*

[331] Consumers Union, #30, 9-10; NCLC, #35, at 6-7.

[332] Consumers Union, #30, at 9. *See also* Regulation Z, 12 C.F.R. §1026.12.

[333] Consumers Union, #30, at 9. *See also* Regulation E, 12 C.F.R. § 1005.6.

[334] *See, e.g.,* Consumers Union, #30, at 9; MFY Legal, #17, at 3. The CFPB, in coordination the state attorneys general and the Federal Communications Commission (FCC), took action against Verizon and Sprint alleging that the companies engaged in unfair practices by operating billing systems that allowed third parties to "cram" unauthorized charges on customers' mobile-phone accounts and ignored complaints about the charges. *See supra* note 139.

[335] *See, e.g.,* CAP, #34, at 2; ("the vast majority of branch closures since 2008 have taken place in zip codes with household incomes below the US median"); CFED, #26, at 5-6; One Financial, #33, at 8.

[336] One Financial, #33, at 8.

[337] *Id.*
[338] *See, e.g.,* ANHD, #12, at 1, 4; AFR, #23, 2-3; CFED, #26, at 5-6.
[339] One Financial, #33, at 3.
[340] ASOC, #40, at 6.
[341] Consumers Union, #30, at 12, n.39.
[342] ASOC, #40, at 3.
[343] FDIC Staff Paper, *supra* note 57, at 33.
[344] *See* Consumers Union, # 30, at 2-4; CAP, #34, at 2; NCLC, #35, at 13-14.
[345] *See also*, NCLC, #35, at 13-14 ("All mobile financial services should be required to provide a toll free number to address problems"); CAP, #34, at 2 ("At a minimum, mobile financial services should include free telephone access to customer service").
[346] CAP, #34, at 2.
[347] AARP, #51, at 5-6; NCLC, #35, at 13-18.
[348] NCLC, #35, at 15. *See also* AARP, #51, at 3 (consumers should have ready access to paper statements and terms and conditions at no or low cost for a period of two years).
[349] NCLC, #35, at 15-16.
[350] AFSA, #18, at 2; NBPCA, #13, at 4.
[351] See discussion earlier in Section 3.
[352] See discussion earlier in Section 3.
[353] See discussion earlier in Section 2.
[354] Javelin, #49, at 6.
[355] *See* CFSI, #6, at 4, 10.
[356] FTC, #11, at 1; NCLC, #35, at 1, 6, 22; PIRG and CDD, #19, at 8.
[357] *See* AFR, #23, at 2-3; PIRG and CDD, #19, at 8.
[358] *See, e.g.,* Deloitte, #44, at 15; EPCOR, #46, at 2; Privacy Rights Clearinghouse, #31, at 1-4.
[359] Appleseed, #41, at 7.
[360] *See generally* Gemalto, #37.
[361] *Id.* at 10.
[362] Appleseed, #41, at 4.
[363] Intuit recommended that CFPB consider the opportunities available to consumers through texting because it may "provide real-time information to consumers in a way that they are most likely to read." Intuit, #21, at 19.
[364] ASOC, #40, at 9.
[365] CFSI, #6, at 8. Some comments referred positively to a mobile device feature that allows consumers to remotely delete information and disable applications or the device itself as a way to prevent loss, referred to as "kill switch." Consumers Union, #30, at 13; EPCOR, #46, at 2; Gemalto, #37, at 5. One commenter suggested federal legislation to require devices to have "kill switch" feature built into all mobile devices. Budnitz, #48, at 5.
[366] *See, e.g.,* Merchant Advisory Group, #39, 1-3 (comments suggested an open and competitive process for security standards creation and enforcement and included its support for guiding principles for the creation, maintenance, and enforcement of tokenization security standards);VISA, #25. See also, Dwolla, #36, at 2 provided a description of its tokenization process. Using an API (Application Programming Interface), it stated that its system removes sensitive banking information and: 1) transparently notifies the sender of the additional information and privileges, which may be needed by the third party in order to complete the service or deliver value; 2) requires explicit authorization from the sender to use said information; 3) provides the receiver with a unique "token" that only the authorized receiver can use; and 4) allows the sender or Dwolla to revoke or invalidate the token at any time. Dwolla suggested that its design helps its community reduce its digital "financial fingerprint," offers greater transparency to its users and improves privacy controls.
[367] *See* AgeCheq, #9, at 1 (commented that "Over the past few years, mobile device manufacturers have systematically removed the ability for a device to be uniquely identified through programming means. This change was prompted by privacy concerns, but ironically the removal of device identification has made it impossible for services such as ours who seek to help users understand and manage their personal privacy"); PrivacyCheq, 8, at 2; Intuit, #21, at 15.
[368] Consumers Union, #35, at 4.
[369] MFY Legal, #17, at 3.
[370] *See, e.g.,* Appleseed, #41; ASOC, #40; CDCUs, 38; #Deloitte, #15; Privacy Rights Clearinghouse, #31.
[371] MFY Legal, #17, at 3.
[372] CFSI, #6, at 4.
[373] See discussion earlier in Section 3.
[374] US Chamber, #42, at 12. *See* ABA, #45, at 10; CFED, #26.
[375] See discussion earlier in Sections 3 and 4.
[376] See discussion earlier in Section 2.

In: Mobile Financial Services …
Editor: Oscar Cortez
ISBN: 978-1-63484-551-9

Chapter 2

ASSESSING THE ECONOMIC INCLUSION POTENTIAL OF MOBILE FINANCIAL SERVICES[*]

Susan Burhouse, Matthew Homer, Yazmin Osaki and Michael Bachman

EXECUTIVE SUMMARY

This white paper considers how mobile financial services (MFS) can help increase financial inclusion among the unbanked and underbanked (collectively, "the underserved"). Although banks are rapidly making MFS available to their customers, additional steps could be taken to implement these services in a way that draws underserved consumers more comprehensively into the banking system.

Key Finding: In the short run, MFS is best positioned to have an economic inclusion impact through its ability to meet the day-to-day financial services needs of underbanked consumers as well as consumers at risk of account closure. The anytime, anyplace, and actionable nature of MFS offers the potential to enhance the sustainability of existing relationships between consumers and banks. MFS also has the potential to help the underserved gain access to the banking system and grow their financial capability. However, the technologies to deliver these benefits are less well-established in the marketplace.

There Are Opportunities to Increase the Use of Banking Services by Underserved Populations. The FDIC has found that approximately 17 million U.S. adults live in households without a checking or savings account.[1] An additional 51 million U.S. adults live in households that have a bank account but rely on nonbank providers for some financial services.[2] Consumers who obtain financial services outside the mainstream banking system may not receive the same level of safety and security provided by deposit insurance and

[*] This is an edited, reformatted and augmented version of a white paper, FDIC-021-2014, issued by the Division of Depositor and Consumer Protection, Federal Deposit Insurance Corporation, last revised June 30, 2014.

various federal consumer protections that are guaranteed by law, ensured by supervision, and enforced through a system of ongoing examination.

In order for underserved consumers to choose financial services in the mainstream banking system, banks must offer products or services that those consumers perceive to meet their needs—and those consumers must be aware of the availability of those products or services. Underserved consumers report using alternative financial services, such as nonbank check cashers or money orders, because of their convenience, speed, and price.[3] Meanwhile, banks report a number of factors that can make it difficult to meet the needs of the underserved. According to the FDIC's 2011 Survey of Banks' Efforts to Serve the Unbanked and Underbanked (2011 FDIC Bank Survey), these factors include the regulatory environment, fraud, a lack of consumer understanding about financial products and services, underwriting, and profitability.[4]

Mobile is a Potential Solution to Some of These Challenges. Although MFS is unlikely to meet all of the needs of the underserved or to ease all of the concerns of banks, it has the potential to address many of these challenges . Sixty-eight percent of American adults connect to the Internet via a mobile device.[5] Ninety percent of underbanked adults own a mobile phone (compared to 83 percent of all adults), of which 71 percent are smartphones (compared to the 67 percent of all mobile phone users who use a smartphone).[6] Underbanked mobile phone users are also more likely to use mobile banking (31 percent) than the fully banked (24 percent).[7] Among the unbanked, mobile phone ownership is less widespread, but it is growing. Sixty-eight percent of unbanked adults have access to mobile phones, 49 percent of which are smartphones.[8] Smartphone adoption among unbanked mobile users is rising quickly, however, and is up from 26 percent in 2011.[9] As a result, although MFS is currently more accessible to the underbanked than the unbanked, it is increasingly more accessible among all populations.

As mobile phone adoption is increasing, so too are the financial services available to consumers through a mobile channel. MFS features now exist that enable consumers to meet many day-to-day transaction needs using a mobile phone, including monitoring account balances, paying bills, and depositing checks. In addition, mobile technology enables consumers to conduct these transactions more conveniently and quickly than through other channels. Also, banks' ongoing operational costs associated with MFS are frequently lower than for other channels, and MFS can increase the engagement and longevity of customer relationships and yield more profitable customers.

Considering underserved consumer preferences regarding convenience, speed, and price alongside the anyplace, anytime, and actionable nature of MFS suggests this channel has the potential to help increase economic inclusion among the underserved. To assess this potential, this paper presents an analytical framework that considers the ability of MFS to draw consumers into the banking system, retain them in safe and sustainable account relationships, and foster financial empowerment to deepen banking relationships and fulfill financial goals. Applying this framework of access, sustainability, and growth to the current MFS landscape yields several observations:

> **Access – Drawing consumers into the banking system.** In the short term, MFS on a standalone basis appears to have a limited role in motivating and facilitating unbanked access to the financial mainstream and in improving unbanked consumer perceptions of banks. However, as smartphone usage among the unbanked expands

and mobile account opening becomes more widely available, MFS could a play a larger role in increasing access to the mainstream banking system. This may be particularly the case for consumers whose primary access to the Internet is through a smartphone. To help MFS fulfill its potential, economic inclusion strategies will need to address some of the most significant underlying economic and institutional reasons why unbanked consumers do not have a bank account, such as limited financial resources or insufficient identification. Then, as consumers are ready to enter the financial mainstream, mobile applications (apps) could be useful for enabling easy account opening and verifying a range of acceptable customer forms of identification. Anecdotal evidence suggests that obstacles to mobile account opening are being overcome and that some institutions are finding significant demand for mobile account opening. As it becomes more widely available, institutions may benefit from coupling the functionality of mobile account opening with broader outreach efforts that include partnerships with organizations, such as community groups, that have established relationships with underserved communities and populations.

Sustainability – Retaining consumers in the banking system by sustainably meeting their day-to-day financial services needs. MFS is particularly well-suited to increase the sustainability of banking relationships. Features that could be particularly effective include account balance and transaction history, near real-time alerts, mobile check deposit with quick access to funds, the ability to transfer money to or from a savings account, and payment functions such as bill pay or person-to-person transfers. However, some of these MFS features are not widely available from banks or require adaptation to more directly meet the needs of the underserved. For example, most banks that offer mobile remote deposit capture (mRDC) do not currently offer immediate funds availability, making this functionality less attractive to underbanked consumers that rely on the immediacy offered by check cashers. Similarly, while many banks offer account alerts, until they develop the capability to provide real-time alerts, banks are missing an opportunity to meet consumers' need for accurate and immediate information regarding availability of funds. In addition, certain industry-wide system upgrades, such as a faster payment system, would be particularly beneficial to underserved consumers who live paycheck-to-paycheck and have little time to spare between being paid and needing to pay others. Although significant short-term upfront investment costs are associated with deploying MFS, the transaction costs of serving customers through this channel is likely to decrease over time and may change the economics of serving the underserved. Also, anecdotal evidence suggests mobile banking customers are more engaged with, and less likely to leave, their financial institutions, which could make underserved consumers more attractive bank customers.

Growth – Fostering financial empowerment to deepen banking relationships and fulfill financial goals. It is also important that consumers have the opportunity to advance from basic transactional services into more advanced services and products that can help them meet important milestones, ranging from development of savings reserves to homeownership. MFS tools that help consumers increase their financial engagement and develop deeper banking relationships could help consumers reach such milestones. These tools include personal financial management (PFM) features that enable consumers to set and monitor financial goals and budgets. Through such functionality, consumers have opportunities to improve their financial condition and qualify for additional products. It may be unrealistic to rely *solely* on MFS to facilitate such results, particularly for consumers with less banking experience who may benefit from more personal interaction, such as coaching by a live person. However, as mobile technology advances, it is possible that MFS could play more of a role in this regard, particularly if banks consider incorporating interactive and personalized features such as personalized text, audio, or video chat functionality into their mobile offerings.

Takeaways. MFS is poised to have the largest impact for the underbanked through its ability to meet day-to-day financial services needs. The anytime, anyplace, and actionable nature of MFS offers the potential to enhance the sustainability of banking relationships. However, certain actions could be taken to further fine-tune MFS for economic inclusion and help position it as a mechanism for access and growth, including the following:

- **Integrate MFS into broader economic inclusion strategies.** Successful economic inclusion strategies that incorporate MFS by raising awareness about this service channel and explaining specific functionalities (e.g., alerts or mRDC) that are most relevant and valuable to the underserved may be particularly useful. For example, MFS could be added into existing financial education curricula. Also, the role of a "trusted party" (e.g., bank teller or community-based organization staff) might be particularly helpful when reaching out to unbanked consumers who might need more coaching on how MFS can be used most appropriately to meet specific financial needs.
- **Integrate MFS with other delivery channels and incorporate one-on-one interactions.** Underserved consumers may benefit from one-on-one interactions that provide coaching and guidance on how to properly use banking products. Personal banking relationships can also help consumers learn about mobile tools and deepen their relationship with the bank.
- **Thoughtfully fine-tune risk management strategies associated with features that meet the needs of the underserved.** Uncertainties about new potential risks may discourage banks from providing certain MFS features. As banks and regulators work to apply regulatory requirements in the mobile environment, the responsible use of data, with an eye to minimizing risk and maximizing accessibility of services to underserved consumers, should be part of the ongoing agenda.
- **Address infrastructure challenges to increase the convenience and speed of MFS.** Modernizing bank core processing systems as well as national payment systems would be costly but important steps toward fulfilling the potential of MFS to better meet the financial needs of underserved consumers.
- **Identify opportunities to enable more mobile functionalities.** In most cases, bank customers must be enrolled in their bank's *online* banking service before they can enroll in *mobile* banking. It is also often necessary to set up and manage certain mobile features online rather than through mobile channels. This can include creating

payees for bill pay and enrolling in alerts. These requirements could be obstacles to MFS use for those who rely on a mobile phone to access the Internet.

- **Identify case studies demonstrating profitable implementation of MFS for economic inclusion.** Banks are often challenged by the relatively high costs of some methods of serving the underserved. Efforts to identify and study examples of successful implementation of products for the underserved could help create a more solid business case for MFS as an economic inclusion tool. In addition, financial regulators could evaluate incentives that could encourage banks to offer and demonstrate the benefits of offering specific MFS features that are relevant to underserved consumers.
- **Bridge mobile service delivery with traditional payment methods.** Many underbanked consumers must make certain payments (e.g., rent payments) using paper instruments such as checks or money orders, and some rely on cash exclusively for most or all of their payment needs. MFS is likely to be a more useful financial tool for the underserved if ways can be found to reconcile and meet the underserveds' needs for electronic transactions with their need for paper payments or cash.

These takeaways are intended to inspire action and discourse, and to serve as guideposts for those designing and deploying MFS as well as for economic inclusion advocates and government stakeholders. As banks implement MFS for their customers generally, they may benefit from considering the preferences of the underserved. In many instances, features that specifically benefit the underserved will also benefit a bank's other customers. Utilizing MFS as a tool of economic inclusion for the underserved does not necessarily require any unique products or services intended for that population alone. Rather, the needs of the underserved can be met as a part of an integrated approach that considers their needs alongside those of all customers. However, additional steps may be needed to connect some segments of the underserved population with mobile banking. Incorporating economic inclusion considerations into MFS features and driving consumer adoption is likely to often require the involvement of many stakeholders, including third-party vendors, community and consumer organizations, and financial regulators, among others.

INTRODUCTION

Mobile devices such as smartphones have the potential to change the way consumers interact with banks. Providing financial services through these devices constitutes a next step in a longer-term and broader trend toward electronic banking, following the widespread adoption of online banking. Mobile financial services (MFS) is not a product in itself, but rather a mode of accessing financial services. Although the rise in MFS usage confirms that many consumers value the features offered through this technology, it is unclear what the implications of MFS are for the millions of people who are unbanked or underbanked. Could this technology help draw them more comprehensively into the mainstream banking system and improve their financial stability? This white paper considers that question.

First, this paper describes the contours of the economic inclusion challenge presented by the unbanked and underbanked, from both the consumer and industry perspectives, and presents a framework for evaluating the economic inclusion potential of a financial product or service. Second, the paper considers the potential benefits of MFS to the underserved and identifies key statistics related to underserved adoption of the technology. Third, it evaluates the economic inclusion potential of MFS using the established framework. Finally, based on that evaluation, the paper discusses opportunities to leverage MFS as a tool for economic inclusion. Throughout this analysis, the paper also identifies research needs and policy questions that could help guide future economic inclusion work on MFS.

I. Economic Inclusion Challenge of the Unbanked and Underbanked

Overcoming economic inclusion challenges is critical to expanding the number of individuals who meet their financial needs safely and securely within the mainstream banking system. Meeting these challenges helps the FDIC in its mandate to maintain public confidence in the nation's fi nancial system, which is enhanced when more consumers gain access to the system; find that banks help meet their basic financial needs through relevant and safe products; and develop deeper banking relationships that enable them to meet financial goals.

The mainstream banking system affords consumers many important benefits. When consumers enter and build direct relationships with federally insured depository institutions, they receive consumer protections and wealth-building opportunities that nonbanks generally do not provide. Consumers in the banking system have a level of safety and security provided by deposit insurance and various federal consumer protections that are guaranteed by law, ensured by supervision, and enforced through ongoing examination. These include disclosures, requirements related to terms and conditions of product offerings, and protection from unfair or deceptive practices and discrimination. In addition, participation in mainstream financial markets improves a consumer's ability to access a range of financial products and services, develop wealth, build a credit history, and access credit products.

Nevertheless, many people do not experience these benefits because they are unbanked or underbanked.[10] Indeed, more than 8 percent of U.S. households do not have any relationship with the banking system.[11] About half of these households had a bank account in the past, implying that the banking relationship was not successfully sustained. In addition, many households— one in five—are underbanked, meaning they have a bank account but also meet some of their fi nancial services needs outside of the mainstream banking system by using alternative financial services (AFS). Altogether, an estimated 68 million adults live in underserved households.

BOX 1
WHO ARE THE UNBANKED?

Unbanked households are those that do not have an account in a federally insured depository institution. Close to 10 million households (8.2 percent) are unbanked.

Certain minority groups, such as blacks and Hispanics, are disproportionately overrepresented among unbanked households. Unbanked households tend to be younger, less educated, and have lower incomes than the U.S. population on average. Almost two out of five unbanked householders are under age 35, three out of four have a high school degree or less, and 82 percent earn less than $30,000 a year. Foreign-born consumers, particularly those that are not U.S. citizens, are also overrepresented among the unbanked (17 percent of the unbanked).

Over half of these households have never had a bank account (53.4 percent). Unbanked households conduct many of their transactions using alternative financial services (AFS) providers. Indeed, 64.9 percent used an AFS in the last 12 months and almost half (45 percent) used an AFS in the past 30 days. Transaction AFS, such as nonbank check cashing, remittances, and money orders, are more commonly used than credit AFS, including pawn shops and rent-to-own stores; 62.1 percent of unbanked households used transaction AFS in the past year, compared to 16.8 percent who used credit AFS. More than one-third of unbanked households have used two or more AFS products in the past 12 months.

Notably, 29 percent of unbanked households do not use any of the AFS products mentioned above, implying that they rely predominantly on cash transactions. Nearly 18 percent (17.8 percent) of unbanked households said they used a prepaid card in the past.

BOX 2
WHO ARE THE UNDERBANKED?

Underbanked households have an account with a federally insured depository institution but *also* use AFS to conduct transaction or credit services. Over 24 million households (20.1 percent) are underbanked. Almost all of these households have a checking account (93.9 percent), and more than two thirds (67.8 percent) have a savings account.

Similar to unbanked consumers, minorities such as blacks and Hispanics are overrepresented in this population. The educational attainment and income levels of underbanked consumers are generally higher than those of unbanked consumers, but lower than those of the fully banked. On average, these householders are older than the unbanked but younger than the fully banked.

By definition, all underbanked households have used an AFS in the last 12 months: 71.2 percent used nonbank money orders, 22.8 percent used check cashing, and 14.4 percent used nonbank remittances. Two-fifths of these households used an AFS in the last 30 days despite having a bank account.

Also, 17.4 percent of underbanked households have used prepaid cards in the past.

A. Framework for Evaluating Economic Inclusion

This paper frames economic inclusion through the lenses of access, sustainability, and growth. Challenges to economic inclusion require not only facilitating and encouraging access to bring unbanked consumers into the financial mainstream, but also engaging them appropriately with relevant and safe products that are sustainable for both consumers and banks. In addition, household financial stability may best be obtained when a full range of bank customers have substantive opportunities and the capability to grow their banking relationships in pursuit of their evolving financial goals. These challenges to achieving economic inclusion are summarized in Box 3, and this paper evaluates the potential of MFS to address each.

BOX 3

ECONOMIC INCLUSION FRAMEWORK AND EVALUATION QUESTIONS FOR ASSESSING THE ECONOMIC INCLUSION POTENTIAL OF FINANCIAL SERVICES OR PRODUCTS

a. Access *– Drawing consumers into the banking system.*

Does the service or product help unbanked consumers connect with banks? Does it make it easier, more convenient, or more appealing for unbanked consumers to open bank accounts? For instance, does it make the onboarding process easier or more efficient?

b. Sustainability *– Keeping consumers in the banking system.*

Does the service or product improve the sustainability of banking relationships with underbanked consumers? Does it facilitate underbanked access to safe, transparent, and affordable services that are feasible for financial institutions? Is account longevity improved? Are consumers' day-to-day financial needs met? Are consumers able to easily and conveniently manage their accounts?

c. Growth *– Fostering financial empowerment to deepen banking relationships and fulfill financial goals.*

Does the service or product create opportunities for consumer banking relationships to evolve? Are consumers able to graduate from basic, entry-level accounts to a wider variety of banking products that help them meet key financial goals or milestones (e.g., build wealth or obtain credit)? Can banks better manage consumer relationships?

Obstacles to access, sustainability, and growth exist from both the perspective of the banking industry and consumers. To assess how MFS can affect economic inclusion along these dimensions, it is important to understand why consumers do not engage, or only partially engage, in the financial mainstream and their preferences regarding service providers. It is also important to understand the challenges that financial institutions face when serving these consumers.

B. Challenges from the Underserved Consumer Perspective

Many households cycle in and out of the banking system. Having a bank account does not guarantee a sustainable relationship. For example, more than half of unbanked households in the United States were previously banked, and almost half of these households (48 percent) report being likely to open an account in the future.[12]

Many unbanked consumers do not access the banking system because of institutional constraints or because they affirmatively choose not to. The 2011 FDIC National Survey of Unbanked and Underbanked Households (FDIC household survey) finds that the largest share of unbanked households report not having an account primarily because they feel they lack sufficient funds (32.8 percent of unbanked households) or because they "do not need or want an account" (26 percent). Fewer than 10 percent of unbanked individuals report identification requirements, credit issues, or banking history issues as a primary obstacle to opening an account, although this was more of a concern among Hispanic households (15 percent).

Other studies suggest that the method by which consumers earn their income or make payments also influences their banking status. A Pew Charitable Trust study (2011) of low-income Los Angeles residents found a strong correlation between bank account ownership and noncash payments (e.g., direct deposit or check) from employers. [13] Barr (2008) found that "only 38 percent of unbanked renters stated that their landlords would accept personal checks for payment of rent, while nearly two-thirds of banked renters stated that their landlords would accept personal checks."[14]

The 2011 FDIC household survey found that less than 2 percent of unbanked households cite inconvenient hours and locations as the main reasons they do not have an account. However, other studies that ask consumers about important considerations in deciding whether or where to open an account or conduct financial transactions find convenience to be an important consideration. For example, according to the Pew study of low-income Los Angeles residents, geographic proximity to home or work was the main reason for selecting a financial service provider (bank or nonbank).[15] The study states that "The vast majority (85 percent) of unbanked AFS users will patronize a provider because it is nearby." Similarly, a Detroit metro area survey (Blank and Barr 2009) asked unbanked consumers which bank account features would make them most likely to open an account. The authors reported that "for 29 percent of the sample, lower fees were perceived as the primary facilitator to opening an account, while 20 percent considered more convenient bank hours and locations as being the most important reason why they might open an account."[16]

The importance of convenient hours and location, as well as price, are also evident when examining the use of nonbank transaction services among both unbanked and underbanked consumers. The FDIC (2011) reports that underserved consumers cite convenience, speed, and price as the main reasons they use nonbank transaction services. For banked consumers that use AFS, the Pew study further reports that hours of operation affect the choice of financial service provider, as 40 percent of these respondents were "very likely" to switch to a financial institution that was open in the evenings or on Sundays. This demonstrates the importance of convenience to both attract and sustain financial relationships with underserved consumers.

Other reports highlight the importance of transparency and predictability of financial services to the underserved. Clear communication of fees and terms, including processing timeframes and confirmation that a transaction has been successfully processed, are valuable to underserved consumers. In its study of low-income families in Los Angeles, the Pew Charitable Trust found that many banked families that use AFS "continue to use check cashers and other nonbank financial services because of concerns over transparency and liquidity."[17] Transparency and predictability of services and fees are important to all consumers but even more so for underserved consumers who often cannot afford unexpected financial transaction delays or fees. A payment or deposit that is not completed timely or successfully could result in a serious penalty, such as phone or electrical service being shut off.

In some cases, underserved consumers that have credit needs rely on alternatives such as payday lenders or pawn shop loans. The main reason these consumers report using credit AFS instead of a bank loan is that it is "easier or faster to qualify" for an AFS loan or because they perceive that "banks do not make small dollar loans" (FDIC 2011). Having a banking relationship could help some of these consumers learn about available credit alternatives or build credit histories to qualify for a loan.

C. Challenges from the Financial Institution Perspective

From the perspective of financial institutions, a number of challenges may impede their ability to serve underserved consumers. According to the 2011 FDIC Survey of Banks' Efforts to Serve the Unbanked and Underbanked, financial institutions view the regulatory environment, fraud, consumers' lack of understanding about financial products and services, underwriting concerns, and lack of profitability as major obstacles to serving unbanked and underbanked consumers (see appendix table 4).[18]

More than one-third of banks cited the regulatory environment as a major obstacle to serving underserved consumers. Among these institutions, 40 percent cited "customer identification-related requirements", while 35 percent mentioned "Bank Secrecy Act (BSA)/Anti-Money Laundering" requirements and "Fair Lending/Compliance" risk. About 30 percent of institutions cited fraud concerns, lack of understanding of financial products and services on the part of underserved consumers, and difficulties with underwriting for unbanked and underbanked populations. One in five institutions mentioned profitability as a major obstacle.

Some policies banks have implemented to mitigate risk can also impede their ability to meet the financial needs of underserved consumers, particularly the unbanked. For example, credit checks that are part of the account opening process may disqualify consumers with negative credit histories—or limited or no credit histories ("thin files")—from opening an account. Also, holding funds from deposited checks for a period of time before clearing to mitigate fraud risk can result in challenges for consumers who need more immediate access to funds. Profitability concerns can also deter financial institutions from marketing to underserved populations, offering accounts with certain features attractive to the underserved (e.g., low cost, low balance requirements), or engaging in more resource-intensive account opening processes for consumers who lack traditional forms of identification (ID) or credit scores.

As previously mentioned, underserved consumers commonly cycle in and out of the banking system. Retaining and deepening banking relationships with these consumers is a challenge for many financial institutions. However, further engaging consumers with appropriate banking products can be difficult. Effective product marketing is also reported as a common challenge. Lack of awareness can lead to low take-up rates and the institution's inability to maintain the product offering. In addition to not knowing about available products, financial institutions also reported that underserved consumers lack a full understanding of products and services, which is commonly a major obstacle to serving them.

These findings are consistent with prior FDIC studies in which banks participated in pilot programs to offer low-cost accounts. Banks in the FDIC's Safe Accounts Pilot, for example, noted challenges with traditional marketing and outreach strategies, in part because of resource constraints. In addition, some banks found it difficult to reach the intended population without being so broad as to lower overall applicant quality. The pilot banks noted that using front-line staff, tellers, or customer service agents to provide information and education about the accounts was a more effective strategy.[19] These findings suggest that increasing the financial education of underserved consumers, as well as increasing their awareness of available banking product options, are important steps to growing the financial health of these consumers.

II. MFS: A Way to Meet the Challenge?

The development of new products, services, and technologies sometimes presents an opportunity to meet economic inclusion challenges in new or more effective ways. One such emerging technology is MFS. Broadly defined, MFS is a set of technologies enabling consumers to access and use financial services from virtually any location using communication-enabled mobile devices such as mobile phones, smartphones, and tablets that have the capacity to access the Internet, send and receive text messages, and run programs or apps specifically developed for the device size and format. As stated earlier, MFS is not a product itself but a means for accessing financial services. These services can include basic transactions such as monitoring account balances, as well as more advanced services such as depositing checks, receiving text or push alerts, and making payments.

In practice, MFS can refer to both bank-provided and nonbank-provided financial services, such as mobile wallets and other mobile payments services, and third-party mobile financial management apps. For purposes of this paper, however, the focus is generally on bank-provided MFS, of which the most common form is mobile banking. While the provision and use of nonbank MFS is an important trend that merits continued study and monitoring, the FDIC's primary interest as insurer of the nation's deposits in insured depository institutions is to understand the opportunities for maximum inclusion in the mainstream banking system, as the inclusiveness of that system is a core element underlying public confidence in it.

The availability of MFS among financial institutions is growing rapidly, and for some financial institutions, it has become one the fastest-growing channels. As of 2013, all of the 26 largest institutions offer key MFS features, such as the ability to view recent transactions, check balances, use bill pay, and transfer funds between accounts intra-bank. Banks are also increasingly offering more advanced features, such as mobile remote deposit capture (77 percent in 2013 vs. 48 percent in 2012), personal financial management (31 percent in 2013 vs. 24 percent in 2012), near-real-time alerts (69 percent in 2013 vs. 44 percent in 2012), and two-way alerts (19 percent in 2013 vs. 8 percent in 2012).[20]

As more financial institutions implement MFS, consumers are also increasingly turning to that channel to conduct their banking. Federal Reserve surveys indicate that in 2013 nearly 33 percent of mobile phone users reported using mobile banking in the past 12 months, up from 28 percent the prior year. Among smartphone owners, 51 percent reported using mobile banking in the past 12 months, compared to 48 percent of smartphone owners in 2012.[21]

A. Potential Benefits of MFS for the Underserved: Anyplace, Anytime, Actionable

MFS can provide the ability to conduct banking transactions or make financial decisions anyplace and anytime. These MFS functionalities could help address some of the factors that have prompted underserved consumers to leave the banking system altogether or seek financial services outside the banking system.

MFS has several strengths relative to other modes of accessing financial services (e.g., in a branch, at an automated teller machine (ATM), or through a personal computer) that can potentially increase convenience and help improve the way consumers interact with banks. First, MFS allows consumers to access account information from virtually any location. Second, consumers can do so at any hour of the day. And third, MFS provides consumers the ability to act on this information conveniently to conduct timely financial transactions that can help them avoid problems such as overdrafts, fraud, and late fees. While many of these features are standard components of online phone-based banking, MFS technology also often incorporates features that are distinct from those available through other channels. For example, smartphone cameras provide the potential to deposit a check remotely through mobile remote deposit capture (mRDC), and location-based services can show consumers, using a map on their smartphone, where nearby ATMs or branches are located.

Although these functionalities may appeal broadly to any type of consumer, they could particularly affect the underserved because they may address some of the factors that have prompted those consumers to look outside of the banking system for financial services. Survey results have shown that the underserved most often turn to nonbank financial providers for transaction services because they view those providers as more convenient than banks. MFS presents an opportunity for banks to provide desired services more conveniently. Depositing a check using mRDC, for instance, can be conducted through a mobile device at virtually any time or location. Further, for underserved consumers without home Internet access, MFS may be the only way they can access electronic banking. According to a 2013 Pew study, 45 percent of adults with incomes below $30,000 use mostly their phone to access the Internet compared to about a third (34 percent) of all adults.[22] For such consumers, online banking might not be a convenient option. In fact, the 2013 FDIC household survey reveals that, relative to fully banked households, the underbanked are less likely to use online banking as their main method to access their account (26 percent vs 35 percent) and more likely to use mobile banking (9.4 percent) than the fully banked (4.7 percent).[23]

B. Adoption of Mobile Phones and MFS

> One element that supports the promise of MFS as an economic inclusion tool is the widespread adoption of mobile phones and MFS activity among underserved populations, particularly the underbanked. Relative to other consumers, including fully banked households, large proportions of the underbanked use mobile banking. For unbanked consumers, access to mobile phones is also common; while access to smartphones is limited, it is likely to increase over time.[24]

The potential benefits of MFS can be realized only if underserved consumers have access to the necessary technology. Mobile phone adoption is widespread among U.S. households overall, with 83 percent owning a mobile phone as of June 2013.[25] Over half (56 percent) of mobile phone users have smartphones.[26] Not surprisingly, data suggest that smartphone ownership is an important driver in the adoption of MFS. While some MFS functions, such as SMS text banking, can be completed using any kind of mobile phone, more advanced features, such as mRDC and push alerts via mobile apps, require smartphones. Mobile banking usage among banked smartphone owners (36 percent) is considerably higher than among the broader group of banked mobile phone users (25 percent)[27] (see Table 1). Even among consumers who currently do not use mobile banking, those who own a smartphone report being "more likely to adopt mobile banking [in the next 12 months] than non-smartphone users."[28] Among the consumers who indicated in 2012 that that they would "definitely" or "probably" adopt mobile banking in the next 12 months, 37 percent ultimately did adopt mobile banking in 2013. Further, of the respondents who in 2012 indicated that they "probably will not" and "definitely will not" use mobile banking in the next 12 months, 19 percent and 5 percent, respectively, used mobile banking in 2013.[29]

The underbanked own mobile phones and use MFS at relatively high rates. The 2013 FDIC Survey of Unbanked and Underbanked Households finds that 90 percent of underbanked householders own a mobile phone, of which 71 percent are smartphones.[30] The survey also highlights the fact that underbanked mobile phone users use mobile banking at higher rates than the fully banked; 31 percent versus 24 percent of these populations, respectively, have used mobile banking.[31]

However, unbanked households' access to mobile phones is more limited, and they use MFS at lower rates compared to the underbanked. About 68 percent of unbanked households have access to mobile phones, 49 percent of which are smartphones.[32] Evidence also exists, however, that smartphone adoption among unbanked mobile users is consistently rising over time.[33] In general, the unbanked are much less likely to use MFS than households with a bank account. The Federal Reserve reported that in 2011, relatively small portions of the unbanked population had experience with mobile banking (10 percent) and mobile payments (12 percent) in the 12 months prior to the survey.[34]

Smartphone and MFS adoption rates are higher among younger, minority, or higher-income households. This pattern could help explain why MFS adoption rates are particularly high among underbanked consumers but low among the unbanked. As previously mentioned, although unbanked consumers tend to be younger or minorities, they have lower incomes, on average, relative to the underbanked.

Table 1. 2013 Access to Mobile Phones and Smartphones, and Use of Mobile Banking for Select Demographic Groups (Percent of Households)

	Access to Mobile Phones	**Access to Smartphones**		**Use of Mobile Banking in the Last 12 Months by Banked Households**	
Demographic Group	**Among all households**	**Among all households**	**Among mobile phone users**	**Among mobile phone users**	**Among smartphone users**
All Households	82.6	55.6	67.2	25.4	35.6
BANKING STATUS					
Unbanked	68.1	33.1	48.6	NA	NA
Underbanked	90.4	64.3	71.1	31.0	41.8
Fully Banked	86.8	58.9	67.8	23.9	33.9
RACE OR ETHNICITY					
Black	79.1	52.3	66.2	25.1	34.3
Hispanic	79.9	55.5	69.5	26.8	35.7

Table 1. (Continued)

Demographic Group	Access to Mobile Phones	Access to Smartphones		Use of Mobile Banking in the Last 12 Months by Banked Households	
	Among all households	Among all households	Among mobile phone users	Among mobile phone users	Among smartphone users
Non-Hispanic Whites	83.6	55.5	66.4	24.8	35.6
Other	85.0	63.5	74.7	29.7	37.3
NATIVITY					
Native-born	83.1	55.5	66.8	25.4	35.9
Foreign-born citizens	80.8	57.4	71.0	23.9	32.3
Foreign-born non citizens	79.2	54.3	68.5	26.7	34.7
AGE					
Age 24 or younger	88.8	76.0	85.5	46.0	49.7
Age 25-34	89.8	76.3	85.0	44.4	49.1
Age 35-44	89.0	72.0	80.9	35.0	40.6
Age 45-54	86.6	62.8	72.6	24.0	31.1
Age 55-64	83.5	48.7	58.3	15.1	23.7
Age 65 or older	67.3	23.2	34.5	6.2	15.6
EDUCATIONAL ATTAINMENT					
Less than high school	67.0	30.0	44.8	10.7	21.9
High school	78.2	44.2	56.5	16.9	28.0
Some college	85.3	59.2	69.4	26.9	36.6
Bachelors degree	89.4	70.8	79.1	32.7	40.1
INCOME					
Less than $15,000	69.2	31.2	45.1	14.3	27.6
Between $15K and $30K	74.4	37.9	50.9	17.1	31.7
Between $30K and $50K	82.2	50.9	61.9	22.0	33.8
Between $50K and $75K	88.3	63.2	71.6	26.1	34.6
$75,000 or more	91.6	77.7	84.9	33.9	39.1

Notes:

Households are identified as unbanked if they answered "no" to the question, "Do you or does anyone in your household currently have a checking or savings account?"

Underbanked households are defined as those households that have a checking and/or a savings account and had used nonbank money orders, nonbank check cashing services, nonbank remittances, payday loans, rent-to-own services, pawn shops, or refund anticipation loans (RALs), or auto title loans in the past 12 months.

The demographic characteristics of a household, such as race, age, and education are taken to be those of the owner or renter of the home (i.e., "householder"), unless the characteristic is one defined at the household level, such as income.

Differences within groups may or may not be statistically significant.

Source: 2013 FDIC National Survey of Unbanked and Underbanked Households

BOX 4
HOUSEHOLDS' USE OF MOBILE BANKING AND OTHER BANKING CHANNELS

Table 2. Banking Methods Used in the Last 12 Months (Percent of Households)

Banking Channel	Underbanked Households			Fully Banked Households		
	Used this channel	Used this channel as their most common banking method	Share of users that use it as their most common banking method	Used this channel	Used this channel as their most common banking method	Share of users that use it as their most common banking method
Bank Teller	79.3	29.2	36.8	78.8	33.1	41.9
ATM/Kiosk	76.3	29.6	38.8	67.9	23.0	33.8
Telephone Banking	32.7	4.6	14.1	24.3	3.0	12.2
Online Banking	52.4	26.4	50.4	56.1	35.0	62.3
Mobile Banking	29.0	9.4	32.4	21.6	4.7	21.5
Other	0.7	0.5	68.1	1.1	0.8	76.1
Unknown	NA	0.4	NA	NA	0.5	NA

Notes:

Underbanked households are defined as those households that have a checking and/or a savings account and had used nonbank money orders, nonbank check cashing services, nonbank remittances, payday loans, rent-to-own services, pawn shops, or refund anticipation loans (RALs), or auto title loans in the past 12 months.

Differences were not tested for statistical significance.

Source: 2013 FDIC National Survey of Unbanked and Underbanked Households

Data from the 2013 FDIC National Survey of Unbanked and Underbanked Households suggest that underbanked households are heavier mobile banking users than fully banked households. Specifically, the survey results show that a higher proportion of underbanked households have accessed their account via mobile banking compared to fully banked households, and that a higher proportion of underbanked households use mobile banking as their most common banking channel, compared to fully banked households.

Among households that have accessed their bank account in the past 12 months, 29.0 percent of underbanked households have accessed their account via mobile banking, compared to 21.6 percent of fully banked households. Also, among those households that have used mobile banking to access their bank account, nearly one-third (32.4 percent) of underbanked households identified mobile banking as their most commonly used banking channel, compared to 21.5 percent of fully banked households. Overall, 9.4 percent of all underbanked households and 4.7 percent of all fully banked households use mobile banking as their primary banking method.

Table 3. Banking Methods Used by Mobile Bankers in the Last 12 Months (Percent of Households)

	Underbanked Households		**Fully Banked Households**	
Banking Channel	**Used this channel**	**Used this channel as their most common banking method**	**Used this channel**	**Used this channel as their most common banking method**
Bank Teller	82.8	7.7	80.8	7.4
ATM/Kiosk	93.0	18.4	91.0	14.2
Telephone Banking	51.7	3.1	45.1	2.0
Online Banking	87.9	37.9	92.0	54.2
Mobile Banking	100.0	32.4	100.0	21.5
Other	0.3	0.0	0.5	0.1
Unknown	NA	0.6	NA	1.6

Notes:

Underbanked households are defined as those households that have a checking and/or a savings account and had used nonbank money orders, nonbank check cashing services, nonbank remittances, payday loans, rent-to-own services, pawn shops, or refund anticipation loans (RALs), or auto title loans in the past 12 months.

Differences were not tested for statistical significance.

Source: 2013 FDIC National Survey of Unbanked and Underbanked Households

Many mobile bankers also access their accounts through different channels. A large majority of households, both underbanked and fully banked, that used mobile banking in the past 12 months also accessed their account through bank tellers, ATM/kiosks, and/or online banking. However, the primary bank method used by underbanked and fully banked mobile bankers differed. Underbanked consumers were more likely than the fully banked to use mobile banking as the primary method for accessing their bank account, while the fully banked were more likely to use online banking primarily.

These data suggest that consumers are using mobile banking to complement other banking channels instead of using it as a replacement for other banking methods, implying that for many consumers mobile may not yet function as a standalone banking product. Underbanked households that want or need to use mobile banking as their primary banking method could benefit as mobile banking offerings evolve and incorporate even more features and functionalities.

III. Evaluating the Economic Inclusion Potential of MFS Considering Access, Sustainability, and Growth

The central purpose of this paper is to understand the economic inclusion potential of MFS. This section evaluates MFS against our established framework of access, sustainability, and growth. Through that lens, we assess the potential of MFS to facilitate the entrance of unbanked consumers into the banking system (access), support sustainable banking relationships between unbanked and underbanked consumers and banks (sustainability), and create opportunities to deepen those relationships by increasing financial capability and more fully integrating the underserved into the banking system (growth). We also consider some of the challenges that may exist to implementing MFS in ways that facilitate economic inclusion and opportunities for overcoming those challenges.

A. Access – Drawing Unbanked Consumers into the Banking System

Although smartphone penetration is limited among unbanked consumers, certain segments of this population are familiar with mobile technologies and report being open to using mobile banking. However, mobile functionalities that could facilitate account opening are still not widely available, in part due to technical and regulatory compliance hurdles. Even when smartphone penetration increases and more relevant mobile functionalities become available, MFS alone is unlikely to address the underlying reasons why consumers do not have bank accounts. Thus, it is likely that MFS will be a more effective tool for bringing unbanked consumers into the banking system if used as part of a more comprehensive outreach strategy that addresses a broader set of unbanked issues and concerns, and also includes a "trusted party" that introduces consumers to MFS. Collaborations with community groups could be one useful approach.

A.1. Unbanked Demand for Joining the Banking System

In examining whether unbanked households are likely to find MFS appealing and a motivation for joining the banking system, it is helpful to examine whether these consumers would be comfortable using MFS and, if so, whether this technology can help address the reasons they do not have a banking relationship.

Survey data indicate that segments of unbanked households appear to be comfortable with MFS technology and open to using MFS. For example, even though the use of smartphones among unbanked households is substantially lower than for banked consumers, it is still sizable at 33 percent.[35] Even though relatively small proportions of these consumers have had experience with MFS (10 percent had used mobile banking and 12 percent had used mobile payments),[36] a much larger share reported being likely to use it in the future. Specifically, Federal Reserve data suggest unbanked consumers might be more open to adopting mobile banking than fully banked consumers. About one in five (19 percent) unbanked households with mobile phones reported being likely to use mobile banking in the next 12 months compared to 9 percent of fully banked households.[37]

As access to smartphones becomes more prevalent, it is likely that more unbanked consumers will become familiar with mobile technology. However, increased familiarity with mobile technology in general does not necessarily imply increased comfort with conducting financial transactions using mobile. A number of obstacles prevent unbanked households with mobile phones from conducting banking or payments using their phones. Not surprisingly, the number one reason why unbanked mobile phone users report not using mobile banking is simply because they do not have a bank account (50.4 percent). The other top reasons are security concerns (25.2 percent) and a lack of trust in the technology (20.7 percent). Security is also a main reason why unbanked mobile phone users choose not to use mobile *payments* specifically, cited by 36.2 percent of unbanked mobile users. Lack of trust in the technology (31 percent) and not having the necessary features on the phone (29.4 percent) were the next most common reasons why unbanked mobile users do not use mobile payments.

Despite concerns about security and technology, other findings imply that the unbanked may be particularly open to using mobile technology to perform financial transactions. The Federal Reserve's 2012 mobile financial services report shows that the "unbanked were the least likely to indicate that they did not see any benefit from using mobile payments, with 15 percent citing this as a reason they do not use mobile payments, relative to 30 percent of the underbanked and 40 percent of the fully banked." This may indicate that the unbanked, even more than other groups, see value in the mobile delivery channel.

Although some of the technological obstacles preventing unbanked consumers from using MFS (e.g., not having the necessary functionalities on the phone) are likely to subside over time, other fundamental obstacles that prevent the unbanked from having an account are not directly affected by MFS. MFS is unlikely to address the top reasons consumers cite for not having a bank account, such as that they "do not have enough money to put in an account" (32.7 percent of unbanked households). In addition, it is unclear how MFS could affect unbanked households who report not needing or desiring an account (21 percent).[38] Other issues such as ID, credit, or banking history problems are also likely to continue to be obstacles. MFS could make banking more appealing for households whose primary reason for not having an account is inconvenient bank hours or location; however, current data show that this segment represents a small percentage of the unbanked population.

Demand by the unbanked for mobile banking also depends on the type of functionalities that are available and the ability of the financial products to meet the needs of the unbanked. For example, 22.8 percent of unbanked households used nonbank check cashing in the past year. For these consumers, having the ability to access deposited funds immediately is likely to be a priority. On the other hand, close to one-third (29 percent) of unbanked households do not use AFS and are likely to rely on cash transactions. It is not clear that unbanked consumers would be well-served by the array of MFS features currently available, so more research is needed to evaluate how these consumers would perceive the usefulness of MFS.

A.2. Account Opening

Another approach to expanding access to banking services for unbanked consumers is by leveraging mobile technology to improve or ease the account opening process. Opening an account with a mobile phone could be particularly helpful for those consumers whose only access to the Internet is through a smartphone. According to the 2011 FDIC Household survey, 81 percent of unbanked households earn less than $30,000 in annual income. Pew estimates that a substantial proportion of consumers in this income bracket (45 percent) who use their mobile phone to access the Internet do so as their primary way of accessing the Internet.[39] The use of mobile technology in account opening is still in the early stages of development and is not widely available at this time, although some banks have implemented this capability or are considering doing so. According to a Javelin survey, just 3 percent of surveyed consumers applied for a checking account with a mobile device in 2012.[40] Some banks that have deployed mobile account opening or are seriously considering it recognize that many consumers use their phone as their primary device to access the Internet.

Mobile account opening has the potential to ease the onboarding process for some unbanked consumers; however, a number of issues make its rapid deployment unlikely in the near term. For example, some banks have reported lower consumer demand for mobile account opening relative to other competing mobile services or functionalities, making investing in this functionality less of a priority (although some have also reported strong consumer demand for mobile account opening). Banks may identify services such as mRDC or person-to-person transfers (P2P) as more desired by their customers. In addition, many banks are still fine-tuning previously deployed account opening methods, such as online account opening, which are more widely desired by consumers. Nevertheless, survey data suggest that 10 percent of consumers chose mobile over both online and in-branch options as the most convenient means for applying for a checking account.[41]

Also, technical challenges can make mobile account opening difficult or costly for some banks. Industry reports, as well as conversations with bank officials, suggest that mobile account opening is possible and is in fact already offered by a handful of banks and nonbank providers. However, technical difficulties can arise from the fact that many of the core processing systems in use by banks today provide little flexibility to easily link with other bank applications to facilitate account opening.

It is often observed that nonbanks are able to offer mobile functionalities that are not commonly offered by banks, such as opening an account with a mobile device. This may be, at least in part, because nonbank financial providers operate in more specialized areas of business, so they are less likely to have interoperability issues with legacy systems and therefore may be more flexible and nimble in deploying technology. Some banks are trying to harmonize their systems, so that their mobile platform and the core systems are one and the same.

Another challenge is optimizing the mobile browsing experience for account opening. Many banks already offer *online* account opening, and thus consumers may be able to open accounts by accessing these sites on their mobile Web browser. However, the experience is likely to be cumbersome and could prevent consumers from completing an application if the Web site is not adapted to the mobile channel. And even when mobile Web sites are so optimized, it may be difficult to create a user-friendly browsing experience that can persuade consumers to enter the required personal information through the small screen of a mobile device.

Mobile account opening for the unbanked also presents real or perceived regulatory compliance issues. For example, displaying account opening disclosures can be challenging on a small screen. Banks considering mobile account opening, or any mobile enrollment process, are challenged with creating a user-friendly experience while providing appropriate disclosures and collecting personal information to identify applicants. However, mobile technology may also create new ways to meet those requirements through innovative tools. For instance, image capture technology has made strides in conveniently capturing ID information and could be helpful in this area.

Compliance with Bank Secrecy Act (BSA) requirements, including Customer Identification Program (CIP) account opening requirements, could present challenges when opening accounts with a mobile device. Collecting and verifying CIP information and conducting customer due diligence may be more challenging when the applicant is unbanked, particularly if the applicant lacks an electronic footprint such as a credit history that a bank could draw upon to verify identity. For mobile account opening to reach such individuals, alternative ways of verifying identity through documentary and nondocumentary methods may need to be considered, such as through rent or phone authentication services or by using a phone's camera to capture alternative identifications such as matricula consular or individual taxpayer identification number (ITIN) documentation. Banks must also have appropriate policies, procedures, and processes in place to monitor, identify, and report suspicious activity. Banks may want to consider incorporating the unique features of mobile devices, such as the ability to determine a phone user's location, in their suspicious activity monitoring systems.

Once technical, regulatory, and security challenges are addressed, mobile account opening could serve as a more effective banking access tool. Mobile account opening capabilities are likely to be a more effective economic inclusion tool when used as part of outreach strategies in which a trusted and knowledgeable live intermediary (e.g., bank tellers or community-based organization staff) walks unbanked consumers through the mobile account application process. Unbanked consumers, especially those who do not trust banks or are uncomfortable providing personal information, may not feel comfortable inputting information into a mobile device. Also, less tech-savvy unbanked consumers may find it difficult to use a mobile phone to navigate through the account opening experience on their own. Mobile account opening at volunteer tax preparation (VITA) sites could be an opportunity to attract unbanked consumers and expose them to mobile banking functionalities, including those that would make it easy to direct some or all of a tax refund into a savings account.

Assisting unbanked consumers with mobile account opening could also be an opportunity to demonstrate how to use a bank's MFS product. For example, one bank showed new customers how to use mobile bill pay by making a small donation to charity from the customers' account. The bank reports that the strategy has led to increased mobile adoption. This personal coaching may be vital to the adoption and use of any mobile account opening platform among underserved consumers, particularly the unbanked. Another bank created a series of YouTube videos demonstrating how to use specific MFS features, and another hosts online discussions on Facebook between customers and product mangers to answer customer questions and provide product managers with feedback.

B. Sustainability – Keeping Consumers in the Banking System

> Current features of MFS suggest it is particularly well-suited to increase the sustainability of banking relationships and could improve economic inclusion for the underbanked and those at risk of becoming unbanked.
>
> However, some features require further adaptation to more directly benefit these consumers. Also, while features are already available that could benefit the underserved, it is unclear how widely underserved consumers are taking advantage of them.

Survey results demonstrate that having a bank account does not guarantee a sustainable banking relationship, suggesting that exiting the banking system is an important concern. The use of financial services outside of the banking system also suggests opportunities to better engage current customers. This section considers the ability of MFS to retain underserved consumers in the banking system by better meeting day-to-day financial needs. Sustainability refers to both the continuity and comprehensiveness of a consumer's relationship with a bank, as well as the bank's ability to feasibly serve the underserved through the mobile delivery channel.

B.1. Safe Underlying Accounts

It is important that accounts for underserved consumers be safe, transparent, and affordable; MFS could help make such accounts even safer and more transparent.

As previously mentioned, underserved consumers are likely to place a high value on transparency and the predictability of fees and services. Therefore, regardless of the delivery channel used, sustainable banking relationships will depend on whether the financial products and services are safe, transparent, and affordable. For MFS to broaden economic inclusion and facilitate sustainable banking relationships with underserved consumers, it is vital that the underlying accounts and services be safe and appropriate for those consumers. Offering affordable accounts with transparent fees and consumer protections afforded by the law is an important part of establishing more sustainable banking relationships. Accounts such as those in the FDIC's Model Safe Accounts Pilot are one example.[42]

Further, MFS technology might present opportunities to make accounts even safer and more transparent. Some of the MFS features and functionalities discussed below could provide opportunities to make disclosures more interactive, make fees more transparent, and help consumers avoid fees or prevent fraud (such as through use of alerts).

B.2. Account Management

MFS could contribute to more sustainable banking relationships by making it easy for consumers to be more aware of the funds available for them to use. This could be accomplished by directly accessing account information or receiving alerts and notifications of specific transactions as they occur. More informed account management could help consumers avoid fees, make timely payments, and prevent fraud. However, adoption of alerts is relatively low among all consumers, and enrollment and management of alerts can be challenging for those who do not use online banking. In addition, real-time information is not often available due to technical challenges. The industry is moving toward updating the systems involved in payments to promote access to more timely information.

Many underserved consumers live paycheck to paycheck, with a relatively thin cushion of funds in their bank accounts. For these consumers, access to accurate account information, including the availability of funds, is critical. An account management tool that raises financial awareness and informs the financial decision-making process may be one of the most effective features of mobile technology for the underserved. MFS could provide consumers with actionable information to facilitate account management in two key ways: (1) monitoring account balance and transaction history and (2) receiving alerts. For both of these features, consumers benefit from the "anytime and anyplace" nature of their smartphone.

Before making a purchase, for instance, consumers could check their account to ensure they have adequate funds or receive an alert notifying them of a low balance.

a. Account Management: Account Balance and Transaction History

Providing underbanked consumers, as well as those at risk of becoming unbanked, with a convenient, fast, and free way to check their account balance and transaction history could help them better manage their money and strengthen their trust in the banking system. These features are widely offered among MFS products and are the most frequently used mobile features among all mobile bankers, including the underserved. As of June 2013, approximately 89 percent of underbanked mobile bankers and 86 percent of those fully banked had used mobile banking to check their account balance or recent transactions in the past 12 months.[43] This feature can help consumers avoid fees and other charges, and it is particularly valuable to those with low balance accounts that may need more frequent monitoring. In addition, consumers can view transaction histories quickly and easily, which can help them monitor spending and guard against fraud.

Consumers without smartphones can use "text banking," which allows them to use a mobile phone to send short text messages (SMS messages) to request account information. The functionalities of text banking are more limited than those available through the Web or through an app on a smartphone, but it can still meet a number of basic account needs. Using text banking, a consumer can view recent transactions, check balances, and transfer funds. In fact, some studies estimate that 27 percent of mobile bankers choose SMS text messaging to conduct mobile banking. Because SMS messaging is a feature unique to mobile phones, enrollment in text banking through a mobile device is more widely available than enrollment in mobile banking through a mobile device (15 percent vs. 4 percent).[44] According to a Javelin study, 77 percent of the 26 largest banks offered SMS text banking in 2013.[45] However, as smartphone ownership continues to grow at the expense of standard feature mobile phones and consumers become more comfortable downloading mobile apps, banks are shifting away from the SMS text banking channel. Indeed, at least one large institution dropped text banking support in 2013.[46]

b. Account Management: Alerts

Alerts offer an additional way to help consumers monitor an account and avoid fees and other charges. For example, some alerts let consumers know when a remotely deposited check has cleared and that those funds are available for withdrawal. This feature could be particularly beneficial to consumers whose ability to meet financial obligations is closely tied to the availability of their funds. Alerts are generally available for a variety of purposes, and consumers can commonly sign up for them through online banking. Alerts can be delivered in the form of text messages, push alerts, or email; one advantage of smartphones is the ability to access all three types of communications on a single device.

Although alerts are one of the most widely available mobile banking features, their use is not widespread. According to the 2013 FDIC Household Survey, less than half (46.8 percent) of the households that engaged in mobile banking had read a text message alert from a bank in the 12 months prior to the survey. Among mobile banking users, the underbanked were somewhat more likely to have done so, relative to fully banked households (52 percent vs. 45 percent).

A survey by Javelin conducted in March 2013 found that only 37 percent of respondents received alerts in the past 12 months,[47] compared to 34 percent of respondents in a survey from March 2012.[48] Of the respondents who received an alert in the past 12 months, just over half received only email alerts, compared to 8 percent who received only SMS alerts and 39 percent who received both email and SMS alerts. It is unclear whether consumers are aware of the capabilities and potential benefits of the alert feature and how to enroll, or whether they have decided that they do not want to use this function. Banks do not seem to widely advertise this functionality, perhaps because it does not distinguish them from their competitors. Clearly, opportunities exist for banks and financial educators to raise awareness among consumers, and particularly underserved consumers, about how to take advantage of the available alert functions, including as a means to avoid overdrafts.

The process for enrolling in and managing mobile alerts may constitute a barrier to using them. Alert enrollment and management generally cannot be done from a mobile phone, and instead may require logging into a bank's Web site. This is particularly problematic for consumers who use their phone as their primary means of accessing the Internet and are less likely to use online banking. As previously mentioned, underbanked consumers are less likely to use online banking as the main method of accessing their bank account than the fully banked.[49] Only 31 percent of the largest 26 banks currently allow consumers to adjust their alert setting on a mobile device. However, both alert enrollment and management via mobile are becoming increasingly available.[50]

Mobile alerts could be improved as an economic inclusion tool by offering something closer to real-time information. As currently deployed, most alerts are not real-time or even near real-time. As previously mentioned, accuracy and reliability of account information is likely to be important for underserved consumers. Conversations with providers suggest that the delay is commonly a result of core processing systems that process transactions in batches. This delay can diminish the value of the information provided through the alert, and have the unintended impact of leading some consumers to misunderstand the status of their account. Although some banks have been able to develop real-time or near real-time alerts that arrive on a consumer's phone within seconds of a transaction, this is still relatively uncommon and can be expensive for banks to implement. The capacity to offer real- or near real-time alerts is growing; the latest studies show an increase from 44 percent to 69 percent among the 26 largest financial institutions.

Underserved consumers, in particular, would benefit from real-time alerts, as such alerts can increase the transparency of banking services. For example, a low-balance alert or notification that is sent at the time a consumer reaches a low threshold, as opposed to the following morning, could inform decisions about purchases or funds transfers, and help consumers avoid fees. This could have important consequences for more financially vulnerable consumers. Financial institutions could also benefit from real-time alerts that would enable them to send consumers timely fraud notifications, thereby saving the institutions the costly resources involved in investigating each fraudulent transaction.

As convenient as alerts can be, banks need to consider the appropriate balance between providing timely and useful information and saturating consumers with too much information. Too many alerts may prompt consumers to disregard them, thereby counteracting any potential benefits. Also, the information contained in alerts must be relevant and useful to the consumer in order for them to find value in receiving them. Providing consumers with the ability to easily select and control their alerts—including the type, frequency, and communication method (e.g., push alert, email, SMS)—may be one way to help achieve the right balance.

Consumers may also be concerned about the potential costs of text alerts. Consumers who do not subscribe to text message plans could incur unexpected fees from receiving these alerts. However, as the cost of unlimited text plans decreases over time, this is likely to be less of a concern. Also, there is a trend toward "push alerts" that are part of the mobile app functionality and therefore do not count against a consumer's text allowance, although they may use data and thus would count against the consumer's data allowance.

In addition, other developments such as two-way alerts could help consumers take more immediate action when they receive information about their accounts. With this functionality, consumers receive an alert notifying them of a development, such as when a bill is due, and would have the opportunity to select an action in response (e.g., pay that bill). Currently, five of the largest 26 banks offer two-way alerts.[51]

Further study would be helpful in understanding specific settings in which alerts can create more sustainable relationships with underserved consumers. For example, research is needed to identify specific alert models and strategies that would be effective and useful to underserved consumers. In addition, efforts could explore whether banks can use alert data to help underserved consumers progress in their relationship with the bank, such as by obtaining additional bank products and services. Finally, further study should be given to understanding the type of information underserved consumers would like to receive through alerts, through what medium (e.g., text, push, or email alerts), and how alerts could be paired with other services to enable those consumers to take relevant actions.

B.3. Day-to-Day Transaction Needs

MFS can increase the convenience of several types of banking transactions, such as depositing checks via mobile remote deposit capture or mobile bill pay, and help underserved consumers meet their day-to-day transaction needs. Some of the features or functions that may be most useful for underserved consumers are not yet widely available. Others are available, but enrolling in and managing these services cannot be done with a mobile phone. In some cases, these limitations are attributable to decisions or actions by financial institutions to manage risks while offering new and evolving mobile services.

Some consumers will continue to prefer or need to rely on cash or money orders, and it is not clear whether MFS could always substitute for those traditional payment methods.

A key element to evaluating whether MFS can enhance the sustainability of banking relationships with underserved consumers is its ability to help these consumers meet their financial needs. Mobile banking technology offers transaction capabilities that can help the underserved access basic financial transaction services, including those that are currently being met by nonbank providers. Some of the functionalities that particularly benefit the underserved are highlighted below.

a. Depositing and Cashing Checks

One common financial need facing the underserved is the ability to cash checks and gain quick access to funds, including cash. Approximately 38 percent of unbanked households use nonbank check cashers. Despite the fact that the underbanked have bank accounts, 23 percent of these households cash checks outside the banking system. Convenient hours and locations are the top reasons underbanked consumers cite for using a provider other than a bank to cash checks. MFS might have the potential to change this dynamic through mRDC, which enables consumers to use their smartphone's camera at any time of the day to take a photo of a check and transmit it electronically to their bank for deposit. The technology addresses the preference of underserved consumers for convenience, as it can be easier than visiting a brick-and-mortar check casher and can be done at any time of the day or night. As of 2013, 77 percent of the 25 largest banks offered mRDC,[52] and about 25.7 percent of mobile banking users have used mRDC in the past 12 months. Similar proportions of underbanked (25 percent) and fully banked (26 percent) mobile banking users indicated having done so.[53] If the service is transparent, reliable, and less costly than using a check casher, underserved consumers could be motivated to obtain this service through a bank.

Underserved consumer preferences for convenient check cashing includes being able to access funds immediately. However, the availability of funds through mRDC varies across banks. Banks commonly require consumers to wait a period of time before their funds become available for withdrawal, which helps mitigate fraud risk. Only a handful of banks are known to allow consumers access to funds immediately; where this is allowed, fees for immediate access are typically 1 percent for payroll checks and up to 5 percent for personal checks.[54]

Concerns regarding fraud, the impact on the consumer experience, and the applicability of regulations are some of the concerns that banks cite as issues that must be addressed when deploying mRDC. In addition, accelerating the availability of funds poses additional risks to banks. To mitigate some of these risks, banks may restrict eligibility to well-established customers or set limits on the number and dollar amount of checks deposited, making the services less useful for, or even inaccessible to, the underserved. Banks and nonbanks that currently provide mRDC with immediate availability of funds also often use check guarantee services to mitigate risk. Check guarantee vendors assess the validity of a check and if deemed valid, the check is cleared and funds are disbursed, often within minutes. The check guarantee service assumes the risk of any losses for bad checks and charges the bank a fee similar to insurance premiums that are pooled to offset the risk of loss from bad checks. In turn, banks charge a fee to consumers who opt for immediate or rapid (same day) availability of funds. Clarifications regarding the application of existing regulations to mobile technologies may be helpful in mitigating risks associated with MFS. For example, the Federal Reserve in early 2014 released a proposed rule that would clarify the responsibilities of certain financial institutions when a check is presented more than once for deposit by a consumer.[55] No rule has yet been issued explicitly clarifying whether the funds availability schedule of Regulation CC, implementing the Expedited Funds Availability Act, applies to mRDC transactions.[56]

Further study is needed to understand how mRDC policies imposed by banks to manage risk affect the availability of these services to underserved consumers. As banks gain experience with this new service and the populations they serve, more data will become available to fine-tune risk management, which could affect pricing. Information that can be provided to banks to help assess and manage the risks of these transactions for underserved consumers could be beneficial. Research could include exploring how to make mRDC a realistic alternative to check cashing, while also maintaining a bank's responsibility to manage risk.

b. Transferring Money between Accounts at the Same Institution

Mobile banking can also provide underserved consumers with an easy and convenient way to transfer funds between checking and savings accounts, a feature not available in nonbank products. As of June 2013, similar proportions of underbanked (55 percent) and fully banked (57 percent) mobile banking users had used their mobile device to transfer money between bank accounts in the past 12 months.[57] Underserved consumers can also benefit from being able to build assets in accounts that accumulate interest and are protected by deposit insurance. Thus, MFS can provide an opportunity to transfer money from a checking account to a savings account. This feature is important to the underserved because it enables them to set money aside from daily use. Although some nonbank mobile products include savings "pockets"—the ability to segregate certain funds and designate them as savings—these do not offer the same benefits and consumer protections as interest-bearing savings accounts that banks offer.

c. Making Payments – Bill Pay, Point-of-Sale Transactions, and Person-to Person Transfers

Like all consumers, the underserved need to be able to pay bills and make other payments, including paying family, friends, or a landlord. For some underserved consumers, even those with a bank account, this can be a time-intensive process that can involve paying in person, purchasing a money order, or using money transfer stores to send money (remittances) or pay bills. Providing bill pay functionality through MFS could help the underserved better manage their finances by enabling them to pay bills anytime and anyplace (e.g., after they receive an alert that a deposited check has cleared). Having access to affordable expedited bill pay options could also help underserved consumers manage the narrow timeframe of their bill payments.

The ability to pay bills through online banking platforms is well-established, and banks are increasingly incorporating that functionality into their MFS products. All of the largest banks offer bill pay services using a mobile device.[58] In 2012, 5 percent of the bill pay transactions that originated through banks were initiated through a mobile device.[59] Based on the 2013 FDIC household survey, similar proportions of underbanked and fully banked mobile banking users (about 60 percent) made a bill payment using a bank's mobile app or mobile Web site.[60] Some banks offer expedited bill pay services through their online platform. Initial research shows that expedited payment fees range from $5.00 to $25.00 depending on the type of payment a payee accepts (electronic vs. check), and when the payment needs to be delivered.[61] Expedited bill pay does not seem to be commonly available through mobile, even among institutions that offer the service through other channels.

Mobile P2P payment functionalities are available through some mobile banking platforms (e.g., using Popmoney or QuickPay).[62] As of June 2013, 27 percent of mobile bankers, including 29 percent of those underbanked, had sent money to other people using their banks' Web site or mobile app in the past 12 months.[63] In fact, more than a third (36 percent) of P2P transactions generated through banks were initiated through a bank mobile app or SMS/text message, while the remaining 64 percent were initiated through a bank's web site.[64]

MFS could also enable underserved consumers to send remittances more conveniently. Similar to domestic P2P payments, MFS creates an opportunity for banks to meet the needs of the underserved regarding international money transfers. This would be particularly beneficial for underserved consumers who frequently send money to friends or family abroad. It would also help them avoid the risks associated with carrying large amounts of cash. Remittances enable consumers to use a payment method such as a bank account or prepaid card to send money electronically to international recipients who can receive the funds via deposit to a bank account or other methods. Some nonbank money transmitters offer consumers the ability to send remittances using a mobile device, but this service is not generally available in bank-sponsored mobile products. Although this functionality appears to be becoming more widespread as a standalone nonbank product, some underserved consumers would benefit from such a feature being incorporated into bank-sponsored MFS channels. This would require institutions to address certain regulatory requirements, including the disclosure requirements under the remittance transfer rules recently issued by the Consumer Financial Protection Bureau.[65]

Despite the availability of mobile payments, such transactions may be too slow to meet the needs of some underserved consumers. Speed is particularly important for the underserved because they are more likely to have lower-balance accounts and therefore may be unable to make important payments until they have adequate funds. If the time between when a consumer receives funds and the payment due date is too short, the consumer may risk overdrafting, or being unable to make a payment on time and incurring late charges. Because check and ACH transactions can take several days to clear, some underserved consumers might prefer services like check cashers that provide immediate availability of funds and allow consumers to pay bills in person using cash or money orders. The Federal Reserve Board is exploring opportunities to make the payments system operate in real time, which could make it more attractive and useful to the underserved.[66]

Mobile payment products could be further tailored with an economic inclusion perspective in mind. For example, when bill pay and P2P mobile banking functionalities are available, users are typically required to access *online* (rather than mobile) banking platforms to enroll in bill pay, or add or make changes to payees or recipients. Indeed, even though all of the 26 largest banks offer mobile bill pay, only 15 percent allowed consumers to add a payee, or change payee information, on a mobile device. For consumers who do not have convenient access to online banking, this limitation could be problematic. Technologies such as mobile photo bill pay are slowly becoming available and are currently offered by two of the 26 largest banks. This technology could provide some flexibility and convenience to make changes to payees using a mobile device. Mobile international remittances could also be a valuable service for underserved immigrant markets. However, these services are a less ubiquitous feature among banks but a functionality that exists among some nonbank providers. Bank security concerns is one reason why these functionalities are not more common. With the risks of fraudsters getting a hold of misplaced or stolen devices, financial institutions might be hesitant to give devices full mobile functionalities, at least without some proven strategies for ensuring legitimacy of customer requests originating on a mobile device.

The availability of money orders and checks as payment instruments should be considered in conjunction with mobile banking. Unbanked and underbanked households sometimes use money orders for purposes such as paying rent. Until electronic payments are more widely accepted, these paper instruments are likely to be an important method of payment for these consumers. Finding ways to safely originate check or money order payments or their equivalent from a mobile device could help meet the financial needs of underserved consumers.

d. Depositing and Withdrawing Cash

Either by preference or necessity, many of the underserved frequently use cash to conduct financial transactions. The FDIC estimates that 29 percent of unbanked households do not use AFS providers and are likely to transact predominantly in cash. Anecdotal evidence suggests that even consumers who use nonbank providers are likely making many payments in cash. In fact, findings from the neighborhood study conducted by the New York City Department of Consumer Affairs revealed that "53 percent of checking account holders could not pay their rent with a check or online; rather, they must pay in cash."[67] Although MFS could result in less reliance on cash for other types of payments, it is possible that some preference or necessity for cash could persist. Therefore, although MFS may provide an attractive channel for meeting the many needs of the underserved, the ability to conveniently withdraw cash remains essential.

Since most bank-sponsored MFS products are tied to debit cards, cash can generally be withdrawn at an ATM or through a point-of-sale PIN transaction. However, depositing cash may pose a more significant challenge for consumers who do not live or work near a bank branch or ATM. Some prepaid providers have addressed this issue by selling loadable cards at convenience stores and other retail locations that consumers can purchase with cash and then load into their accounts. In meeting the needs of the underserved through MFS, banks without an ATM or branch presence may need to think about innovative ways to allow underserved consumers to deposit cash to their accounts. The issue of cash also highlights a more general point, which is that in order for MFS to be a sustainable product for the underserved, consumers must be provided with some linkages to the nonelectronic world until electronic payments are ubiquitous among underserved consumers.

B.3. Feasibility for Banks

MFS offers potential cost savings and can increase the profitability of serving the unbanked and underbanked. However, implementing any new delivery channel comes with upfront costs and uncertainties. Banks looking to maximize recovery of their investment costs in the short term might prioritize serving more profitable, less risky customers. Over time, the lower costs and efficiencies associated with mobile transactions could change the economics of serving the underserved.

Relationships with underserved consumers also need to be sustainable from the financial institution's perspective. Therefore, it is important to examine whether MFS can increase the feasibility for institutions serving unbanked and underbanked consumers through, for example, cost savings or by addressing other barriers, such as fraud. As previously mentioned, profitability and fraud are two of the barriers to serving underserved consumers reported by financial institutions.

a. Potential for Cost Savings and Profitability

In the short term, banks are investing resources to implement and update MFS functions. Some MFS features, including those that might be particularly beneficial to the underserved, like real-time notifications and transactions, may require additional large-scale investments to modernize processing systems and other technologies beyond the scope of mobile banking. Conversations with financial institutions confirm that the deployment of MFS has increased their total costs. Aside from investment costs, consumer use of MFS has thus far been primarily additive in nature, meaning consumers continue to use other channels in addition to mobile (see Box 4).

In addition, as a new delivery channel, MFS is introducing new types of risks and uncertainties into the banking business. In light of investment costs and lack of experience with these services, some banks have focused their initial efforts on delivering MFS to their more established, profitable, and less risky customers. Therefore, current banking business models may not consider the costs and benefits of serving underserved segments, making early MFS offerings impractical for the underserved (e.g., restricting the use of mobile banking to online banking customers).

Although short-term costs and uncertainties are associated with MFS, many industry reports indicate it has the potential to reduce the cost of providing banking services. For example, Forrester Research has estimated that offering mobile banking results in a return on investment of 15.7 percent. As more consumers choose to switch to, or increase reliance on, the mobile channel relative to other, higher-cost, delivery channels (e.g., bank teller, phone-based customer service), banks may be better positioned to realize cost savings by reassigning resources to meet changing consumer demand. For instance, Javelin has calculated that the average cost of an in-branch transaction is $4.25, whereas the average cost of a mobile transaction is $0.10. Also, a survey by BAI found that banks that have high MFS adoption rates experience 50 percent fewer teller transactions than peer banks that do not.[68]

Reduced volumes of basic financial transactions at the teller could result in changes in the way banks reconfigure their delivery channels. For instance, if MFS and other electronic channels become a primary method for conducting day-to-day transactions, branch resources could be transformed to handle more services that are likely to require one-on-one interactions, including managing complex services and cross-selling products. For financial institutions with a focus on serving underserved consumers, an increase in MFS could also present opportunities for banks to use resources more efficiently to better engage underserved consumers through one-on-one interactions that provide information on available products, or on how to use lower-cost channels for everyday transactions.

In addition to a potential reduction in overall banking costs in the longer term, anecdotal evidence also suggests increased customer engagement among mobile banking customers. Consumers who use mobile banking tend to engage with their banks more frequently, albeit for much shorter sessions, than they do through other channels (including online). Some report that mobile banking customers are also more profitable than other customers through reduced attrition and higher account balances. Increased consumer engagement could also create cross-selling opportunities for banks. In addition, it can provide banks with better customer data, which can contribute to a better understanding of the traits of different customer segments, cross-selling opportunities, improved underwriting, and improved fraud protection. Additional research could focus on evaluating the extent to which mobile banking contributes to higher retention rates, as opposed to it being a reflection of the characteristics of early adopters who might already tend to be more engaged and have higher-balance accounts.

Some banks are also finding that MFS provides opportunities to generate new revenue through fee income (e.g., faster funds availability). However, if MFS is to be a tool of economic inclusion for the underserved, any new fees related to it must be carefully considered so as not to discourage underserved consumers from engaging with the mainstream banking system. Additional study could monitor bank costs and consumer fees associated with MFS. Monitoring and analyzing these trends, and considering them alongside underserved consumer preferences and price sensitivity, could be helpful in identifying MFS products and services that can be feasible for banks and attractive to the underserved. Also, it would be useful to understand how cost structures vary depending on the size of banks and how smaller banks might be able to deploy MFS in a way that serves this population.

b. Security and Fraud

As previously mentioned, financial institutions cite fraud as one of the major obstacles to serving underserved consumers. Besides the risks associated with fraudsters obtaining access to misplaced or stolen devices, security risks of this emerging delivery channel are less understood. The rapid development and dissemination of mobile apps that do not incorporate high-security features increases the vulnerability of a mobile device. To cope with these concerns, financial institutions have established processes and policies that may help explain why some of the mobile features that are most relevant to underserved consumers are not widely available.

Importantly, however, industry reports argue that mobile applications have the potential to be more secure than online applications for at least three reasons. First, some vendors are developing features that can use a mobile device's camera to scan photographs of documents and automatically insert needed information into the application. The photograph also helps banks assess the authenticity of the documents used. Second, by using the location-tracking capabilities of mobile devices, banks can identify an applicant's actual location, which helps prevent fraud. Third, banks can use biometric authentication—including facial, voice, and fingerprint recognition—to enhance security.[69] Banks are beginning to pilot multi-factor authentications and voice biometric solutions to increase security and detect fraud.[70] Moreover, consumers may become more educated about and experienced with about mobile security practices (e.g., using passwords to lock or access their device). These developments could play a role in addressing some of the concerns that limit the functionalities available through mobile banking. Additional research could be devoted to ways in which these security innovations can specifically help address concerns about deploying the services and functionalities that could be most relevant to underserved consumers. Potential cost savings related to improving the ability to identify fraud more quickly through mobile banking could also be explored and considered in the cost-benefit equation.

C. Growth – Fostering Financial Empowerment to Deepen Banking Relationships and Fulfill Financial Goals

Economic inclusion involves not only bringing consumers into the banking system and establishing sustainable relationships, but also helping customers increase their financial engagement, develop deeper banking relationships, and pursue financial goals. Mobile technology can potentially foster growth in these ways, in part by using personal financial management (PFM) tools and similar functionalities to help consumers track and achieve financial goals and improve financial capabilities. Further, by increasing the amount of interaction between customers and banks, mobile devices could ultimately help customers become more fully integrated into the banking system.

> As MFS continues to emerge as a banking delivery channel, further study is needed to better understand the type of mobile financial capability tools that underserved consumers would find useful. In addition, as more services and resources shift to electronic (including mobile) methods, it is important to consider the impact on underserved consumers, many of whom value personal interactions to learn about and better use banking products. Given that mobile interactions tend to be brief and can lack a human connection, clear challenges are associated with relying on mobile banking alone to grow banking relationships with these consumers. Successful strategies to deepen banking relationships with the underserved are likely to leverage the advantages of mobile while incorporating the strengths of other delivery channels, including those involving human interaction.

C. 1. Financial Capability

Financial capability combines financial education with sound financial decision making to improve behaviors and outcomes. Many mobile tools could help advance financial capability. As previously discussed, account management tools like alerts and the ability to check balances and account information at anytime, from anyplace can help can help increase consumers' awareness of their finances and allow them to interact more with their bank. Beyond this, mobile technology could provide convenient, basic PFM functions, including tracking expenses; setting, monitoring, and achieving savings goals; and monitoring credit reports and scores. For example, savings trackers could help consumers visualize the progress they are making toward their savings goals, and embedded alerts and messages could motivate them to keep up with their savings plans. Or, tools that set up automatic transfers between accounts could help consumers set money aside for different purposes, without having to regularly repeat the transaction.

Many providers are including PFM tools in their mobile banking suites, but the levels of customer demand for and satisfaction with these tools is unclear. Only 21 percent of respondents to a Javelin survey conducted in August 2012 reported using at least one type of PFM tool (PFM software, bank PFM, or Web PFM).[71] The Federal Reserve found that 28 percent of mobile phone users are interested in using their phones to track their finances.[72] However, some anecdotal evidence suggests that many consumers do not wish to use their phones for relatively complicated PFM tasks. Instead, they prefer to use mobile banking for simple, quick transactions while using online banking for more involved activities such as budgeting and expense tracking, to the extent that these are desired. In fact, only 10 percent of mobile phone users currently use their phones for active financial management by tracking purchases and expenses. When mobile financial management tools are used, though, some evidence suggests that they may be effective in shaping financial behaviors and outcomes. For example, the 2014 Federal Reserve survey revealed that a relatively high proportion (over two-thirds) of mobile bankers are already using their phones to check their account balances or available credit before making a large purchase. In fact, half of these consumers reported deciding not to make a purchase upon learning how much money or credit they had available in their accounts.[73]

Concerns about the complexity and usability of mobile PFM tools may be particularly relevant to underserved consumers and new entrants to the banking system, who are often less familiar than fully banked customers with financial products and services. By including a variety of features and functions that may appeal to other market segments, sophisticated PFM tools could become overwhelming for consumers with more straightforward financial needs.

It may also be possible for mobile devices to be used to deliver more traditional financial education. The devices' small screen size would make it difficult to deliver a comprehensive curriculum on a mobile phone, but brief financial education messages or tips might be effective if delivered based on specific consumer actions or locations.

Further study would be helpful to explore whether financial education and PFM tools can be effectively offered through MFS and to gauge consumer demand for such tools. If MFS is not an optimal standalone channel for financial education, research could also be conducted to advance our understanding of how MFS could integrate or connect with other channels to increase effectiveness. Further study could also examine how personal financial management tools that may be suitable for the underserved have been implemented by nonbank entities. Such an effort could determine how or whether mainstream banks could benefit from these technologies, and how they could be integrated into bank systems.

C.2. Customer Relationships

By increasing customers' ability to conduct transactions and access information without needing to call or speak directly to bank staff, mobile technology is likely to fundamentally change the nature of the banking relationship. It is also likely to change the way banks locate and use physical branches. While many of the benefits of mobile's self-service functions are clear, the technology could have unintended negative consequences as well. Customers who do not interact with bank tellers or customer service staff may not receive one-on-one education or guidance at account opening, may have fewer opportunities to learn about and qualify for other bank products, and could find it more difficult to develop the connections that underpin relationship lending. In both the FDIC's Small Dollar Loan Pilot and the Model Safe Account Pilot, for example, one-on-one financial counseling and guidance provided by tellers and bank customer service staff were reported to be vital to the success of the loans and accounts opened by underserved consumers.[74]

Regarding mobile banking specifically, anecdotal evidence suggests that some underserved consumers may need or strongly prefer one-on-one, personal assistance to set up their mobile profiles, or to learn how to use specific features. In some cases, a teller or customer service representative may provide this type of assistance at account opening or during other in-person contacts with the bank. In other cases, though, it may be difficult for underbanked consumers to gain access to individual guidance. Although customers can use their mobile phone to call customer service, it can be challenging to find live support contact information from within mobile apps or mobile Web sites. Even if consumers do reach a bank staff member, not all staff members are consistently trained on how to inform and teach customers about the bank's mobile offerings, so some consumers are not made aware of the mobile options. A practical constraint also exists in that it may be difficult to access the MFS functionality on the phone at the same time the phone is being used to talk to a customer service representative. Thus, it is more difficult for the customer service representative to walk the consumer through the necessary steps than it would be if the consumer were calling while using a separate computer interface. An ATM "virtual teller" is one option banks are beginning to implement to add the human touch to transactions.[75] In a Javelin survey conducted in July 2013, 25 percent of consumers who do not use mobile banking stated that one of the top three reasons they do not was that they preferred to deal with people.[76]

Concerns exist among industry observers that the use of mobile banking is leading to a decrease in the availability of bank branches. This could be detrimental to customers who prefer to use bank branches for everyday transactions, and could make it more difficult for customers to access branches when they need to complete the more complex banking activities that are not well-suited to online or mobile banking.

Numerous sources indicate that branch accessibility remains important to customers, including underbanked consumers. The 2013 FDIC household survey found that about a third of all banked consumers reported using bank tellers as their main banking channel.[77] In the case of underserved consumers, bank tellers, along with ATMs/kiosks are the primary ways they access their account.[78] Mintel's October 2012 Retail Banking report found that half of consumers chose their bank because there is a branch near their home, which was by far the most popular reason. Overall, Mintel found that nine of ten consumers feel having a branch nearby is important.[79] Also, a survey conducted by Javelin in August 2012, revealed that 40 percent of mobile bankers chose depositing funds in person at a branch as their most preferred channel, whereas only 6 percent of mobile bankers chose mobile banking as their most preferred channel.[80] A separate survey by Novarica found that more than half of consumers say their primary concern when choosing a new bank is branch locations. Even the young, who are perceived to be more "connected" and ready to forgo branches in favor of mobile, still found nearby branches to be important (58 percent of those under 30 would not consider opening an account at a bank without a branch nearby).[81]

Opportunities exist for banks to re-envision the concept of the bank branch to complement digital channels. While it is unlikely that branches will disappear anytime soon, the ways branches are used may well evolve. Some industry observers believe that branches will shrink in both size and number, and will incorporate more technology. It is also thought, though, that the branch will remain the best place for banks to grow through sales, and to conduct complicated transactions. Some have suggested that consumers are now visiting branches primarily for advice rather than routine transactions that can be conducted online or through MFS. In fact, industry reports indicate that mobile bankers who visit a branch are less likely than general consumers to conduct basic transactions, such as deposits or withdrawals. Instead, mobile bankers are slightly more likely to visit the branches for activities, such as learning about products and services (13 percent vs. 10 percent for all consumers), buying a money order (9 percent vs. 7.5 percent for all consumers), or addressing potential fraud (8 percent vs. 6 percent for all consumers). To address this shift, some banks have begun experimenting with branches that are more technology-focused and specialized in offering advice. Restructuring branches could provide banks an opportunity to improve efficiency but also better meet the needs of customers and do so in way that blends technology and personal relationships.

C.3. Integration into the Banking System

A successful banking relationship can be thought of as one in which the customer is fully integrated into the banking system. For the purpose of this paper, a fully integrated bank customer is one that has access to, or information about, the full range and level of products and services offered by his or her bank and an ability to graduate to other products, including credit.

With frequent, but brief, customer interactions over mobile, banks face the challenge of delivering relevant and appropriate cross-selling opportunities to deepen the banking relationship with consumers. At this point, it is unclear how or whether consumers who interact with their banks exclusively, or predominantly, using mobile banking will learn about and access other bank products to the same extent as online and/or branch banking customers. This raises potential challenges for banks seeking to ensure that these customers will have the same opportunities to progress to new or more complex banking products as their financial needs mature. Thus, mobile may not suffice as a standalone tool for integrating consumers into the mainstream banking system. However, it can serve as one valuable piece of a model for such integration, a model that also includes human connections and other types of banking touch points.

D. Access, Sustainability, and Growth Findings

Considering MFS through the lenses of access, sustainability, and growth allows for an assessment of where and how MFS might best facilitate economic inclusion, and where significant obstacles remain. In the short run, the attributes of MFS discussed in the sustainability portion of the framework hold the most potential for the underserved. The anytime, anyplace, and actionable nature of MFS features offers the potential to enhance the sustainability of banking relationships with underbanked consumers through added convenience and value.

Further, these features could also be helpful in improving the banking relationships of those who are at risk of becoming unbanked, including younger consumers who may not automatically view banks as the primary place to meet their financial services needs. MFS features that help consumers better manage their accounts and avoid fees could make it easier and more appealing for them to remain in the banking system. However, some of the features that could most directly appeal to underserved consumers and encourage more sustainable banking relationships are not commonly offered. For example, features such as real-time alerts, mobile check cashing, and enrollment in and management of bill pay using a mobile device are not generally available at this time.

MFS appears to have a relatively small role in motivating and helping the unbanked access the financial mainstream and in increasing demand for banking products among the unbanked. This is in part because of the lower penetration of smartphones among unbanked households. Also, many unbanked consumers face severe economic challenges and have deeply ingrained reasons for being unbanked that are unlikely to be addressed by MFS. Still, mobile account opening functionalities could be a useful tool for banking the unbanked when deployed as part of broader outreach efforts, such as mobile account opening at VITA sites or in conjunction with social services. As smartphone usage among the unbanked expands and mobile account opening becomes more widely available, MFS could play more of a role in increasing access.

More work needs to be done in exploring how to realize the potential that mobile tools, such as expense and savings trackers, have in helping underserved consumers make better financial and banking decisions and achieve financial goals. Also, relying exclusively on a mobile device for a relationship with a bank is unlikely to fully achieve the economic inclusion objectives of fostering financial empowerment, growing banking relationships, and fulfilling financial goals. Instead, other delivery channels, particularly human interaction, are likely to be important for providing consumers the support and guidance they need to learn about and properly evaluate and engage in additional banking products.

In short, further work is needed to understand the factors that affect the adoption of mobile banking and the specific features that could potentially improve the value of the banking relationship.

IV. Takeaways

MFS is on its way to becoming a standard banking delivery channel for bank customers generally. Banks are investing in the technology and continuing to expand mobile services. As part of this effort, banks must make important choices regarding the specific services and functionalities to offer along with risk management strategies that have the potential to affect the availability of those options. This paper encourages financial institutions and other stakeholders to consider the impact that these choices could have on expanding access to financial services, maintaining banking relationships, and expanding services to underserved consumers.

When choosing to conduct financial services, underserved consumers highly value convenience, speed, cost, transparency, and predictability. Convenience is the top reason why many underserved consumers use nonbank providers for basic financial transaction needs. Many of these consumers live paycheck to paycheck, which leaves little room for the standard multi-day transaction clearing process, unanticipated delays, or posting errors. Their tight budgets also make underserved consumers price-sensitive.

MFS has the potential to enhance banking services along the dimensions that are important to the underserved. For example, convenience can be addressed through the "anytime and anyplace" attribute of the mobile technology and its potential to provide consumers with clear, real-time, actionable information about their accounts. However, this potential is not being fully realized.

This section identifies opportunities to make MFS an increasingly useful tool for economic inclusion along all three dimensions. The ideas presented are meant to inspire action and discourse that can help increase the availability and accessibility of MFS offerings with features that are likely to be particularly beneficial for the underserved, and to encourage the adoption of those features. The concepts are deliberately broad in scope in order to be flexible for future developments or advancements that may occur in MFS technology. They might serve as guideposts for those designing, deploying, regulating, and/or supervising MFS products, as well as for helping consumers use the technology. Economic inclusion proponents, both within and outside of banks, may use these ideas to help bring economic inclusion objectives to the forefront as MFS tools continue to be developed and implemented.

- **Integrate MFS into broader economic inclusion strategies**
  Although MFS is a promising channel for increasing economic inclusion, it is likely to be more effective when thought of as part of a specific outreach strategy. Successful economic inclusion strategies that incorporate MFS are likely to include efforts to create awareness about this service channel, explain its features and benefits, and demonstrate how it can be most appropriately used to meet specific financial needs. Targeted marketing or outreach activities geared toward specific underbanked segments and their unique needs or pain points are important since underbanked consumers have some unique concerns relative to the general population. Highlighting specific MFS functionalities (e.g., alerts) that are most relevant and valuable to the underserved may be particularly useful.
  In addition, pilot studies and surveys document the importance of including a "trusted party" or "trusted intermediary" that can introduce underserved consumers to MFS, help them enroll, and coach them on how to properly use specific functionalities.[82] Bank staff can certainly play this role, but some providers might find it helpful to partner with community groups or other stakeholders that already work closely with the unbanked and underbanked. The role of a "trusted intermediary" is even more imperative when using MFS to help the unbanked open bank accounts. For example, unbanked consumers are more likely to benefit from mobile account opening functionalities when the service is provided as part of an outreach strategy in which a trusted and knowledgeable intermediary (e.g., community-based staff) guides them through the mobile account application process. Incorporating MFS topics into financial education curricula and outreach could also help the underserved better understand the value and appropriate use of mobile products.
  Institutions of different sizes may take different approaches to using MFS for economic inclusion. For example, large banks may be able to realize the benefits of scale more quickly for mobile products, but community banks might be better suited to supplement mobile with certain other approaches and use their relationships within the community to attract and retain underserved consumers.
- **Integrate MFS with other delivery channels and incorporate one-on-one interactions** Mobile technology presents a promising channel for delivering financial services in a manner that advances economic inclusion, but MFS is likely to be more effective when combined with other approaches or channels. Although MFS can enable consumers to conduct many transactions on their own, the underserved in particular may benefit from periodic one-on-one interactions that provide the consumer with coaching and guidance on how to properly use banking products and mobile tools. In-person delivery channels can also help consumers learn about other relevant products and services, deepening their relationship with the bank. Different channels may continue to have relative strengths and weaknesses for conducting specific tasks. For instance, MFS may allow for quick and easy basic account management, but branches might continue to be helpful for on-boarding or more involved inquiries.
  Fitting MFS into a larger integrated delivery approach is complicated because it involves, paradoxically, both enhancing the mobile channel so it can provide more functionality independent of other channels, and preserving consistency and

accessibility across a variety of touch points. While it may be very useful for underserved consumers to be able to use a mobile device to complete basic transactions, such as setting up alerts, without needing to go online or speak to bank staff, it is also important that mobile technology not dehumanize the banking experience for those who prefer personal interactions.

- **Thoughtfully fine-tune risk management strategies associated with features that meet the needs of the underserved**
  Because MFS is an emerging technology, many providers are working to continually fine-tune their risk management approach. Banks that have less experience meeting the needs of the underserved may face new uncertainties regarding how to safely offer mobile products that are useful to these populations. In some cases, these uncertainties about new potential risks may inhibit the availability of or access to specific features. For example, meeting underserved consumers' demand for immediate access to funds through mobile check cashing may require banks to consider new approaches to guaranteeing those funds and allowing consumers to access funds sooner than is typical for most transaction accounts.
  Addressing risk challenges related to security may help increase consumer comfort and trust related to using MFS. As previously noted, one of the primary reasons consumers (including the underserved) report for not adopting MFS is concern about security. Many experts in this field have discussed the potential for MFS to be safer and more secure than other delivery channels, due to several unique features of mobile devices, such as the ability to determine a phone user's location. Consumers may also benefit from greater awareness of ways they can secure their phone and use MFS safely.
  Banks may benefit from engaging regulators early in the process as they work to identify solutions to novel risk challenges. As banks and regulators work to apply regulatory requirements in the mobile environment, the responsible use of data, with an eye to minimizing risk and maximizing accessibility of services to underserved consumers, should be part of the ongoing agenda. Pilot programs, information sharing, and close communications between banks and their regulators could be helpful. Within the financial regulatory arena, an inclusive approach that brings together the perspectives of various functions within regulatory organizations, including economic inclusion and supervisory issues, could help bring awareness to banking services that are safe, sound, and accessible to underserved consumers.
- **Address infrastructure challenges to increase the convenience and speed of MFS**
  Current survey data show that convenience and speed are leading reasons why underserved consumers use nonbank transaction services. The potential of MFS to improve the convenience and speed of banking services includes the ability to provide real-time or near real-time, actionable information (e.g., account balances checks or low balance alerts), as well as quick processing of transactions (e.g., expedited bill pay, immediate funds availability). Nevertheless, banking processing systems do not typically process transactions in real time, which could potentially limit the accuracy and usefulness of information delivered through the mobile channel.
  In many cases, fulfilling the promise of delivering financial information and processing transactions in real-time requires costly investments and industry-wide

policies that go beyond the scope of an MFS strategy. Modernizing core processing systems within banks is an important step, but other efforts are also needed to expedite the way financial institutions verify available funds in transactions and settle payments. Therefore, the modernization of the payment system that the Federal Reserve is exploring could play a key role in increasing the ability of financial institutions to provide more timely transaction information to consumers and banks, as well as to offer faster payment and deposit clearing.[83]

Investments in payment and processing infrastructure improvements, especially systemwide, are likely to take time.[84] Meanwhile, financial institutions could continue exploring solutions that can help increase the accuracy of account information available to consumers. For example, consumers could be provided the ability to conduct "virtual check-booking," whereby they could reduce their available balance for payments that have not yet reached the bank (such as check payments or ACH payments they have scheduled with a utility company).

- **Identify opportunities to enable more mobile functionalities**

  For some of the underserved, a mobile phone may serve as their primary point of access to the Internet, and online banking using a computer might not be a convenient banking option. In fact, relative to fully banked households, underbanked consumers are less likely to use online banking and more likely to use mobile banking as the main method of accessing their bank account.[85]However, most MFS services are not set up to be accessible or practical for these individuals. It is not widely possible to open new accounts via mobile. And, in most cases, bank customers need to already be enrolled in their bank's online banking service before they can enroll in mobile banking. In addition, to use some MFS features, consumers may be required to first set them up online (e.g., creating payees in bill pay or enrolling in alerts); managing these features must also often be done online, not through a mobile device. Banks may consider exploring ways to serve those consumers who rely on mobile banking as their main form of banking, which may require modifying existing mobile platforms. For some banks, especially smaller institutions, this may require working with third-party vendors who manage the platform a bank uses for its online or mobile banking.

  Risk management concerns and compliance with the regulatory framework may also need to be addressed to facilitate mobile enrollment. For example, the ability to add a payee or external account on a mobile phone could be exploited by fraudsters to transfer money out of an account. Banks have found ways to address these risks in the online banking environment and are increasingly adopting methods for doing so in the mobile environment as well. Anecdotal evidence indicates that mobile account opening is growing, which suggests that banks are indeed finding ways to address some of these challenges. For unbanked consumers, additional obstacles such as lack of ID or banking history can come into play regardless of the channel. In the case of MFS, though, opportunities may exist for using technology in creative ways to capture information from consumers with alternative IDs or limited credit histories, perhaps by integrating alternative data sources like rent payment history or phone records.

- **Identify case studies demonstrating profitable implementation of MFS for economic inclusion**
  Cost and profitability are important factors that banks need to evaluate when considering economic inclusion strategies. Banks are often challenged by the relatively high cost of some methods of serving the underserved. Should MFS help lower the cost of providing basic financial services, it has the potential to change the economics of how banks provide services to underserved consumers. At this relatively early stage, banks may view the cost of deploying MFS as an investment that is additive in nature (in that consumers continue to use other channels as well), with any overall savings being realized over time. Over the long run, as consumers rely more on MFS for their banking needs, cost savings are likely to become larger, and opportunities are likely to emerge for reconfiguring service channels in ways that lower the costs of serving all consumers. As previously noted, underserved consumers are price sensitive; therefore, new business models may be most effective if they do not carry prohibitively high fees that would discourage obtaining financial services through a bank. Efforts to study examples of successful implementation for the underserved would help create a more solid business case for MFS as an economic inclusion tool.
  In addition, banks could receive an incentive to design and deploy MFS in ways that meet the needs of underserved low- and moderate-income (LMI) individuals and needs in underserved geographies through application of the Community Reinvestment Act (CRA). CRA consideration could be contemplated for banks that demonstrate they are meeting underserved needs through MFS. However, MFS should not be viewed as a substitute for bank branches in LMI communities.
  Banks may benefit from engaging a variety of internal and external stakeholders in exploring how best to tailor products to meet underserved preferences. Involving persons with expertise in areas such as product design, mobile technology, economic inclusion, compliance, and risk management may be helpful in designing solutions related to convenience, speed, and price.
- **Bridge mobile service delivery with traditional payment methods**
  It is important to bridge offline and online service delivery for underserved consumers. As noted in this paper, underserved consumers frequently prefer to use cash and therefore require the ability to deposit cash into an account and to withdraw it. In addition, many of the underbanked must make payments (e.g., rent payments) using paper instruments such as checks or money orders. MFS is likely to be a more useful financial tool for the underserved if ways can be found to reconcile and meet the need for electronic transactions with their need for paper payments or cash.

CONCLUSION

New technology is continually creating opportunities to change the way consumers interact with products and services. These changes sometimes present opportunities to expand a product or service to more consumers. This is the case with MFS. In the short term, MFS has the most potential for a subset of the underserved, primarily the underbanked and those in the banking system that might otherwise experience account closure. Over the long run, however, it could draw many more into the mainstream banking system. The unbanked in particular are more likely to adopt MFS as their ownership of smartphones increases and as MFS more directly meets their needs.

As banks implement MFS for their customers, they may benefit from considering the preferences of the underserved. It will be important to understand how needs and preferences vary among different segments of the underserved, and how they change over time. This will help providers and economic inclusion stakeholders more carefully fine-tune strategies for using MFS for economic inclusion.

In many instances, features that specifically benefit the underserved will be valuable to a bank's other customers as well. Serving the underserved with MFS does not necessarily require any unique products or services intended for that population alone. Rather, the needs of the underserved can be met as a part of an integrated approach that considers their needs alongside those of all customers. For MFS to be truly successful as a tool of economic inclusion, it must benefit banks and consumers alike. In addition, incorporating economic inclusion considerations into MFS features and driving consumer adoption is likely to require the involvement of many stakeholders, including third-party vendors, community and consumer organizations, and financial regulators, among others.

APPENDIX TABLES

Appendix Table 1. 2011 Distribution of Households by Banking Status and Household Characteristics (Percent Of Households)

	Access to Mobile Phones	**Access to Smartphones**		**Use of Mobile Banking in the Last 12 Months by Banked Households**	
Demographic Group	**Among all households**	**Among all households**	**Among mobile phone users**	**Among mobile phone users**	**Among smartphone users**
All Households	82.6	55.6	67.2	25.4	35.6
BANKING STATUS					
Unbanked	68.1	33.1	48.6	NA	NA
Underbanked	90.4	64.3	71.1	31.0	41.8
Fully Banked	86.8	58.9	67.8	23.9	33.9
RACE OR ETHNICITY					
Black	79.1	52.3	66.2	25.1	34.3
Hispanic	79.9	55.5	69.5	26.8	35.7
Non-Hispanic Whites	83.6	55.5	66.4	24.8	35.6
Other	85.0	63.5	74.7	29.7	37.3

Demographic Group	Access to Mobile Phones	Access to Smartphones		Use of Mobile Banking in the Last 12 Months by Banked Households	
	Among all households	Among all households	Among mobile phone users	Among mobile phone users	Among smartphone users
NATIVITY					
Native-born	83.1	55.5	66.8	25.4	35.9
Foreign-born citizens	80.8	57.4	71.0	23.9	32.3
Foreign-born non citizens	79.2	54.3	68.5	26.7	34.7
AGE					
Age 24 or younger	88.8	76.0	85.5	46.0	49.7
Age 25-34	89.8	76.3	85.0	44.4	49.1
Age 35-44	89.0	72.0	80.9	35.0	40.6
Age 45-54	86.6	62.8	72.6	24.0	31.1
Age 55-64	83.5	48.7	58.3	15.1	23.7
Age 65 or older	67.3	23.2	34.5	6.2	15.6
EDUCATIONAL ATTAINMENT					
Less than high school	67.0	30.0	44.8	10.7	21.9
High school	78.2	44.2	56.5	16.9	28.0
Some college	85.3	59.2	69.4	26.9	36.6
Bachelors degree	89.4	70.8	79.1	32.7	40.1
INCOME					
Less than $15,000	69.2	31.2	45.1	14.3	27.6
Between $15K and $30K	74.4	37.9	50.9	17.1	31.7
Between $30K and $50K	82.2	50.9	61.9	22.0	33.8
Between $50K and $75K	88.3	63.2	71.6	26.1	34.6
$75,000 or more	91.6	77.7	84.9	33.9	39.1

Notes:

Households are identified as unbanked if they answered "no" to the question, "Do you or does anyone in your household currently have a checking or savings account?"

Underbanked households are defined as those households that have a checking and/or a savings account and had used nonbank money orders, nonbank check cashing services, nonbank remittances, payday loans, rent-to-own services, pawn shops, or refund anticipation loans (RALs) in the past 12 months.

Appendix Table 2. 2011 Use of Transaction Alternative Financial Services by Banking Status

	All Households		Unbanked	Underbanked	Fully Banked
Timing of AFS Use	Numbers (1000s)	Pct of Col	Pct of Col	Pct of Col	Pct of Col
All Households	120,408	100.0	100.0	100.0	100.0
ANY AFS PRODUCTS					
In last 30 days	14,470	12.0	45.5	41.2	-
In last 2-12 months	16,139	13.4	19.4	58.8	-
Not in the last 12 months	21,002	17.4	9.4	-	23.6
Never used	65,335	54.3	20.6	-	76.4
Unknown	3,461	2.9	5.1	-	-
NON-BANK MONEY ORDER					
In last 30 days	9,952	8.3	32.1	28.0	-
In last 2-12 months	12,127	10.1	17.0	43.2	-
Not in the last 12 months	17,592	14.6	9.8	8.3	17.2
Never used	77,817	64.6	35.6	20.2	82.8
Unknown	2,920	2.4	5.5	0.3	-
NON-BANK CHECK CASHING					
In last 30 days	4,626	3.8	25.0	8.9	-
In last 2-12 months	4,646	3.9	13.1	13.9	-
Not in the last 12 months	6,745	5.6	9.2	8.7	4.3
Never used	101,889	84.6	48.1	68.2	95.7
Unknown	2,501	2.1	4.6	0.4	-
NON-BANK REMITTANCES					
In last 30 days	1,758	1.5	3.9	5.7	-
In last 2-12 months	2,640	2.2	5.3	8.8	-
Not in the last 12 months	2,678	2.2	3.2	3.6	1.7
Never used	110,431	91.7	81.9	81.5	98.3
Unknown	2,901	2.4	5.7	0.5	-

Notes:

- = For this table cell there were so few sample respondents (in some cases zero) reporting that the estimated universe proportion round to 0.0 percent. It is estimated that the true value is only slightly greater than zero.

[a]Households were not asked whether they used these AFS products in the last 30 days.

Households are identified as unbanked if they answered "no" to the question, "Do you or does anyone in your household currently have a checking or savings account?"

Underbanked households are defined as those households that have a checking and/or a savings account and had used nonbank money orders, nonbank check cashing services, nonbank remittances, payday loans, rent-to-own services, pawn shops, or refund anticipation loans (RALs) in the past 12 months.

Refer to 2011 FDIC National Survey of Unbanked and Underbanked Households and FDIC Technical Notes for terms, definitions, and methodological notes. Figures do not always reconcile to totals because of rounding. Differences between groups may or may not be statistically significant.
Source: 2011 FDIC National Survey of Unbanked and Underbanked Households

Appendix Table 3. 2011 Use of Credit Alternative Financial Services by Banking Status

	All Households		Unbanked	Under Banked	Fully Banked
Timing of AFS Use	Numbers (1000s)	Pct of Col	Pct of Col	Pct of Col	Pct of Col
PAYDAY LENDING					
In last 30 days	814	0.7	0.5	3.2	-
In last 2-12 months	1,249	1.0	1.2	4.7	-
Not in the last 12 months	3,559	3.0	5.7	6.8	1.6
Never used	111,772	92.8	86.6	84.6	98.4
Unknown	3,014	2.5	6.0	0.7	-
PAWN SHOPS					
In last 30 days	911	0.8	2.7	2.7	-
In last 2-12 months	2,609	2.2	7.8	7.6	-
Not in the last 12 months	5,438	4.5	10.0	9.2	2.6
Never used	108,283	89.9	72.9	79.7	97.4
Unknown	3,166	2.6	6.5	0.8	-
RENT-TO-OWNa					
In last 2-12 months	1,814	1.5	5.1	5.4	-
Not in the last 12 months	3,821	3.2	6.7	7.6	1.6
Never used	111,551	92.6	81.6	86.3	98.4
Unknown	3,222	2.7	6.6	0.7	-
REFUND ANTICIPATION LOANSa					
In last 2-12 months	1,449	1.2	3.4	4.6	-
Not in the last 12 months	3,020	2.5	5.4	5.9	1.3
Never used	112,614	93.5	84.7	88.6	98.7
Unknown	3,324	2.8	6.6	0.8	-

Notes:

- = For this table cell there were so few sample respondents (in some cases zero) reporting that the estimated universe proportion round to 0.0 percent. It is estimated that the true value is only slightly greater than zero.

[a]Households were not asked whether they used these AFS products in the last 30 days.

Households are identified as unbanked if they answered "no" to the question, "Do you or does anyone in your household currently have a checking or savings account?"

Underbanked households are defined as those households that have a checking and/or a savings account and had used nonbank money orders, nonbank check cashing services, nonbank remittances, payday loans, rent-to-own services, pawn shops, or refund anticipation loans (RALs) in the past 12 months.

Refer to 2011 FDIC National Survey of Unbanked and Underbanked Households and FDIC Technical Notes for terms, definitions, and methodological notes. Figures do not always reconcile to totals because of rounding. Differences between groups may or may not be statistically significant.

Source: 2011 FDIC National Survey of Unbanked and Underbanked Households.

Appendix Table 4. obstacles to providing financial products and services to Underserved Consumers (Percent of Financial Institutions)

	Total	Major Obstacle	Minor Obstacle	Not An Obstacle	Don't Know
Regulatory Environment	7,034	34.9	29.5	22.7	12.7
Fraud	6,968	31.8	47.2	13.6	7.2
Lack of Consumer Understanding	7,056	31.4	43.1	10.2	15.1
Underwriting	7,030	28.4	41.7	16.6	13
Profitability	7,076	24.4	39.2	25.4	10.8
Effective Product Marketing	5,624	19.1	55.2	25.5	0
Lack of Consumer Demand	7,056	17.9	37.3	19.3	25.3
Nonbank Competition	7,035	15.8	38.5	28.1	17.4
Product Development	7,035	11.7	44.9	30.2	13
Lack of Familiarity with Banking Products	7,056	5.7	42	40	12.2

Source: 2011 FDIC Survey of Banks' Efforts to Serve the Unbanked and Underbanked.

Appendix Table 5. 2013 Unbanked Households' Access to Mobile Phones and Smartphones (Percent of Households)

	Access to Mobile Phones	Access to Smartphones	
Demographic Group	**Among all households**	**Among all households**	**Among mobile phone users**
All Households	68.1	33.1	48.6
RACE OR ETHNICITY			
Black	69.9	35.1	50.2
Hispanic	66.1	32.9	49.8
Non-Hispanic Whites	68.1	31.9	46.8
Other	65.3	26.2	40.2
NATIVITY			

Demographic Group	Access to Mobile Phones	Access to Smartphones	
	Among all households	Among all households	Among mobile phone users
Native-born	70.2	34.9	49.7
Foreign-born citizens	50.1	25.1	50.2
Foreign-born non citizens	64.1	28.0	43.8
AGE			
Age 24 or younger	77.6	49.5	63.7
Age 25-34	77.7	48.0	61.8
Age 35-44	71.8	36.4	50.8
Age 45-54	65.1	26.7	41.1
Age 55-64	59.6	14.7	24.7
Age 65 or older	43.6	7.6	17.4
EDUCATIONAL ATTAINMENT			
Less than high school	64.7	27.4	42.3
High school	69.7	34.0	48.8
Some college	74.4	42.6	57.2
Bachelors degree	54.0	28.1	51.9
INCOME			
Less than $15,000	67.7	28.4	42.0
Between $15K and $30K	68.6	37.7	54.9
Between $30K and $50K	73.4	42.8	58.3
Between $50K and $75K	60.8	39.8	65.5
$75,000 or more	54.3	26.9	49.6

Notes:

Households are identified as unbanked if they answered “no” to the question, “Do you or does anyone in your household currently have a checking or savings account?”

The demographic characteristics of a household, such as race, age, and education are taken to be those of the owner or renter of the home (i.e., “householder”), unless the characteristic is one defined at the household level, such as income.

Differences within groups may or may not be statistically significant.

Source: 2013 FDIC National Survey of Unbanked and Underbanked Households.

Appendix Table 6. 2013 Underbanked Households’ Access to Mobile Phones and Smartphones and Use of Mobile Banking (Percent of Households)

Demographic Group	Access to Mobile Phones	Access to Smartphones		Use Of Mobile Banking in the Last 12 Months by Banked Households	
	Among all households	Among all households	Among mobile phone users	Among mobile phone users	Among smartphone users
All Underbanked Households	90.4	64.3	71.1	31.0	41.8
RACE OR ETHNICITY					
Black	89.9	64.5	71.7	28.8	38.7

Appendix Table 6. (Continued)

Demographic Group	Access to Mobile Phones	Access to Smartphones		Use Of Mobile Banking in the Last 12 Months by Banked Households	
	Among all households	Among all households	Among mobile phone users	Among mobile phone users	Among smartphone users
Hispanic	89.7	67.3	75.0	30.1	38.8
Non-Hispanic Whites	90.6	62.8	69.3	32.2	44.4
Other	93.0	68.9	74.1	31.3	40.0
NATIVITY					
Native-born	90.4	63.6	70.3	31.5	42.8
Foreign-born citizens	91.9	66.7	72.6	28.2	38.2
Foreign-born non citizens	89.3	68.6	76.8	30.0	37.6
AGE					
Age 24 or younger	94.2	83.0	88.2	48.5	53.3
Age 25-34	95.2	83.0	87.1	47.0	52.1
Age 35-44	94.2	75.5	80.1	38.5	45.9
Age 45-54	91.3	63.4	69.5	24.6	34.1
Age 55-64	89.9	51.6	57.3	15.3	25.9
Age 65 or older	74.3	25.2	33.9	8.9	21.9
EDUCATIONAL ATTAINMENT					
Less than high school	80.0	42.4	53.0	15.4	27.4
High school	88.7	57.7	65.1	23.3	34.3
Some college	92.5	69.8	75.4	34.9	44.2
Bachelors degree	95.8	77.8	81.2	42.6	50.6
INCOME					
Less than $15,000	81.6	41.0	50.2	17.9	31.0
Between $15K and $30K	87.0	52.9	60.8	24.3	37.9
Between $30K and $50K	91.5	66.4	72.5	31.3	41.7
Between $50K and $75K	94.5	75.0	79.4	36.2	43.6
$75,000 or more	97.1	85.4	88.0	42.7	47.8

Notes:

Underbanked households are defined as those households that have a checking and/or a savings account and had used nonbank money orders, nonbank check cashing services, nonbank remittances, payday loans, rent-to-own services, pawn shops, or refund anticipation loans (RALs), or auto title loans in the past 12 months.

The demographic characteristics of a household, such as race, age, and education are taken to be those of the owner or renter of the home (i.e., "householder"), unless the characteristic is one defined at the household level, such as income.

Differences within groups may or may not be statistically significant.
Source: 2013 FDIC National Survey of Unbanked and Underbanked Households.

Appendix Table 7. 2013 Mobile Banking Activities (Percent of Households)

Mobile Banking Activity	Banked Households That Used Mobile Banking in the Last 12 Months		
	All	Underbanked	Fully Banked
Downloaded or used bank's mobile app	68.7	69.6	68.5
Checked account balance or recent transaction	86.8	89.0	86.0
Made a bill payment using bank's mobile app or website	60.0	59.5	60.2
Read a text message alert from the bank	46.8	51.6	44.9
Sent money to other people using your bank's website or mobile app	26.9	29.2	26.0
Transferred money between accounts owned by the same person	56.1	55.2	56.6
Deposited a check electronically using the mobile phone's camera	25.7	24.9	26.2
Located the closest in-network ATM or bank branch	33.4	38.1	31.5
Other (Specify)	2.9	2.0	3.2

Notes:
Underbanked households are defined as those households that have a checking and/or a savings account and had used nonbank money orders, nonbank check cashing services, nonbank remittances, payday loans, rent-to-own services, pawn shops, or refund anticipation loans (RALs), or auto title loans in the past 12 months.
Differences within groups may or may not be statistically significant.
Source: 2013 FDIC National Survey of Unbanked and Underbanked Households.

Appendix Table 8. 2013 Most Common Ways Banked Households Access Accounts (Percent of Households)

Banking Channel	Banked Households That Used Mobile Banking in the Last 12 Months		
	All	Underbanked	Fully Banked
Bank Teller	32.3	29.2	33.1
ATM/Kiosk	24.4	29.6	23
Telephone Banking	3.3	4.6	3
Online Banking	32.8	26.4	35
Mobile Banking	5.7	9.4	4.7
Other	0.8	0.5	0.8
Unknown	0.7	0.4	0.5

Notes:
Underbanked households are defined as those households that have a checking and/or a savings account and had used nonbank money orders, nonbank check cashing services, nonbank remittances, payday loans, rent-to-own services, pawn shops, or refund anticipation loans (RALs), or auto title loans in the past 12 months.
Differences were not tested for statistical significance.

Figures for households whose underbanked status is unknown are not presented in the table but are included in the statistics for all banked households.
Source: 2013 FDIC National Survey of Unbanked and Underbanked Households.

End Notes

[1] Federal Deposit Insurance Corporation, "2011 FDIC National Survey of Unbanked and Underbanked Households," September 2011.
[2] Ibid.
[3] Ibid.
[4] Federal Deposit Insurance Corporation, "2011 Survey of Banks' Efforts to Serve the Unbanked and Underbanked," December 2012.
[5] Pew Research Center, "The Web at 25 in the U.S.," February 2014.
[6] Federal Deposit Insurance Corporation, "2013 FDIC National Survey of Unbanked and Underbanked Households," forthcoming in October 2014.
[7] Ibid.
[8] Ibid.
[9] Matthew B. Gross, Jeanne M. Hogarth and Maxmilian D. Schmeiser, Federal Reserve Bulletin, "Use of Financial Services by the Unbanked and Underbanked and the Potential for Mobile Financial Services Adoption," September 2012, Vol.98, n.4.
[10] In this paper, the unbanked and underbanked are collectively referred to as "the underserved."
[11] Unless otherwise noted, statistics related to unbanked and underbanked households are from the 2011 FDIC National Survey of Unbanked and Underbanked Households. Underbanked households own a bank account, but in the past year have used nonbank check cashers, nonbank money orders, nonbank remittances, payday lenders, pawn shops, refund anticipation loans, or rent-to-own agreements.
[12] Federal Deposit Insurance Corporation, "2011 FDIC National Survey of Unbanked and Underbanked Households," September 2011.
[13] Pew Charitable Trust, "Unbanked by Choice: A look at how low-income Los Angeles households manage the money they can," July 20, 2010.
[14] Michael Barr, "Financial Services, Saving and Borrowing Among Low- and Moderate-Income Households: Evidence from the Detroit Area Household Financial Services Survey," March 2008.
[15] Pew Charitable Trust, July 2010.
[16] Rebecca Blank and Michael Barr, "Insufficient Funds: Savings, Assets, Credit and Banking Among Low-Income Households," March 2009.
[17] Pew Health Group, "Slipping Behind- Low-Income Los Angeles Households Drift Further from the Financial Mainstream," October 2011.
[18] Federal Deposit Insurance Corporation, December 2012.
[19] Federal Deposit Insurance Corporation, "Model Safe Accounts Pilot - Final Report," April 2012.
[20] Javelin Strategy & Research, "2012 Mobile Banking Financial Institution Scorecard," November 2012, and "2013 Mobile Banking Financial Institution Scorecard," November 2013. In these reports, Javelin Strategy examined mobile banking offerings of the largest 26 financial institutions ranked by deposit size, limited to institutions that are primarily retail-banking-focused. One-way alerts provide information, but require the customer to log in to the mobile banking app or browser if they wish to take action. Two-way alerts allow customers to take more immediate action (i.e., make transactions or financial decisions) by simply responding to the alert.
[21] Federal Reserve Board, "Consumers and Mobile Financial Services 2014," March 2014. The FDIC began collecting data on mobile financial services in the 2013 FDIC National Survey of Unbanked and Underbanked Households.
[22] Pew Research Center, "Cell Internet Use 2013," September 16, 2013.The study reported that 63% of adult mobile phone owners used the internet on their phone. The estimate is 55 percent for those with income below $30,000.
[23] Federal Deposit Insurance Corporation, "2013 National Survey of Unbanked and Underbanked Households," Forthcoming in October 2014. Results exclude banked households that did not access their account in the past 12 months.

[24] Federal Reserve Board, March 2014. Mobile banking and mobile payment estimates refer to use within the last 12 months.
[25] Federal Deposit Insurance Corporation, October 2014 (forthcoming).
[26] Ibid.
[27] Ibid.
[28] Federal Reserve Board, "Consumers and Mobile Financial Services 2013," March 2013.
[29] Federal Reserve Board, March 2014.
[30] Federal Deposit Insurance Corporation, October 2014 (forthcoming).
[31] Ibid. Mobile banking and mobile payment estimates refer to use within the last 12 months.
[32] Ibid.
[33] Federal Reserve Board, March 2014. Based on Federal Reserve Consumer and Mobile Financial Services surveys, mobile phone access among unbanked adults increased from 59 percent in November 2012 to 69 percent in December 2013, while smartphone ownership among mobile phone owners remained constant at approximately half over the same time period.
[34] Federal Reserve Board, "Consumers and Mobile Financial Services 2012," March 2012. The estimate of mobile banking use among the unbanked may reflect usage by households that were previously banked or mobile banking linked to prepaid cards.
[35] Federal Deposit Insurance Corporation, October 2014 (forthcoming).
[36] Federal Reserve Board, March 2012. Ten percent of the unbanked use mobile banking, and 12 percent use mobile payments. Mobile banking estimates may reflect usage by households that were previously banked, or mobile banking linked to prepaid cards.
[37] Ibid.
[38] Federal Deposit Insurance Corporation, December 2012.
[39] Pew Research Center, September 16, 2013.
[40] Javelin Strategy & Research, "How to Upgrade Online and Mobile Account Opening for an Omnichannel Era," September 2013.
[41] Javelin Strategy & Research, September 2013.
[42] For more information about the FDIC's Model Safe Accounts Pilot, please visit http://www.fdic.gov/consumers/template/.
[43] Federal Deposit Insurance Corporation, October 2014 (forthcoming).
[44] Javelin Strategy & Research, "2013 Mobile Banking Financial Institution Scorecard," November 2013.
[45] Ibid.
[46] Ibid.
[47] Javelin Strategy & Research, "Financial Alerts Forecast 2013," December 2013.
[48] Javelin Strategy & Research, "Road Map to Alerts 3.0," October 2012.
[49] Federal Deposit Insurance Corporation, October 2014 (forthcoming).
[50] Javelin Strategy & Research, November 2013.
[51] Ibid.
[52] Ibid.
[53] Federal Deposit Insurance Corporation, October 2014 (forthcoming).
[54] Based on Regions Bank and Ingo publicly posted pricing schedules as of March 2014. For full pricing schedule visit: http://www.regions.com/personal banking/now banking.rf#Check-Cashing or http://ingomoney.com/how-it-works.html.
[55] Federal Reserve Board, "Availability of Funds and Collection of Checks," February 4, 2014.
[56] If Regulation CC funds availability were deemed to apply, banks would have to ensure that they made funds from checks deposited via mRDC available no later than the timeframes specified in Regulation CC. This would be a further consideration banks would have to weigh in evaluating whether to offer mRDC at all, and at what cost.
[57] Federal Deposit Insurance Corporation, October 2014 (forthcoming).
[58] Javelin Strategy & Research, November 2013.
[59] Federal Reserve, "2013 Federal Reserve Payments Study," December 19, 2013. Does not include transactions generated using the mobile Web browser.
[60] Federal Deposit Insurance Corporation, October 2014 (forthcoming).
[61] Examples: http://www.unitedbank-wv.com/personalservices/expedited bill pay faq.asp, http://www.fmfcu.org/eservices/billpayer.htm, http://www.bankatunion.com/home/about/news/expedited bill payments, BBVA.
[62] Federal Reserve Board, December 19, 2013. P2P services are also commonly offered outside the mobile banking environment.

[63] Federal Deposit Insurance Corporation, October 2014 (forthcoming). The survey question did not specify domestic vs. international transfers.

[64] Federal Reserve Board, December 19, 2013. "Person-to-person transfers (P2P) excluded transactions between consumers using a depository institution's online bill payment platform."

[65] For more information see the following *Federal Register* notices issued by the CFPB: https://www.federalregister. gov/articles/2012/12/31/2012-31170/electronic-fund-transfers-regulation-e

[66] Federal Reserve Financial Services, "Payment System Improvement- Public Consultation Paper," September 10, 2013.

[67] New York City Department of Consumer Affairs, "Neighborhood Financial Services Study: An Analysis of Supply and Demand in Two New York City Neighborhoods," June 2008.

[68] Banking Strategies Daily, "Scoring Remote Deliver Impact," November 8, 2013.

[69] Javelin Strategy & Research, September 2013.

[70] Mobile Payments Today, "U.S. Bank pilots voice biometrics for credit card access," February 13, 2014.

[71] Javelin Strategy & Research, "21st Century PFM for a Mass Audience," February 2013.

[72] Federal Reserve Board, March 2014.

[73] Ibid.

[74] Federal Deposit Insurance Corporation, "Model Safe Accounts Pilot - Final Report," April 2012; and "A Template for Success: The FDIC's Small-Dollar Loan Pilot Program," 2010 Q2.

[75] Ben Bradford, "Banks Try To Save Big With 'ATMs Of The Future,'" January 1, 2014.

[76] Javelin Strategy & Research, November 2013.

[77] Federal Deposit Insurance Corporation, October 2014 (forthcoming).

[78] Ibid.

[79] Susan Menke, "Branch Matters: the Importance of Bank Branches," July 27, 2012.

[80] Javelin Strategy & Research, "Leveraging an Omnichannel Approach to Drive $1.5 B in Mobile Banking Cost Savings," July 2013.

[81] Novarica, "Bank Shopper Snapshot Survey Volume 3," January 2013.

[82] Federal Deposit Insurance Corporation, April 2012.

[83] Federal Reserve Financial Services, September 10, 2013.

[84] Ibid.

[85] Federal Deposit Insurance Corporation, October 2014 (forthcoming).

In: Mobile Financial Services …
Editor: Oscar Cortez
ISBN: 978-1-63484-551-9

Chapter 3

CONSUMERS AND MOBILE FINANCIAL SERVICES 2015[*]

Alexandra Brown, Sam Dodini, Arturo Gonzalez, Ellen Merry and Logan Thomas

EXECUTIVE SUMMARY

Mobile phones have increasingly become tools that consumers use for banking, payments, budgeting, and shopping. Given the rapid pace of developments in the area of mobile finance, the Federal Reserve Board began conducting annual surveys of consumers' use of mobile financial services in 2011. The survey examines trends in the adoption and use of mobile banking, payments, and shopping behavior and how the emergence of mobile financial services affects consumers' interaction with financial institutions.

This report presents findings from the 2014 survey, fielded in December, which focused on consumers' use of mobile technology to access financial services and make financial decisions. Where applicable, the findings from the current survey are also compared with the findings from the 2011, 2012, and 2013 surveys. Topics include consumer access to bank services using mobile phones ("mobile banking"), consumer payment for goods and services using mobile phones ("mobile payments"), and consumer shopping decisions facilitated by use of mobile phones. Details about the survey, its methodology, and limitations can be found in the body of the report and in a methodological appendix.

Key Findings

Key findings of the 2014 survey include:

[*] This is an edited, reformatted and augmented version of a paper prepared by the Consumer and Community Development Research Section of the Federal Reserve Board's Division of Consumer and Community Affairs (DCCA), issued March 2015.

- **Mobile phones are in widespread use.**
  - Eighty-seven percent of the U.S. adult population has a mobile phone, consistent with 2013.
  - Seventy-one percent of mobile phones are smart-phones (Internet-enabled), up from 61 percent a year earlier.
- **The ubiquity of mobile phones is changing the way consumers access financial services.**
  - Thirty-nine percent of all mobile phone owners with a bank account have used mobile banking in the 12 months prior to the survey, up from 33 percent in 2013 and 29 percent in 2012.
  - Fifty-two percent of smartphone owners with a bank account have used mobile banking in the 12 months prior to the survey, up from 51 percent a year earlier.
  - Among those mobile phone users with bank accounts who do not currently use mobile banking, 11 percent think that they will probably or definitely use it within the next 12 months, down from 12 percent a year earlier.
  - The most common use of mobile banking is to check account balances or recent transactions (94 percent of mobile banking users).
  - Among mobile banking users, transferring money between an individual's own accounts (61 percent) and receiving an alert (e.g., a text message, push notification, or e-mail) from their bank (57 percent) are the second- and third-most common uses of mobile banking.
  - Fifty-one percent of mobile banking users have deposited a check using their mobile phone in the 12 months prior to the survey, up from 38 percent in 2013.
  - Among mobile banking users, the frequency of use has increased slightly, from a median of four times per month in 2013 to five times per month in 2014. This frequency was five times per month in 2012.
  - Residents of more rural areas have a lower incidence of mobile banking use than residents of more urban areas.
- **Mobile phones are also changing the way consumers make payments.**
  - Twenty-two percent of all mobile phone owners reported having made a mobile payment in the 12 months prior to the survey, up from 17 percent in 2013 and 15 percent in 2012.
  - The share of smartphone users who reported having made a mobile payment in the 12 months prior to the survey has increased to 28 percent, up from 24 percent in both 2013 and 2012.
  - Among mobile payment users with smartphones, the most common type of mobile payment was bill payment through an online system or mobile app (68 percent, up from 66 percent in 2013).
  - Thirty-nine percent of all mobile payment users with smartphones have made a point-of-sale payment using their mobile phone in the 12 months prior to the survey, in line with the 39 percent reporting such payments in 2013.
  - Of mobile payment users with smartphones who made point-of-sale mobile payments, 31 percent did so by scanning a barcode or QR code displayed on

their phone's screen at check out (down from 39 percent in 2013), while 22 percent used an app that did not require tapping their mobile phone or scanning a barcode (up from 17 percent in 2013).
- Residents of more rural areas have a lower incidence of mobile payments use than residents of more urban areas.

- **A preference for other methods of banking and making payments, as well as concerns about security, continue to be the main impediments to the adoption of mobile financial services cited by some consumers.**
    - Of those not using mobile banking, the primary reason respondents cited was a belief that their banking needs were being met without the use of mobile banking (86 percent).
    - The primary reason non-mobile payment users gave for not using mobile payments was that they believe it is easier to pay with cash or credit/debit cards (75 percent).
    - Concern about the security of the technology was a common reason given for not using mobile banking or mobile payments (62 percent and 59 percent, respectively, of non-users).
- **Smartphones are changing the way people shop and make financial decisions.**
    - Forty-seven percent of smartphone users have comparison shopped with their phone while at a retail store, and 33 percent have used their phone to scan a product's barcode to find the best price for the item.
    - Of those consumers who used their phones to comparison shop in a retail store, 69 percent have changed where they purchased a product as a result of the information they found.
    - Forty-two percent of smartphone users have used their phone to browse product reviews or get product information while shopping at a retail store, and 79 percent of them changed the item they purchased based on this information.
    - Sixty-three percent of mobile banking users have checked their account balance on their phone before making a large purchase in the previous 12 months leading up to the survey, and over half (53 percent) of them decided not to purchase an item as a result of their account balance or credit limit.
    - Twenty-nine percent of all mobile phone users and 38 percent of smartphone users have used their phone to track purchases and expenses.
- **Mobile phones are prevalent among unbanked and underbanked consumers.**
    - The share of consumers who are unbanked is 13 percent, and the share who are underbanked is 14 percent.
    - Sixty-seven percent of the unbanked have access to a mobile phone, 65 percent of which are smartphones.
    - Ninety percent of the underbanked have access to a mobile phone, 73 percent of which are smartphones.
    - Forty-eight percent of underbanked consumers had used mobile banking in the 12 months prior to the survey.

INTRODUCTION

In 2011, the Federal Reserve Board's Division of Consumer and Community Affairs conducted its first Survey of Consumers' Use of Mobile Financial Services. Since that time, the adoption of mobile financial services has continued to increase, along with the range of services offered. As part of its ongoing efforts to monitor developments in the mobile financial services arena and to gain insights into consumers' usage of, and attitudes toward, mobile financial services, the Board has continued to conduct the survey annually.[1] The fourth survey, conducted in December 2014, included a random sample of respondents to the previous survey in 2013, as well as a random sample of new respondents. The sub- sample of respondents who voluntarily completed both the 2013 and 2014 waves of the survey allows for the analysis of changes in behavior over the past year among these individuals.

Survey Background

The original survey instrument and subsequent waves of the survey were designed in consultation with a mobile financial services advisory group made up of key Federal Reserve System staff with relevant consumer research and payments backgrounds. The 2012, 2013, and 2014 survey samples were all composed of a mix of a randomly selected respondents to the previous year's survey and new survey respondents.

The 2014 survey was again administered by GfK, an online consumer research company, on behalf of the Board. The survey was conducted using a sample of adults ages 18 and over from KnowledgePanel®, a proprietary, probability-based web panel of more than 50,000 individuals from randomly sampled households; the sample was designed to be representative of the U.S. population. After pretesting, the data collection for the survey began on December 5, 2014, and concluded on December 21, 2014.

For the results presented in the main body of this report, the sample was drawn following the method used for the 2012 and 2013 surveys. As shown in table 1, e-mails were sent to 2,308 randomly selected respondents to the 2013 survey and 2,657 randomly selected respondents from the remaining members of KnowledgePanel®. The respondents completed the survey in approximately 12 minutes (median time). Of the 2,925 respondents, 1,489 had responded to the 2013 survey one year before, while 1,436 were new survey respondents drawn from the general population.[2] Further details on the survey methodology are included in appendix 1.

Table 1. Key survey response statistics: Main interview

	Number sampled for main survey	Qualified completes	Completion rate
2013 re-interviews	2,308	1,489	64.5%
Fresh cases	2,657	1,436	54.0%
Total primary sample	4,965	2,925	58.9%

As with any survey method, Internet panels can be subject to biases resulting from undercoverage or nonresponse and, in this case, potential underrepresentation of adults who may be uncomfortable with technology. Not everyone in the United States has access to the Internet, and there are demographic (income, education, age) and geographic (urban and rural) differences between those who do have access and those who do not. These concerns are addressed by GfK providing Internet access to respondents who do not have it in order to include the portion of the population that does not have Internet access in KnowledgePanel®, and using sample weights to ensure that the Internet usage and key demographics of the sample population matches the adult U.S. population. See appendix 1 for a more detailed discussion. While care has been taken to ensure the survey results are generalizable to the adult U.S. population, the usual caveats regarding surveys nevertheless apply.

The full survey questionnaire is presented in appendix 2 and the responses to all the categorical survey questions are presented in appendix 3 in the order that the questions were asked of respondents. Tables of summary statistics for the respondent demographics by mobile phone usage are also included as tables C.66 to C.69. Beginning at table C.70, cross-tabulations are presented of consumers' use of mobile phones, mobile banking, and mobile payments by age, race, gender, education, and income.

The following sections of this report summarize key findings from the Federal Reserve Board's survey of consumers conducted by GfK, with a focus on how consumers use mobile phones to conduct their banking, make payments, enhance information gathering while shopping, and manage their finances. The numbers cited in this report are derived from the Board survey unless otherwise noted. All data were weighted to yield estimates for the U.S. adult population. Only questions pertaining to these topics are discussed in the report; however, the complete survey questionnaire and the results of the entire survey are summarized in appendix 2 and appendix 3.

Consumer Access to Mobile Phones

As of December 2014, 87 percent of the U.S. population ages 18 and above owned or had regular access to a mobile phone. While the percent of the adult population with mobile phones has remained constant over the previous two years, an increasing proportion of those own smartphones: this survey's 71 percent smartphone ownership rate among those with mobile phones is a substantial increase over the 61 percent rate reported in 2013,[3] 52 percent rate in 2012, and 44 percent rate in 2011.

Rates of mobile phone usage remain high and consistent across demographic and socioeconomic groups. The prevalence of mobile phones demonstrates the extent to which they have become engrained in modern culture. Mobile phone usage is approximately 91 percent for persons ages 18 to 44, and declines only slightly to 87 percent for persons ages 45 to 59 and to 80 percent for persons ages 60 and over. Smartphone adoption is also higher among younger generations, with the differences being more pronounced among age groups: 84 percent of those ages 18 to 29 and 86 percent of those ages 30 to 44 who own a mobile phone have a smartphone, while 67 percent of mobile phone owners ages 45 to 59 and 47 percent of mobile phone owners ages 60 and over have a smartphone.

Table 2. Smartphone usage by race/ethnicity Percent, except as noted

Race/ethnicity	Smartphone usage			
	2011	2012	2013	2014
White, non-Hispanic	41	50	57	68
Black, non-Hispanic	47	54	63	66
Other, non-Hispanic	45	54	76	83
Hispanic	55	60	72	82
2+ races, non-Hispanic	43	59	64	65
Total	44	52	61	71
Number of respondents	**2,002**	**2,291**	**2,341**	**2,603**

Note: The denominator is all respondents with a mobile phone.

Mobile phone ownership varies slightly by race and ethnicity, with non-Hispanic whites, Hispanics, and non-Hispanic blacks having rates of 88 percent, 85 percent, and 83 percent, respectively. However, adoption of smartphones varies in a somewhat more pronounced way: 82 percent of Hispanic mobile phone users have a smartphone, compared to 68 percent of non-Hispanic whites and 66 percent of non- Hispanic blacks (table 2).

Mobile phone and smartphone usage does vary with the level of household income. In households earning less than $25,000 per year, 74 percent of adults have a mobile phone of some type, and 53 percent have a smartphone. Use of both mobile phones and smart-phones increases with income, reaching 95 percent and 85 percent, respectively, for adults in households earning more than $100,000 per year.

The relatively high prevalence of mobile phone and smartphone use among younger generations, minorities, and those with low levels of income—groups that are more likely to be unbanked or under-banked—makes mobile phones a potential platform for expanding financial access and inclusion.

In 2014, the share of consumers who were unbanked rose to 13 percent from 10 percent in 2013.[4] The share of consumers who would be described as underbanked—defined as having a bank account but also using an alternative financial service such as a money order, check cashing service, pawn shop loan, auto title loan, paycheck advance/deposit advance, or a payday loan—was 14 percent in 2014.[5]

Among individuals who are unbanked, 67 percent have access to a mobile phone and 65 percent of these are smartphones. Smartphone ownership has been increasing among the unbanked. The share of the unbanked with access to a mobile phone was 69 percent in 2013 and 59 percent in 2012, approximately half of which were smartphones.

Among the underbanked, 90 percent have a mobile phone, 73 percent of which are smartphones. Further, 48 percent of the underbanked with mobile phones reported using mobile banking in the 12 months prior to the survey, while 32 percent reported making mobile payments.

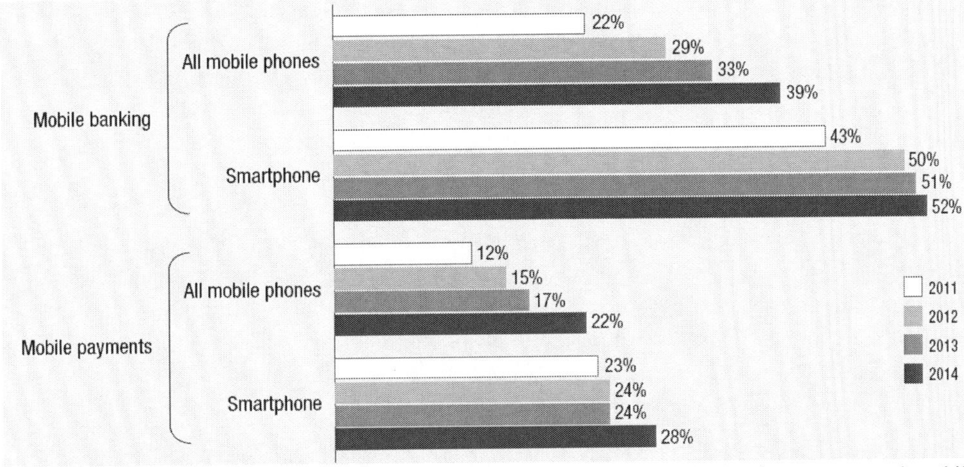

Note: For mobile banking, the results are derived from respondents with bank accounts and mobile phones and all respondents with bank accounts and smartphones, respectively. For mobile payments, the results are derived from respondents with mobile phones and all respondents with smartphones, respectively.

Figure 1. Usage of mobile banking and mobile payments by mobile phone type, 2011–14.

Trends in the Utilization of Mobile Banking and Payments

Services that allow consumers to obtain financial account information and conduct transactions with their financial institution ("mobile banking") and that allow consumers to make payments, transfer money, or pay for goods and services ("mobile payments") have become increasingly prevalent. Over the past several years, these services have become available at a broader range of institutions and the types of services continue to evolve. With increased dissemination of technology and a broadening array of options, consumer adoption of mobile financial services has risen. In the 2011 survey, for instance, 22 percent of mobile phone users with bank accounts and 43 percent of smartphone users with bank accounts reported that they had used mobile banking in the previous 12 months.[6] These proportions have increased in each year of the survey. In the 2014 survey, the prevalence of mobile banking continued to increase, reaching 39 percent of mobile phone users with bank accounts and 52 percent of smartphone users with bank accounts (figure 1).

Use of mobile payments has also increased. In 2011, 12 percent of mobile phone users and 23 percent of smartphone users reported using mobile payments. By 2014, usage of mobile payments had increased to 22 percent for mobile phone users and increased to 28 percent for smartphone users. The steady increases in the adoption rate among all mobile phone users, but more gradual rise in the adoption rate among smartphone users, suggest that smartphone adoption substantially contributed to the increased use of mobile payments.

A continuing impediment to adoption of either mobile banking or mobile payments appears to be consumers' limited demand for them: many consumers said their needs were already being met without mobile banking or payments, that they were comfortable with non-mobile options, and that they did not see a clear benefit from using either service. In addition, around one in five (22 percent) of those with mobile phones and bank accounts indicated they do not know if their bank or credit union offers mobile banking, which may be consistent with a lack of interest in these services among a portion of the population. That said, the share who do not know if mobile banking is available from their bank decreased from 28 percent in the 2013 survey, and the share that said their bank does not offer the service decreased as well—from 6 percent in 2013 to 4 percent in 2014. These results suggest an increase in availability and consumer awareness of mobile banking services.

Concerns about the security of mobile banking and mobile payment technologies are also frequently cited as reasons why consumers chose not to adopt these technologies. Consumers appear to be more cognizant of the need to protect the personal information stored on their phones, as they are increasingly using passwords to protect their smartphones. The share of smartphone owners who password protect their phone increased to 69 percent in 2014, from 61 percent in 2013 and 54 percent in 2012.[7]

Box 1. Use of Mobile Financial Services among Rural Respondents

Mobile financial services may offer convenience or access in different ways to different subpopulations. One group that could especially benefit from mobile services is rural residents. Because rural residents may have to travel longer distances to visit financial institutions compared to urban consumers, mobile banking services may be particularly convenient. However, there are also countervailing factors that could make usage less likely. To learn more, the 2014 survey included an oversample of residents in rural areas.

Thirty-three percent of residents in non-metropolitan (non-metro) areas reported using mobile banking services in the prior 12 months, compared with 39 percent of respondents in metropolitan (metro) areas. Similarly, a smaller percentage (17 percent) of non-metro respondents reported using mobile payments in the prior 12 months relative to respondents in metro areas (23 percent).

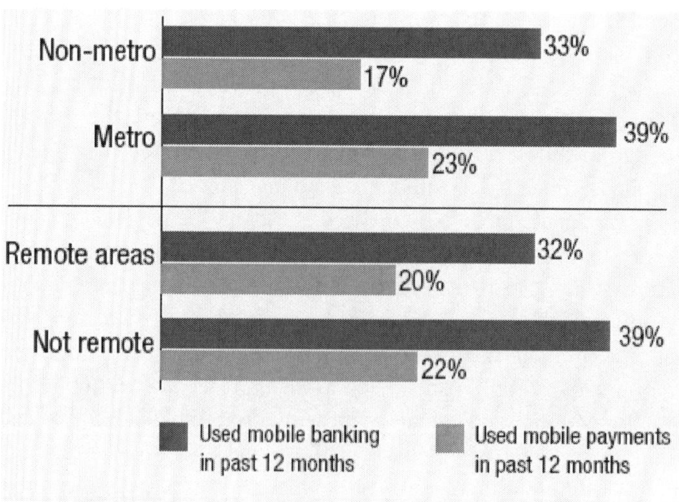

Figure A. Mobile banking and mobile payments, by Geography..

This commonly used metropolitan/non-metropolitan distinction, however, has some limitations as a way to identify rural areas. In particular, non-metro areas include some places that are connected to urbanized areas and have a diversity of access to financial services. To provide an alternate measure of usage of mobile financial services for rural respondents, the survey results were also analyzed using a more narrow definition, measuring as "remote areas" only the respondents who live in small towns and rural areas with low commuting flows to urban places.[1] Fairly similar patterns persisted using this definition: 32 percent used mobile banking in remote rural areas, compared to 39 percent for everyone else, and 20 percent of those from remote rural areas used mobile payments, compared to 22 percent of the rest of respondents (figure A).

If, by either measure, rural residents appear to use mobile financial services at least somewhat less than those in non-rural areas, why would this be? Results from this survey point to some combination of differing technology, access to broadband services, services offered by financial institutions, and consumer awareness of those services.

Non-metro residents are slightly less likely than metro residents—84 versus 88 percent—to own a mobile phone, but considerably less likely to own a smartphone—54 versus 63 percent. They are also less likely to report near-constant access. When asked to characterize their Internet access on a mobile phone through wifi or a wireless network, 57 percent of non-metro respondents described it as "nearly always available," compared to 64 percent of respondents in metro areas (table A).[2] This relative lack of smartphone ownership and constant mobile Internet access may make use of certain mobile services less attractive or perhaps not possible.

When it comes to mobile banking, the supply of services also appears to differ. When asked whether mobile banking was offered by their financial institution, 65 percent of respondents in non-metro areas said yes, compared to 75 percent in metro areas (figure B).

Table A. Internet access on mobile phone through wifi or a wireless network (3G, 4G, LTE) is…

	Almost always available	Not always available, but is available at convenient locations	Available only at locations that require extra effort or planning to get to	Not available	I do not need access to the Internet on my mobile phone
Non-metro	57%	12%	2%	10%	20%
Metro	64%	8%	1%	7%	18%
Remote areas	59%	10%	1%	10%	19%
Not remote	63%	9%	1%	8%	18%

Note: Here and elsewhere in this report, totals may not add to 100 percent due to rounding and question non-response.

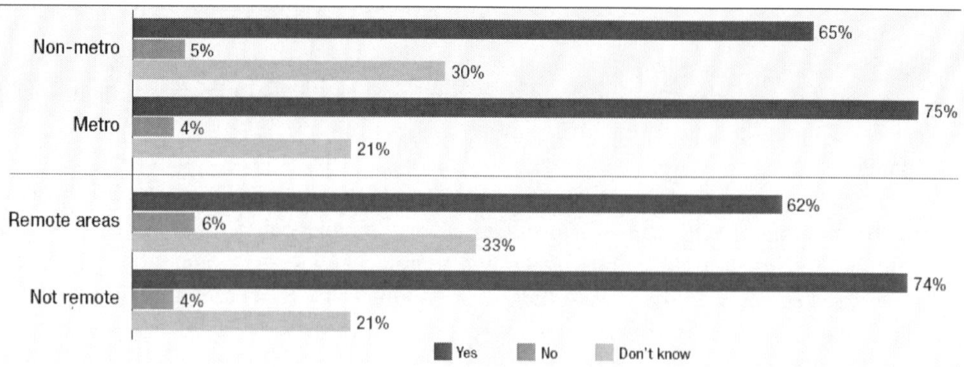

Figure B. Bank or credit union offers mobile banking, by geography.

A higher share (30 percent) of respondents in non-metro areas also reported not knowing if mobile banking was offered by their financial institution, compared to 21 percent in urban areas. Whether this represents a lack of interest by rural consumers or simply a lack of awareness, it would seem that fewer rural residents have access to mobile banking or are aware of available mobile banking services relative to residents of more urban areas.

Demographic differences between residents of metro and non-metro areas also may be a factor in any observed differences in the use of technology or the adoption of mobile financial services across areas.[3] In addition, preferences regarding technology use may be correlated with residential location apart from these other demographic factors. Overall, respondents from non-metro areas are as likely to be "banked" as metro area respondents—86 versus 87 percent, respectively—but somewhat less likely to use either mobile banking services or mobile payments. The lower usages may be associated with lower availability of or consumers' knowledge about mobile banking services by their financial institution, lower levels of smartphone adoption, and less continuous mobile broadband access. They could also be attributed to other factors, including differences between urban and rural residents in preferences, demographic characteristics, or demand for these services. These results indicate that the promise of mobile technology as a way to bridge some challenges of living in rural areas may have not yet been fully realized.

[1] This alternate measure uses Rural-Urban Commuting Area (RUCA) codes, developed by the Department of Agriculture. The "Remote areas" correspond to small towns (less than 2,500 people) and rural areas with low urban commuting in RUCA code categories 7.0, 7.2, 8.0, 8.2, 9.0, 10.0, 10.2, and 10.3. (See www.ers.usda.gov/data-products/rural-urban-commuting-area-codes.aspx.) The companion category "Not remote" includes most portions of metropolitan and micropolitan areas, as well as small towns and rural areas that have a substantial secondary commuting flow (30–50 percent) to urban areas. This narrower definition of rural areas is very similar to a definition developed by the WWAMI Rural Health Research Center (http://depts.washington.edu/uwruca/ruca-maps.php). See appendix 1 for additional information on the sampling methods used for the primary sample and rural oversample included in this analysis.

[2] Nearly 1.3 million people in rural areas lacked access to mobile broadband in 2012, and rural residents generally face greater challenges with mobile coverage than urban residents. See https://apps.fcc.gov/edocs_public/attachmatch/FCC-13-34A1.pdf.

[3] For example, estimates from the 2013 American Community Survey show that the median age of the population in non-metro areas is higher than in metro areas. Mobile banking use is lower among older consumers, as noted in this report.

ACCESSING FINANCIAL SERVICES

Survey respondents were given a set of screening questions that asked if they had access to a bank account, the Internet, and a mobile phone. They were further asked about the various ways in which they access their financial accounts. Of the 87 percent of American consumers who have a checking, savings, or money market account, the majority use some form of technology to interact with their financial institution.

As shown in figure 2, the most common way of interacting with a financial institution remains in-person at a branch, with 87 percent of consumers who have a bank account reporting that they had visited a branch and spoken with a teller in the 12 months prior to the survey. The second-most common means of access in the previous 12 months was using an automated teller machine (ATM) at 75 percent, followed by online banking at 74 percent.[8] Onethird of all consumers with bank accounts used telephone banking, while 35 percent used mobile banking, up from 30 percent the previous year.[9] (For additional information on the use of various banking channels by mobile banking users, see box 2.)

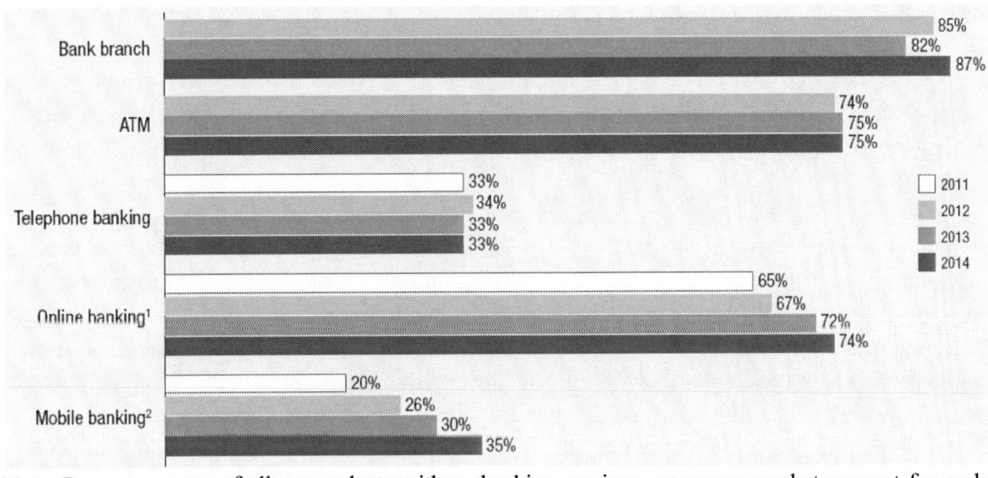

Note: Percentages are of all respondents with a checking, savings, or money market account for each banking channel, regardless of mobile phone ownership or access to the Internet. Questions about usage of bank branches and ATMs were not included on the 2011 survey.

1. For online banking, respondents who reported that they did not have regular access to the Internet other than that provided by GfK were not asked the online banking question in the 2011–2013 surveys. In the 2014 survey, all respondents with bank accounts were asked the question about online banking, which raised the measure for 2014 to 74 percent—2 percentage points higher than if these respondents had been excluded as in prior years.
2. For mobile banking, the percentages here may differ from the incidence rates elsewhere in this report because the latter are computed for those with mobile phones and bank accounts.

Figure 2. Usage of different means of accessing banking services, 2011–14.

Mobile Banking

The Federal Reserve survey defines mobile banking as "using a mobile phone to access your bank or credit union account. This can be done either by accessing your bank or credit union's web page through the web browser on your mobile phone, via text messaging, or by using an app downloaded to your mobile phone."[10]

Adoption Rates

The adoption of mobile banking has continued to increase in the past year. When asked about usage in the previous 12 months, 39 percent of mobile phone users with a bank account reported that they used mobile banking, a proportion that has been steadily climbing (figure 1). Mobile banking among smart- phone users with a bank account is substantially higher at 52 percent, up modestly from earlier surveys. The higher incidence of mobile banking adoption among smartphone users suggests that as smart-phone adoption continues to increase, mobile banking usage may also increase.

A significant fraction of mobile banking users have only recently adopted the technology. Although the majority of mobile banking users reported that they started using it more than one year ago, 15 percent reported that they adopted mobile banking in the last six months, and 12 percent reported that they adopted mobile banking between six and twelve months ago. Among those consumers with mobile phones who do not currently use mobile banking, 11 percent reported that they will "probably" or "definitely" use mobile banking in the following 12 months.

Although previous surveys suggest that the reported adoption intentions of the respondents do not perfectly reflect subsequent behavior, there is an association between the planned use of mobile banking and subsequent adoption. Using the panel of respondents to both the 2013 and 2014 Board surveys, it is possible to compare the reported mobile banking adoption intention over the next 12 months from the 2013 survey to the reported use of mobile banking in the 2014 survey. Of those consumers who reported in 2013 that they would "definitely" or "probably" adopt mobile banking in the following 12 months, only 28 percent had, in fact, adopted mobile banking one year later. Nonetheless, this is a higher proportion than those who said they did not expect their activity to change. Among those who indicated that they "probably will not" and "definitely will not" adopt mobile banking, 15 percent and 2 percent, respectively, had adopted mobile banking in 2014.

In total, 11 percent of those who reported that they were not mobile banking users in 2013 reported being mobile banking users in 2014.[11] However, 14 percent of those who were mobile banking users in 2013 reported that they had not used mobile banking in 2014.[12] Among panel respondents overall, mobile banking usage increased from 33 percent of mobile phone users with bank accounts in 2013 to 35 percent in 2014.

For the group of respondents in the 2013 survey who believed they "definitely" or "probably" would use mobile banking in the coming year, the most notable difference between those who actually did adopt mobile banking by the 2014 survey and those who did not was that the adopters were more likely to own a smartphone. Of this likely-to-adopt group, 42 percent with smartphones in 2014 used mobile banking, while 3 percent with feature phones used mobile banking. In both the panel and cross-sectional data, smartphone users were more likely to engage in mobile banking than non-smartphone users.

BOX 2. CHANNEL USE AMONG MOBILE BANKING USERS

Mobile banking can provide convenient access to some banking services. However, consumers may still need or want to use other banking channels. For example, a visit to an automated teller machine (ATM) or branch may be necessary to withdraw cash, and visiting a branch or talking with a customer service representative may be preferred ways of resolving a problem. Respondents to the survey were asked about their use of five banking channels (branch, ATM, telephone, online banking, and mobile banking), and the answers provide a fuller picture of how mobile banking users interact with their bank or credit union.

Users of mobile banking services generally access them frequently, but not to the exclusion of other kinds of bank services. In general, mobile banking users reported using multiple channels to conduct banking business: 82 percent reported using four or five of these channels; only 2 percent used one or two channels. In the prior 12 months, 95 percent of mobile banking users also used online banking, 92 percent used an ATM, 85 percent visited a branch and spoke with a teller, and 36 percent used telephone banking (table A).

Most mobile banking users (90 percent) reported accessing mobile banking in the preceding month, and the median number of uses for those who used it in that month was five. Similarly, among mobile banking users who accessed online banking, 97 percent used online banking in the prior month, and the median number of uses of online banking was six. The FDIC has noted that many banks have required their customers to be enrolled in online banking before they can enroll in mobile banking, and some mobile banking features, such as setting up payees for bill payment and enrolling in alerts, may require an online setup.[1] These types of bank policies would contribute to the high level of online banking use we observed among mobile banking users. For mobile banking users who accessed ATMs and bank branches, the likelihood of having used those channels in the past month was lower (85 and 72 percent, respectively), and the median number of uses was lower as well (three for ATM and two for branch). These responses suggest that many mobile banking users use online and mobile banking quite consistently for their banking needs, and access other bank channels on a periodic basis.

In a separate question, respondents were asked to rank the three main ways they interact with their bank or credit union. Twenty-one percent of mobile banking users ranked the mobile channel first—a lower share than those who chose online banking (35 percent) or ATM (30 percent), but a higher share than for the branch (13 percent) or telephone banking (1 percent).[2] Tallying the share of mobile banking users who ranked each of the channels in their top three, the ATM channel had the largest share (80 percent), followed by online banking (73 percent), mobile banking (60 percent), branch (56 percent), and telephone banking (17 percent).

Taken together, these estimates indicate that while mobile banking users are utilizing technological platforms at a high rate and on a consistent basis, they have also maintained connections to their banks through the more traditional branch and ATM channels.

Table A. Channel access among mobile banking users

Percent, except as noted			
	MB users who used channel in the past 12 months	MB users who used channel in the past month[1]	Median frequency of channel use past month[2]
Mobile banking	100	90	5
Online banking	95	97	6
ATM	92	85	3
Branch/teller	85	72	2
Telephone banking	36	68	2

[1] Of those who used channel in the past 12 months.
[2] Of those who used channel in the past month.

[1] For the full FDIC white paper "Assessing the Economic Inclusion Potential of Mobile Financial Services," see www.fdic.gov/ consumers/community/mobile/Mobile-Financial-Services.pdf.
[2] The 2013 FDIC National Survey of Unbanked and Underbanked Households reported the primary banking method for house-holds who used mobile banking and accessed their account in the last 12 months as follows: online banking (50 percent), mobile banking (25 percent), ATM/Kiosk (15 percent), bank teller (7 percent), and telephone banking (2 percent). For the full report on the survey, see www.economicinclusion.gov/surveys/2013household/ documents/2013_ FDIC_ Unbanked_HH_Survey_ Report.pdf.

In every year of the survey, older consumers have consistently been less likely to use mobile banking than have younger consumers (table 3). For those with a mobile phone and a bank account, results from the 2014 survey indicate that mobile banking use is 60 percent for those in the 18-to-29 age range and 54 percent for those in the 30-to-44 age group. By comparison, only 13 percent of individuals ages 60 or older reported having used mobile banking. Usage has generally increased from year to year for all age groups.

Consistent with the data from previous surveys, minorities continue to be more likely to use mobile banking than non-Hispanic whites. In particular, Hispanic mobile phone users with bank accounts show a higher rate of use of mobile banking (53 percent) relative to mobile phone users with bank accounts overall (39 percent) (table 4).

Table 3. Use of mobile banking in past 12 months by age

Percent, except as noted				
Age group	2011	2012	2013	2014
18–29	45	54	63	60
30–44	29	37	43	54
45–59	12	21	25	32
60+	5	10	9	13
Total	22	29	33	39
Number of respondents	**1,859**	**2,180**	**2,187**	**2,437**

Note: Percentages are of those in each group who have a mobile phone and a bank account.

Table 4. Use of mobile banking in the past 12 months by race/ethnicity

Percent, except as noted				
Race/ethnicity	**2011**	**2012**	**2013**	**2014**
White, non-Hispanic	19	26	30	34
Black, non-Hispanic	35	39	42	43
Other, non-Hispanic	23	31	35	48
Hispanic	29	36	45	53
2+ races, non-Hispanic	21	36	31	41
Total	22	29	33	39
Number of respondents	**1,859**	**2,180**	**2,187**	**2,437**

Note: Percentages are of those in each group who have a mobile phone and a bank account.

Among those with a mobile phone and bank account, mobile banking use is more common for those with higher levels of education. Usage for those with a college degree or some college (44 percent) is greater than for those with a high school degree or less (29 percent). In addition, mobile banking usage for those mobile phone users with bank accounts with household incomes of $40,000 and above (41 percent) is greater than for those with incomes below $40,000 (34 percent).

Common Mobile Banking Activities

Among those who reported using mobile banking in 2014, the most common mobile banking activity was checking financial account balances or transaction inquiries, with 94 percent of mobile banking users having performed this function in the 12 months prior to the survey (figure 3). This was followed by transfer ring money between accounts, performed by 61 percent of users. In addition, 57 percent of mobile banking users received an alert from their financial institution through a text message, push notification, or e-mail. Depositing a check to an account electronically using a mobile phone camera (known as remote deposit capture) and making an online bill payment from a bank account using a mobile phone were the next most common activities (done by 51 percent and 48 percent of mobile banking users, respectively). Mobile banking users appear to be using mobile applications to conduct their banking transactions, as 71 percent of mobile banking users have installed their bank's application on their phones.

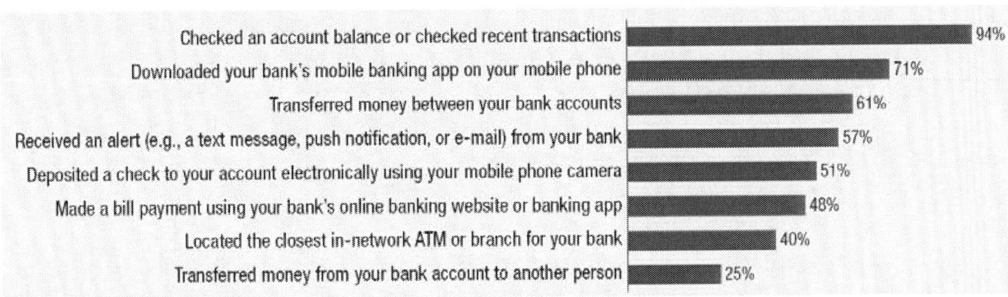

Note: The number of respondents who were mobile banking users was 829.

Figure 3. Using your mobile phone, have you done each of these in the past 12 months? (Among mobile banking users)..

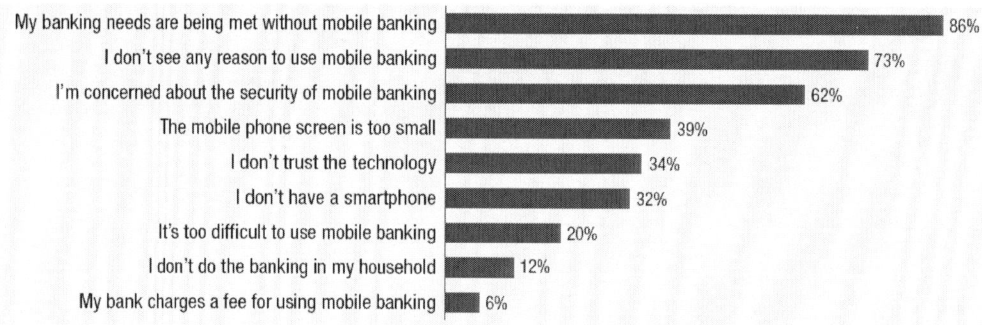

Note: The number of respondents was 945.

Figure 4. Please tell us if each of the reasons below are why you do not use mobile banking.

Among all mobile banking users, the frequency of mobile banking use has increased slightly over the past year. The median reported usage increased from four times per month in 2013 to five times per month in 2014. Median usage for those with bank accounts who reported using mobile banking in 2011 and 2012 was also five times per month.

Among mobile bankers, there is variation in how frequently people use mobile banking services, and what types of activities they engage in. A relatively small share of mobile bankers (6 percent) indicated that they had used mobile banking in the previous year but had not used mobile banking in the previous month. These low-intensity users have a lower likelihood of engaging in all types of mobile banking activities, relative to mobile banking users overall. Like all mobile banking users, the most common task for low-intensity users is checking account balances or recent transactions (84 percent). Forty-three percent of the low-intensity users have downloaded their bank's mobile banking app—a sizeable share, but lower than the 71 percent of all mobile banking users who have done so. A greater proportion of low-intensity mobile banking users are non-Hispanic white (78 percent) compared to all mobile banking users (62 percent). Further, a greater proportion of low-intensity mobile banking users are ages 45 or older (49 percent), relative to all mobile banking users (31 percent).

In contrast, high-intensity users—defined here as mobile banking users who have conducted mobile banking tasks more than 10 times during the month prior to the 2014 survey—tend to conduct all mobile banking tasks at the same or higher rates than the larger group.[13] In particular, high-intensity users reported making bill payments using their bank's online banking website or banking app and transferring money between their own accounts at higher rates than all mobile banking users. Overall, high- intensity users are demographically similar to the larger group of mobile banking users but include slightly greater shares of younger and black or Hispanic mobile banking users.

Reasons for Using—or Not Using—Mobile Banking

Convenience continues to be the most common reason consumers give for adopting mobile banking. Indeed, 35 percent of consumers indicated that the convenience was the main reason they started using mobile banking. Thirty-three percent of consumers said getting a smartphone was the main reason for using mobile banking. A further 20 percent of consumers indicated that the timing of their adoption of mobile banking was driven by their bank starting to offer the service.

Among those consumers with mobile phones and bank accounts who do not currently use mobile banking, several reasons for not using the service pre-dominated—namely, they believed that their banking needs were being met without mobile banking (86 percent), they did not see any reason to use mobile banking (73 percent), and they were concerned about security (62 percent) (figure 4). The small size of the mobile phone screen was cited by 39 percent of consumers as the reason they do not use mobile banking. This was followed by a lack of trust in the technology (34 percent) and not having a smartphone (32 percent) as reasons for not using mobile banking. Less commonly cited reasons included the difficulty associated with using mobile banking (20 percent) and not doing the banking in the household (12 percent). The incidence of reasons for not using mobile banking was generally consistent between the 2013 and 2014 surveys. However, in the 2014 survey, concerns about the security of mobile banking decreased from 69 percent in 2013. Also, fewer respondents reported that the small size of the mobile phone screen (44 percent in 2013) and not having a smartphone (44 percent in 2013) were reasons why they had not used mobile banking.

Consumers who expressed concerns about the security of mobile banking were asked to specify what aspect was of greatest concern (figure 5). Some reported fears of data interception (22 percent), phone "hacking" (17 percent), and lost or stolen phones (9 percent). While additional specific concerns were noted by small numbers of respondents, the most common response was that they were concerned with all of those security risks occurring (43 percent).

When consumers who do not use mobile banking were asked what mobile banking activities they would be interested in performing if their concerns were addressed, their responses largely mirrored those of current users. Checking financial account balances or recent transactions was the most commonly cited (32 percent), followed by downloading their bank's mobile banking app (21 percent), transferring money between accounts (20 percent), receiving alerts from their bank (19 percent), locating the closest in-network ATM or branch (18 percent), depositing checks electronically (17 percent), and making bill payments (15 percent). However, 59 percent of those who do not use mobile banking indicated that they had no interest in performing any mobile banking activities even if their concerns were addressed.

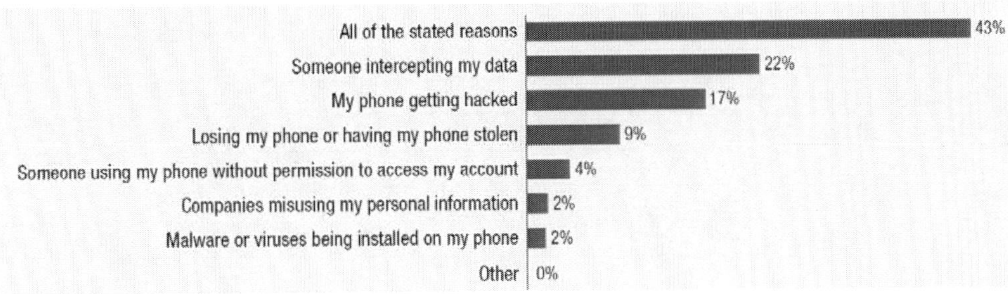

Note: The number of respondents was 600.

Figure 5. Which one of the following security aspects are you most concerned with?

Mobile Payments

For purposes of this survey, mobile payments are defined as "purchases, bill payments, charitable donations, payments to another person, or any other payments made using a mobile phone. You can do this either by accessing a web page through the web browser on your mobile device, by sending a text message (SMS), or by using a downloadable app on your mobile device. The amount of the payment may be applied to your phone bill (for example, Red Cross text message donation), charged to your credit card, deducted from a prepaid card, or withdrawn directly from your bank account."

Adoption Rates

Mobile payments continue to be less common than mobile banking. Based on the responses to the broad definition of mobile payments listed above, 22 percent of those with access to a mobile phone reported that they made a mobile payment in the 12 months prior to the survey, up from 17 percent in 2013, 15 percent in 2012, and 12 percent in 2011. Rates of mobile payment usage are somewhat higher among smartphone users. The share of smartphone users who reported having made a mobile payment in the previous 12 months increased to 28 percent, up from 24 percent in 2013 and 2012, and 23 percent in 2011.

Table 5. Use of mobile payments in the past 12 months by age

Percent, except as noted				
Age group	**2011**	**2012**	**2013**	**2014**
18–29	20	26	28	34
30–44	16	18	21	31
45–59	8	9	13	16
60+	5	8	7	7
Total	12	15	17	22
Number of respondents	**2,002**	**2,291**	**2,341**	**2,603**

Note: Percentages are of those in each group who have a mobile phone.

Table 6. Use of mobile payments in the past 12 months by race/ethnicity

Percent, except as noted				
Race/ethnicity	**2011**	**2012**	**2013**	**2014**
White, non-Hispanic	10	13	12	17
Black, non-Hispanic	14	18	34	34
Other, non-Hispanic	15	17	16	24
Hispanic	20	18	26	32
2+ races, non-Hispanic	9	13	31	23
Total	12	15	17	22
Number of respondents	**2,002**	**2,291**	**2,341**	**2,603**

Note: Percentages are of those in each group who have a mobile phone.

Of current mobile payment users, 16 percent had started using mobile payments in the prior six months, while 13 percent began using mobile payments six to twelve months prior to the survey. A further 21 percent reported that they started using mobile payments in the prior one to two years, and 26 percent reported that they began using mobile payments more than two years prior to the survey. Twenty-two percent of users are unable to recall when they began using mobile payments.

Younger consumers are more likely to make mobile payments (table 5). Of those with a mobile phone in 2014, 34 percent of individuals ages 18 to 29 and 31 percent of individuals ages 30 to 44 had made mobile payments. By comparison, only 7 percent of those ages 60 or over reported making mobile payments. This pattern of use by age has been evident across all four years of the survey.

Among those owning a mobile phone, minorities are more likely to make mobile payments (table 6). In 2014, 34 percent of non-Hispanic blacks with mobile phones and 32 percent of Hispanics with mobile phones had made mobile payments, while only 17 percent of non-Hispanic whites reported making mobile payments. The pattern of minorities making mobile payments at a higher rate than white, non-Hispanic consumers has persisted over time.

There is no clear relationship between mobile payment usage and income or education level among those who own a mobile phone.

Common Mobile Payment Activities

Focusing only on those smartphone owners who reported that they had made a mobile payment in the prior 12 months, the most common mobile payment activity was paying bills (68 percent), followed by making online or in-app purchases (54 percent). The next most common activities reported by mobile payment users were paying for a product or service at a store (39 percent) and transferring money directly to another person in the United States (36 percent). Receiving money from another person using a mobile phone (31 percent) and using an app to receive loyalty or reward points (30 percent) were also relatively common activities for mobile payment users with smartphones. Less common activities were paying for parking, a taxi, or public transit using a mobile phone (16 percent), making a payment by text message (11 percent), and sending a remittance overseas (9 percent). (See box 3 for a research note on measuring the use of mobile payments and mobile banking.)

Although using a mobile phone to pay for a retail purchase at the point-of-sale (POS) is less common than paying bills or making an online or in-app purchase, it is becoming less rare of an occurrence. Developments in technology, the entrance of new market participants, and increased familiarity with mobile payments may be contributing to this trend. As noted above, in 2014, 39 percent of all mobile payments users with smartphones made POS purchases with their mobile phone in the 12 months prior to the survey—a figure in line with the 39 percent who reported such payments in 2013. However, among those POS users, less than half (41 percent) had made a POS payment in the preceding month, and less than a quarter had made more than two such payments.

Box 3. Research Note: Measuring the Use of Mobile Payments and Mobile Banking

Over the four years that the Federal Reserve has been conducting this survey, respondents have consistently been asked to gauge whether they had used mobile banking or mobile payments in the preceding 12 months based on general descriptions of these mobile financial services. Responses to those questions provide a baseline for how usage has changed over the course of the survey. However, the number or respondents reporting that they use mobile banking and mobile payments based on the general descriptions is lower than the number reporting that they engage in specific banking or payment activities. This indicates that actual usage may be somewhat higher than the general questions would indicate, and may indicate that more specific questions may prompt respondents to remember details about their usage in a different way. These results also illustrate the challenges for both researchers and respondents in how to categorize mobile banking and payment activities as technologies continue to emerge and evolve and as consumers move from exploration to adoption of new ways of using their smartphones.

For example, mobile payment users were identified by a general question about whether they have engaged in any mobile payments activities over the past 12 months.[1] In addition, mobile phone users were asked whether they had used their phone for particular mobile payments tasks. Some respondents who answered "no" to the mobile payments question indicated they have done one or more of these mobile payments tasks, implying the share of people making mobile payments may be higher than the measure of mobile payments users based on the general definition. In the 2014 survey, 28 percent of smartphone owners were identified as mobile payments users based on their response to the general question. By comparison, 47 percent of smartphone owners reported completing at least one mobile payments task, regardless of their answer to the general question about mobile payments.[2]

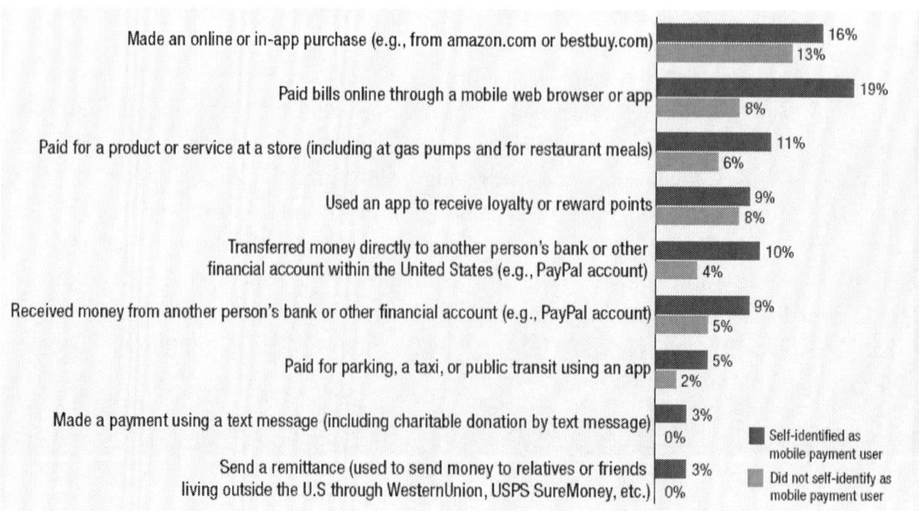

Figure A. Mobile payment tasks for smartphone users, by mobile payment self-identification.

Figure A shows the share of respondents with a smartphone who reported completing mobile payments tasks, grouped by whether they indicated they used mobile payments. The lighter bars represent respondents who said they had used a particular form of mobile payment but had answered "no" to the more general question about whether they had used any form of mobile payment.

A similar pattern is evident with the questions on mobile banking. Thirty-nine percent of those with mobile phones and bank accounts reported using mobile banking in the prior 12 months based on the general question. By comparison, 50 percent of respondents with mobile phones and bank accounts reported completing one or more specific mobile banking tasks, regardless of their answer to the general question about mobile banking.

These results illustrate that technology adoption can be viewed as a continuum, both in terms of the types and frequency of activities involved and in terms of how respondents view and report their activities. The majority of respondents were consistent in providing responses indicating they were either users or non-users of these services in their answers to both the general questions and the specific task questions, although there was less consistency in the responses for mobile payments use than for mobile banking use.[3] Those respondents who provided seemingly anomalous answers did report less frequent use of the specific services cited than respondents who said "yes" to the general question as well as the more specific ones. For this reason, it is possible that some consumers are "dabblers" in mobile services but do not consider themselves more general users of the technology. It is also possible that different questions simply prompted different responses or that some respondents misremembered and answered incorrectly.

[1] See the explanation of mobile payments earlier.

[2] For all those with mobile phones, including both feature phones and smartphones, 22 percent reported making mobile payments based on the general definition and 36 percent reported completing at least one mobile payments task, regardless of their answer to the general question about mobile payments.

[3] Overall, 73 percent of smartphone owners provided consistent responses on the mobile payments questions: 25 percent self-identified as mobile payments users in response to the general question and also reported at least one mobile payments task, while 49 percent self-identified as not using mobile payments based on the general question and reported no mobile payments tasks. Overall, 86 percent of those with mobile phones and bank accounts provided consistent responses to the mobile banking questions: 38 percent self-identified as mobile banking users in response to the general question and reported at least one mobile banking task, while 48 percent self-identified as not using mobile banking based on the general question and reported no mobile banking tasks.

Scanning a QR code displayed on a mobile phone is the most common method that consumers use to make mobile payments at the point of sale, used by 31 percent of those mobile payment users with smartphones who had made mobile POS payments.[14] While this remains the most common POS mobile payment, it is a decrease from 39 percent a year ago. The next most common POS methods were making a payment using a mobile app that does not require scanning a barcode or tapping their device (22 percent), and making a payment by waving or tapping their mobile phone at the POS terminal (14 percent).[15]

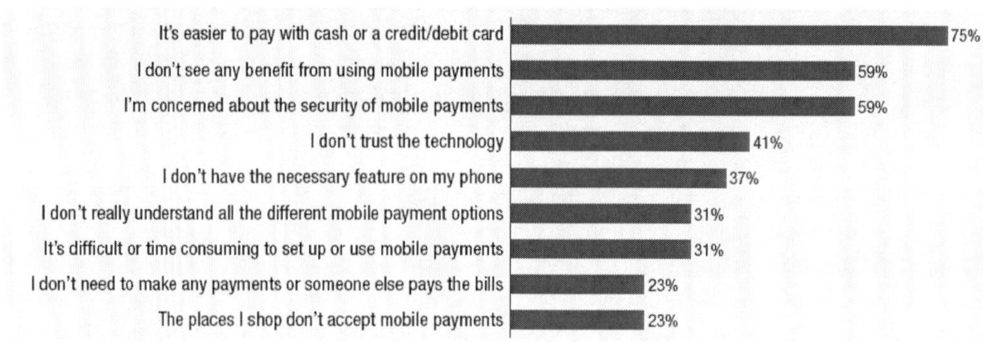

Note: The number of respondents was 2,137.

Figure 6. Please tell us if any of the reasons below are why you do not use mobile payments.

Mobile payments are most commonly funded using debit cards (55 percent), credit cards (51 percent), directly from a bank account (41 percent), or from an account at a non-financial institution such as PayPal (15 percent). Only 8 percent of mobile payment users reported that they used a prepaid debit card, and 4 percent had the charge directly applied to their phone bill. The type of payment used to fund the mobile purchase has implications for the consumer protections that the payer is afforded on the transaction, as different payment sources are covered by different consumer regulations and regulatory agencies.[16]

Among all mobile payments users, the median reported frequency of using mobile payments was two times in the month prior to the survey. As with mobile banking, there is variation among mobile payments users in how frequently they use the service and in types of activities. Twenty-seven percent of mobile payments users reported they had used mobile payments in the past 12 months but not in the month prior to the survey. Like the overall group of mobile payments users, the most common mobile payment activity reported by these low-intensity users was paying bills (31 percent).

Eighteen percent of mobile payments users reported that they had used mobile payments more than five times in the month prior to the survey. Compared to all mobile payment users, these high-intensity mobile payment users had higher rates of engaging in all mobile payments activities and tended to engage in a few mobile payment activities at much higher rates.[17] High-intensity users more frequently made an online or in-app purchase, paid their bills online through a mobile web browser or app, paid for a product or service at a store, and transferred money directly to another person's bank or other financial account.

Reasons for Using—or Not Using—Mobile Payments

Getting a smartphone is the most common reason given by consumers who have newly adopted mobile payment activity (34 percent). Convenience is the second-most common reason people started using mobile payments (29 percent). The ability to make mobile payments becoming available to them was cited by 16 percent of users, while 9 percent indicated that they began using mobile payments because they became comfortable with the security.

Among those who do not use mobile payments, the main reason they have not adopted the technology is that they prefer to use other means of making payments: 75 percent reported that it is easier to pay with other methods. Fifty-nine percent did not see a benefit from using mobile payments; the same proportion cited security concerns (figure 6). The incidence of reasons for not using mobile payments was generally consistent between the 2013 and 2014 surveys. However, in the 2014 survey, concerns about the security of mobile payments decreased from 63 percent in 2013. Also, fewer respondents reported that not having the necessary features on their phone (46 percent in 2013), not understanding mobile payment options (37 percent in 2013), and the places they shopped not accepting mobile payments (27 percent in 2013) were reasons why they had not used mobile payments.

For those worried about the security of mobile payments, the concerns roughly mirror those about mobile banking. The main fears associated with mobile payments include the interception of payment information (21 percent), phone "hacking" (13 percent), lost or stolen phones (10 percent), misuse of personal information (3 percent), and malware or viruses installed on their phone (2 percent). As with mobile banking, the most common response was that respondents were concerned with all of those security risks (51 percent).

When consumers who do not use mobile payments were asked to indicate all the mobile payment activities they would have an interest in using if their concerns were addressed, 65 percent indicated that they simply had no interest in using mobile payments even if their concerns were addressed. This is similar to the responses regarding mobile banking, indicating that some consumers simply have no interest in utilizing the new technology under any circumstances. Of the potential activities of interest to others, receiving/ using coupons on their phone was the most commonly cited (20 percent), followed by using a mobile phone to pay for purchases at a store (18 percent) (figure 7).

When those with a smartphone who did not report making POS payments were asked if they plan to use their mobile phone to make a payment in a store in the next 12 months, 5 percent said they "definitely will" and 16 percent said they "probably will." The majority of smartphone users said that they "probably will not" (44 percent) or "definitely will not" (35 percent) use their phone to make an in-store payment.

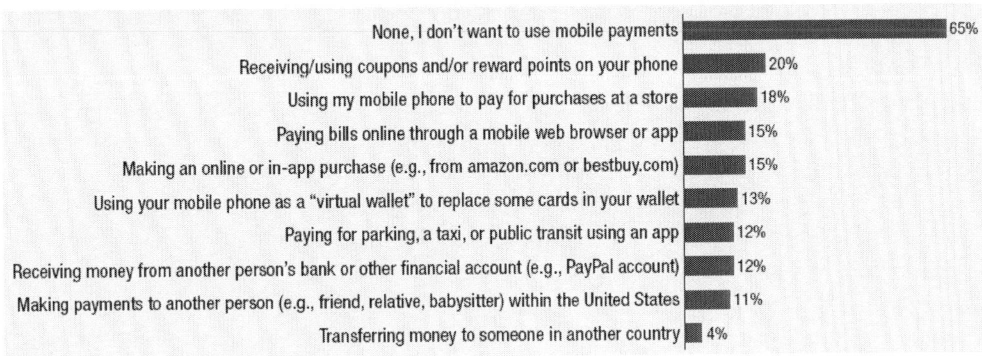

Note: The number of respondents was 2,137.

Figure 7. Activities you would be interested in doing if concerns about mobile payments were addressed.

Mobile Security

One of the main reservations consumers have with adopting mobile banking and mobile payments is concern about the security of the technology. Despite the increased prevalence of mobile banking and mobile payments, a significant share of consumers believe the technology to be unsafe or do not know how safe it is (see box 4 for a discussion of industry developments in securing mobile payments). Among all mobile phone users, 25 percent believed that people's personal information is "somewhat unsafe" when using mobile banking and 19 percent believed that it is "very unsafe." A further 15 percent of mobile phone users simply did not know how safe it is to use mobile banking. Only 7 percent said it is "very safe" to use mobile banking (table 7).

When mobile phone users were asked how safe they believe people's personal financial information is when they use a mobile phone to pay for a purchase at a store, 28 percent said it was "somewhat unsafe" and 21 percent said it was "very unsafe." As with mobile banking, there exists significant uncertainty about the security of POS mobile payments, with 15 percent saying they "don't know" whether people's personal financial information is safe when making such a payment. The share of consumers who said that POS mobile payments were "very safe" was only 5 percent, while 30 percent said that it was "somewhat safe" (table 8).

Box 4. Industry Developments in Securing Mobile Payments

Interest and adoption of mobile payment services may be poised for growth as a number of developments in technology and security take hold in the mobile financial marketplace. In this and preceding surveys, concerns about the security of mobile payment technologies are frequently cited by non-users as reasons for not using mobile payments. Consumers have also cited, to a lesser extent, the lack of necessary features on their phone and the lack of acceptance of mobile payments at places where they shop as reasons for not using mobile payments.[1] Recent efforts to enhance the security of mobile payment transactions and to apply emerging technologies to a payments context could shape consumers' attitudes about and use of mobile payments in the coming years.

This survey's results confirm that security concerns are on the minds of many consumers. The payments industry is taking steps to enhance transaction security at various points in the process, including by working toward conversion to EMV (named after its founders Europay, MasterCard, and Visa), a standard payment specification for authorizing credit and debit chip-card transactions. (This technology is also referred to as "chip and pin" or "chip and signa- ture.") In order to accept in-person EMV transactions, merchants install EMV-compliant checkout terminals in their stores, and card issuers provide consumers with new cards containing microchips that meet the EMV standard. To encourage merchants and card issuers to adopt this technology, the card networks have set a deadline of October 2015, after which they intend to shift liability for fraudulent transactions to the party that is not EMV-compliant. While not a mobile-specific development, EMV conversion ought to decrease the forms of certain types of payment fraud, and could influence consumer preferences over time.

Increasingly, smartphone manufacturers are also equipping devices with hardware and software to provide more payment options—such as Near Field Communications (NFC) antennas to interact with in-store check-out NFC-enabled terminals—and security features—such as fingerprint authentication technology. Many new EMV terminals are likely to also support NFC technology. Security-minded consumers may have more confidence making a mobile payment from a device that uses multiple layers of security, complies with EMV standards, and/or offers new or additional features. While these efforts are largely undertaken by the private sector, an October 2014 Executive Order establishing EMV as the standard for federal government payments may reinforce private actions.[2]

The changes in the marketplace may ultimately better protect customers' data by reducing the amount of data accessed and stored by merchants. New payment card technology that replaces the real card number with a substitute value (also known as a token) may also make it more difficult to use card information—on mobile devices or in other forms— fraudulently. If successful, these efforts could improve consumer confidence in newer payments technology in general, possibly affecting the related use of mobile payments.

[1] In the 2014 survey, 37 percent of non-mobile payments users cited the lack of necessary features on their phone and 23 percent cited the lack of acceptance of mobile payments at places where they shop as reasons for not using mobile payments.

[2] See www.whitehouse.gov/the-press-office/2014/10/17/fact-sheet- safeguarding-consumers-financial-security.

Table 7. How safe do you believe people's personal information is when they use mobile banking?

Percent, except as noted	2013	2014
Very safe	6	7
Somewhat safe	32	34
Somewhat unsafe	25	25
Very unsafe	18	19
Don't know	17	15
Number of respondents	**2,341**	**2,603**

Table 8. How safe do you believe people's personal information is when they use a mobile phone to pay for a purchase at a store?

Percent, except as noted	2013	2014
Very safe	4	5
Somewhat safe	30	30
Somewhat unsafe	27	28
Very unsafe	19	21
Don't know	18	15
Number of respondents	**2,341**	**2,603**

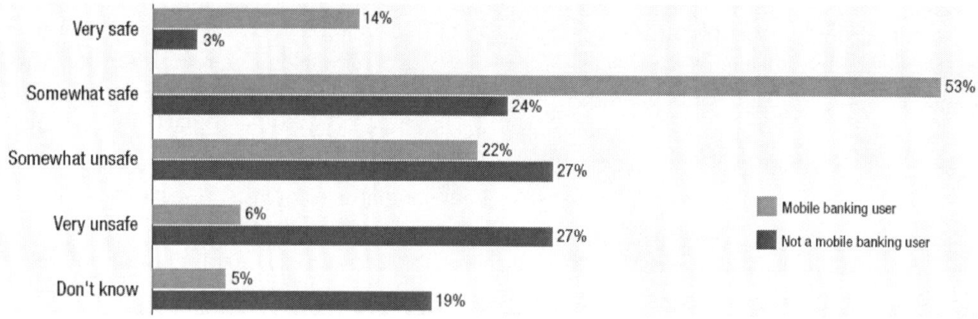

Note: The number of respondents was 829 mobile banking users and 1,584 non-users of mobile banking.

Figure 8. How safe do you believe people's personal information is when they use mobile banking?

In addition, there is a dichotomy in perceived security among users and non-users of mobile banking services. Among mobile phone owners who do not use mobile banking, only 3 percent rated the overall security of mobile banking as "very safe," while 24 percent rated it "somewhat safe." Nineteen percent of non-users indicated that they "don't know" how safe it is to use mobile banking. Mobile banking users, however, rated mobile banking as "very safe" (14 percent) or "somewhat safe" (53 percent) in maintaining their personal information. Only 5 percent of mobile banking users indicated that they "don't know" how safe mobile banking is at protecting their personal information (figure 8).

How Mobile Phones Affect Shopping Behavior

Interest in Mobile Services

Mobile phone users expressed significant interest in expanding the range of functions they could perform with their phones. Consumers were asked to select the types of activity they would be interested in performing with their mobile phones, assuming the function were made available to them (figure 9). Some consumers appear to be open to greater use of their phones as a tool to get the best prices in their shopping activities: 24 percent expressed an interest in using their mobile phones to compare prices while shopping; 26 percent indicate that they would like to receive and manage discount offers and coupons; and 24 percent would like to receive location-based offers. They also expressed an interest in using their phones to store gift cards or track loyalty/reward points (19 percent) and to manage their personal finances (13 percent).

Although consumers might be willing to use their phones to improve shopping experiences, many are resistant to sharing their current location and personal information with companies they shop with regularly (figure 10). Smartphone users were asked about their level of agreement with the statement "I am willing to allow my mobile phone to provide my location to companies I shop with regularly so that they can offer me discounts, promotions, or services based on where I am." There appears to be significant discomfort with providing one's location to companies, as 33 percent indicated that they "disagree" and 26 percent "strongly disagree."

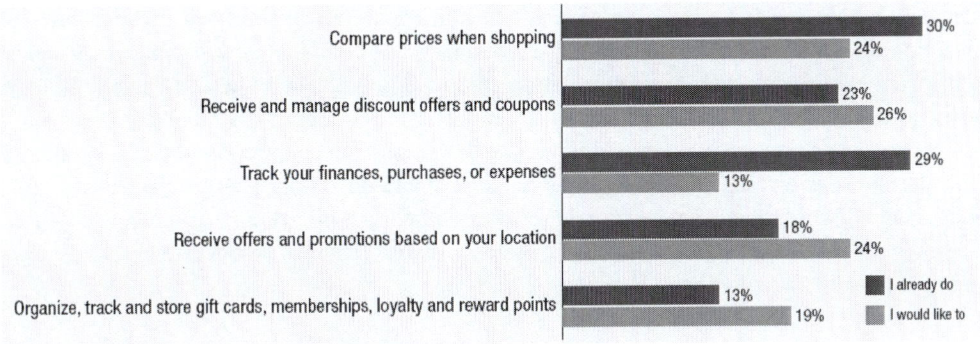

Note: The number of respondents with mobile phones was 2,603.

Figure 9. Share of respondents that already do or would like to use mobile phones for any the following purposes.

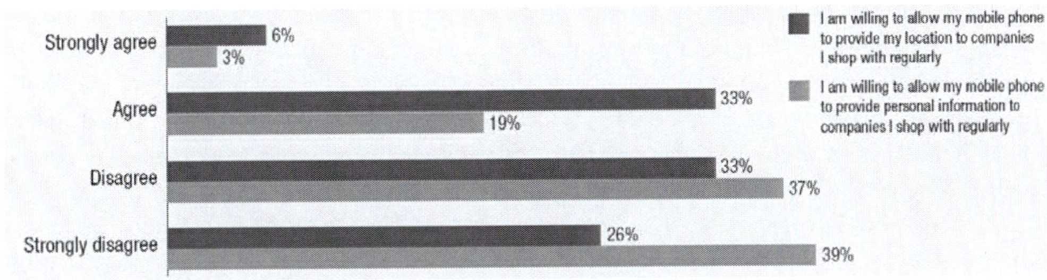

Note: The number of respondents with smartphones was 1,775.

Figure 10. Willingness to allow mobile phones to provide information.

Consumers reported being even less willing to allow their phones to be used to provide companies with their personal information in order to receive targeted discounts, promotions, and offers. When smart- phone owners were asked about their level of agreement with the statement "I am willing to allow my mobile phone to provide personal information such as my sex, age, friends, and shopping history to companies I shop with regularly so that they can offer me targeted discounts, promotions, or services," 37 percent chose "disagree" and 39 percent chose "strongly disagree."

In-Store Product Research and Price Comparison

Consumers are using their mobile phones to comparison shop and obtain product information while in retail stores. The prevalence of smartphones with barcode scanning software and Internet access has altered consumer behavior in the retail environment. With this technology, consumers can compare prices across retailers while in a store or online, or locate an item that is out of stock. Retailers have coined the term "showrooming" to describe the practice of consumers going to retail stores to examine products and then purchasing them online.

Among smartphone owners, 47 percent said that they have used their mobile phone to comparison shop on the Internet while at a retail store, and 33 percent have used a barcode scanning application for price comparisons. Consumers are also using their smart-phones to obtain product information: 31 percent have scanned a QR code in a newspaper, magazine, or billboard advertisement to obtain information about a product, and 42 percent have used their phone to get product reviews or product information while shopping at a retail store.

Many consumers who use their smartphone to comparison shop reported that they altered their decisions as a result: 69 percent who have comparison shopped in a store reported that they changed where they made a purchase after comparing prices, and 79 percent reported that they changed what they purchased as a result of reading product reviews on their smartphone while at a retail store.

Use of Mobile Phones in Financial Decisionmaking

As the use of mobile banking increases, mobile phones are increasingly becoming tools for managing personal finances and controlling spending. For example, 63 percent of mobile banking users with smartphones report using their mobile phone to check account balances or available credit before making a large purchase in the 12 months prior to the survey. Of those who checked their balance or available credit, 53 percent reported that they decided not to buy an item because of the amount of money in their bank account or the amount of available credit. Many consumers have near-constant access to their mobile phones, and these results illustrate that these devices have the potential to provide "just-in- time information" that can influence consumer financial behavior.

In addition, mobile phones can provide readily accessible and timely prompts that may help consumers make different, and perhaps smarter, financial decisions. The actions consumers take in response to the receipt of text message or e-mail notices from their financial institutions demonstrate some of the potential effects of this technology for encouraging consumers to engage in different financial behaviors that may prove to have beneficial outcomes.

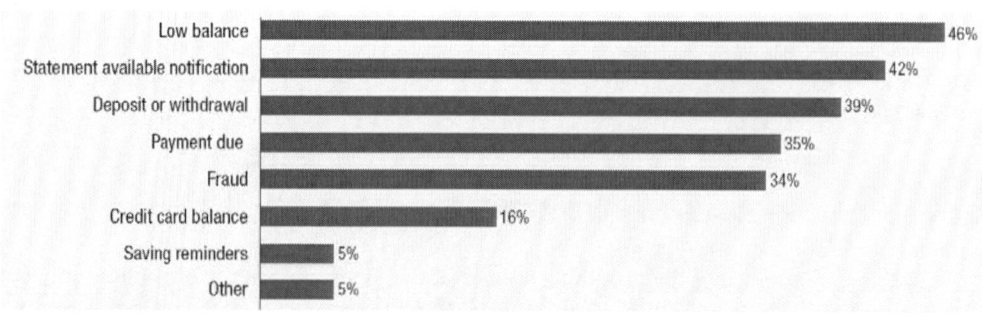

Note: The number of respondents who were mobile banking users was 459. Respondents may receive alerts from their financial institution via push notification, text message, or e-mail.

Figure 11. Do you receive each of the following kinds of alerts?

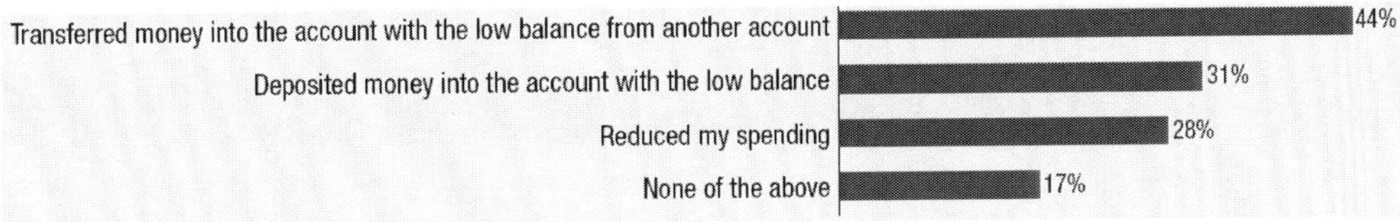

Note: The number of respondents who were mobile banking users was 211.

Figure 12. Thinking of the most recent low-balance alert you received, which of the following actions did you take after receiving the alert?

More than half (57 percent) of people who use mobile banking receive alerts from their bank (figure 11). Nearly all mobile banking users who received a low-balance alert from their bank reported taking some action in response: transferring money into the account with the low-balance (44 percent), reducing their spending (28 percent), or depositing additional money into the account (31 percent) (figure 12). Only 17 percent reported taking no action in response to receiving a low-balance alert.

CONCLUSION

As smartphones become more common and more versatile, they can play an increasingly large role in the interactions between consumers and financial service providers, retailers, and other businesses. The near-constant presence of mobile phones in consumers' lives also makes them a potentially useful tool for the delivery of just-in-time financial information or as an aid in decisionmaking. Given the prevalence of mobile phones—particularly smartphones—among minorities, low-income individuals, and younger persons, mobile technology has the potential to empower consumers and expand access to financial services for underserved populations. However, consumers will need to understand and weigh the perceived benefits and potential risks to their security and privacy presented by the use of this evolving technology.

The use of mobile banking has increased substantially in the past year and appears likely to continue to increase as more consumers use smartphones or recognize the convenience of this service, and as more financial institutions offer mobile banking. The most common tasks for mobile banking users continue to be checking account balances and transferring funds. Use of the remote deposit capture feature continues to grow steadily. The use of mobile payments, broadly defined, also increased from 2013 to 2014. Paying bills online and making online or in-app purchases are the most common mobile payment activities, followed by making a POS payment. Among mobile payments users with smartphones, the use of mobile phones to make payments at the POS is essentially unchanged from the 2013 survey.

The main factors limiting consumer adoption of mobile banking and payments are a preference for using other methods for banking or making payments and security concerns. In terms of the value proposition to consumers, the significant number of mobile users who reported an interest in using their phones to receive discounts, coupons, and promotions or to track rewards and loyalty points suggests that tying these services to a mobile payment service may increase the attractiveness of mobile phones as a means of payment.

APPENDIX 1: TECHNICAL APPENDIX ON SURVEY METHODOLOGY

In order to create a nationally representative probability-based sample, GfK's KnowledgePanel® has selected respondents based on both random digit dialing and address-based sampling (ABS). Since 2009, new respondents have been recruited using ABS. To recruit respondents, GfK sends out mailings to a random selection of residential postal addresses. Out of 100 mailings, approximately 14 households respond to GfK and express an interest in joining the panel. Of those who express an interest in joining, around 64 percent complete the process and become members of the panel.[18] If the person contacted is interested in participating but does not have a computer or Internet access, GfK provides him or her with a laptop and Internet. Panel respondents are continuously lost to attrition and added to replenish the panel, so the recruitment rate and enrollment rate may vary over time.

For the 2014 mobile survey, a total of 6,892 KnowledgePanel® members received e-mail invitations to complete the survey, including both the primary sample and a rural oversample. The primary sample included a random selection of 2,308 out of the 2,657 KnowledgePanel® respondents who participated in the Board's 2013 mobile survey and an additional 2,657 randomly selected KnowledgePanel® respondents who did not participate in the Board's previous survey. (See table 1 in main text.) From these two components of the primary sample, a total of 2,925 people (excluding breakoffs) responded to the e-mail request to participate and completed the survey, yielding a final stage completion rate of 58.9 percent. The recruitment rate for the primary sample, reported by GfK, was 14.6 percent and the profile rate was 64.0 percent, for a cumulative response rate of 5.5 percent. Answers from these respondents were used to compute statistics presented in the main body of the report, as well as in the tables in appendix 3.

The 2014 survey also included an oversample of respondents residing in rural areas as defined by Rural Urban Commuting Area (RUCA) codes.[19] Respondents were selected for inclusion in the rural oversample if the ZIP code for their residence was classified as being in RUCA codes 7.0-10.3. Because RUCA codes are assigned at the Census tract level, ZIP codes meeting this criteria were identified based on the crosswalk available from the Center for Rural Health at the University of North Dakota. (See ruralhealth.und.edu/ruca.) All members of KnowledgePanel® residing in rural areas based on this definition, but not already included in one of the other two samples, received an invitation to respond to the survey. Of these additional 1,927 KnowledgePanel® members who received invitations as a part of the rural oversample, 1,298 people (excluding breakoffs) responded to the e-mail request to participate and completed the survey, yielding a final stage completion rate of 67.4 percent for the oversample. The recruitment rate for the rural oversample, reported by GfK, was 14.4 percent and the profile rate was 63.3 percent, for a cumulative response rate of 6.1 percent. Answers from these respondents were combined with answers from the other two samples and used to compute statistics presented in box 1 of the report.

To enhance the completion rate, GfK sent e-mail reminders to non-responders on days three and ten of the field period. GfK maintains an ongoing modest incentive program to encourage KnowledgePanel® members to participate. Incentives take the form of raffles and lotteries with cash and other prizes. KnowlegePanel® members who were a part of the rural oversample in the 2014 survey were offered an additional $5 incentive for completion of the survey.

Significant resources and infrastructure are devoted to the recruitment process for the KnowledgePanel® so that the resulting panel can properly represent the adult population of the United States. Consequently, the raw distribution of KnowledgePanel® mirrors that of the U.S. adults fairly closely, baring occasional disparities that may emerge for certain sub-groups due to differential attrition rates among recruited panel members.

The selection methodology for general population samples from the KnowledgePanel® ensures that the resulting samples behave as an equal probability of selection method (EPSEM) samples. This methodology starts by weighting the entire KnowledgePanel® to the benchmarks secured from the latest March supplement of the Current Population Survey (CPS) along several dimensions. This way, the weighted distribution of the KnowledgePanel® matches that of the U.S. adults. Typically, the geo-demographic dimensions used for weighting the entire KnowledgePanel® include gender, age, race/ethnicity, education, Census region, household income, home ownership status, metropolitan area status, and Internet access.

Using the above weights as the measure of size (MOS) for each panel member, in the next step a probability proportional to size (PPS) procedure is used to select study specific samples. Since this survey includes a rural oversample, the departure caused by this oversample from an EPSEM design are corrected by adjusting the corresponding design weights accordingly with the CPS benchmarks serving as reference points.

Once the sample has been selected and fielded, and all the study data are collected and made final, a post-stratification process is used to adjust for any survey non-response as well as any non-coverage or under- and over-sampling resulting from the study- specific sample design. The following variables were used for the adjustment of weights for this study: gender, age, race/ethnicity, education, Census region, residence in a metropolitan area, access to the Internet, and residence in a rural area according to the definition used for the rural oversample. Demographic and geographic distributions for the non-institutionalized, civilian population ages 18 and over from the March 2014 CPS are used as benchmarks in this adjustment. For the geographic distribution of residence in a rural setting, the full set of members of KnowledgePanel® was used to generate the bench- mark since the CPS does not provide statistics on rural status according to the criteria used to select the oversample.

Although weights allow the sample population to match the U.S. population based on observable characteristics, similar to all survey methods, it remains possible that non-coverage or non-response results in differences between the sample population and the U.S. population that are not corrected using weights.

There are several reasons that a probability-based Internet panel was selected as the method for this survey rather than an alternative survey method. The first reason is that these types of Internet surveys have been found to be representative of the population.[20] The second reason is that the ABS Internet panel allows the same respondents to be re-interviewed in subsequent surveys with relative ease, as they remain in the panel for several years. The third reason is that Internet panel surveys have numerous existing data points on respondents from previously administered surveys, including detailed demographic and economic information. This allows for the inclusion of additional information on respondents without increasing respondent burden. Lastly, collecting data through an ABS Internet panel survey is cost effective, and can be done relatively quickly.

There are possible questions about the extent to which results from an online survey of technology use can be interpreted as being representative of the technology use of the U.S.

population. As with any survey method, Internet panels can be subject to biases resulting from undercoverage or nonresponse and, in this case, potential underrepresentation of adults who are physically or cognitively impaired or who may prefer not to use some forms of technology. Not everyone in the United States has access to the Internet and there are demographic (income, education, age) and geographic (urban and rural) differences between those who do have access and those who do not. These concerns are partially corrected by GfK providing Internet access to respondents who do not have it in order to include the portion of the population that does not have Internet access in KnowledgePanel®. They are further corrected by the use of post-stratification weights to ensure that the Internet usage and key demographics of the weighted sample population matches the entire U.S. population. That said, participation in this type of survey may require a certain level of skill and interest in responding online, which could limit coverage of some groups, particularly among those in the population who are less likely to use computers or the Internet. As a result, to the extent that these differences cannot be incorporated into the sample weights, technology usage among survey respondents may differ along key dimensions from that of the overall U.S. population.

APPENDIX 2: SURVEY OF CONSUMERS' USE OF MOBILE FINANCIAL SERVICES 2014—QUESTIONNAIRE

Below is a reproduction of the survey instrument in its entirety. The bracketed text are programming instructions that (1) indicate whether or not a question is single choice [SP] or multiple choice [MP] and (2) represent any skip pattern used to reach that question and which questions should be grouped together on a page. The respondents only saw the questions and response options; they did not see the program code.

[DISPLAY]

OMB Control Number: 7100-0359
Expiration Date: 04/30/2017
For more information, click here.

The Federal Reserve Board is interested in learning more about how people manage their finances, shop, and make payments. We are also interested in how people interact with financial institutions, and how mobile phones and other technology facilitate these interactions. The information collected in this survey will be used for research, analysis, and policymaking. A dataset containing anonymized responses may also be released publicly on the Federal Reserve Board's website. We appreciate your participation in this survey.

To begin, we are going to ask a few questions about the types of financial products and services that you use.

[PROGRAM INSTRUCTION]
[If "For more information…" clicked, display this text in a new tab or window]

The Federal Reserve may not conduct or sponsor, and an organization is not required to respond to, a collection of information unless it displays a currently valid OMB control number. Public reporting burden for this information collection is estimated to average 0.18 hours, including the time to gather data in the required form and to review instructions and complete the information collection. Send comments regarding this burden estimate or any other aspect of this collection of information, including suggestions for reducing this burden to: Secretary, Board of Governors of the Federal Reserve System, 20th and C Streets, NW, Washington, DC 20551, and to the Office of Management and Budget, Paperwork Reduction Project (7100-0359), Washington, DC 20503.

Banking Section

[SP][SAME AS Q1 IN S16674]

1. Do you or does your spouse/partner currently have some type of bank or credit union account such as a checking, savings, or money market account?
   a. Yes
   b. No

[SP, IF Q1 = B][SAME AS Q2 IN S16674]

2. Have you or your spouse/partner ever had some type of bank or credit union account such as a checking, savings, or money market account?
   a. Yes
   b. No

[SP]

4a. A prepaid debit card, also known as a general purpose prepaid card, is loaded with money and can be used to make payments in stores and online. It works much like a debit card except that it is not connected to a traditional bank account. A prepaid debit card is NOT a credit card.
Have you used a prepaid debit card in the past 12 months?
   a. Yes
   b. No

[SP]

5. Remittances are used to send money to relatives or friends living outside the U.S. For example money can be sent through a bank, WesternUnion, or an app on your mobile phone.
Have you sent a remittance in the past 12 months?
   a. Yes
   b. No

[SP]

5a. In the past 12 months, have you used a money order, check cashing service, pawn shop loan, auto title loan, paycheck advance/deposit advance, or a pay-day loan?
   a. Yes
   b. No

[IF Q1 = A; DISPLAY; SHOW ON THE SAME SCREEN AS Q16]

In this section we would like to ask you about how you interact with your bank or credit union.

[IF Q1 = A; NUMBER BOXES; RANGE: 1-3; UNIQUE VALUES; SHOW ON SAME SCREEN AS DISPLAY]

16. What are the three main ways you (or your spouse/partner) interact with your bank or credit union when you use your accounts? Use number 1 for most often, 2 for 2nd most often, 3 for 3rd most often used. (You can stop numbering below if all the ways you interact with your bank or credit union are covered in less than three responses).
   a. ATM/Cash machine
   b. A teller in person at a branch
   c. Mail
   d. Phone – Talking or using touchtone service
   e. Over the Internet using a computer/tablet
   f. Mobile phone app, mobile web browser, or SMS/text message
   g. Family member, friend, or neighbor does the banking for me
   h. Other (please specify): **[TXT]_______**

[SP, IF Q1 = A]

6. Have you visited a bank branch and spoken with **a teller or a bank employee** in the past 12 months?
   a. Yes
   b. No

[IF Q6=A; NUMBER BOX; RANGE: 0-99]

7. In the past **month,** about how many times have you visited a branch and spoken with a teller or a bank employee? If none enter "0". ____times in the past month

[SP, IF Q1=A]

8. Which of the following best describes the location of your bank or credit union branch that you typically visit when you need to speak with a teller or bank employee?
   a. I visit a branch close to my home, work, school or other place I go to frequently.
   b. I must go out of my way or travel for a while to visit a branch.

c. I am not able to visit a branch because my bank does not have a branch in my area.
d. I do not need to visit a branch.

[IF Q8= A OR B; NUMBER BOX; RANGE: 0-999]

9. About how long does it take you to travel to the branch you typically visit (one way)?
_______minutes

[SP, IF Q1 = A]

10. Have you used an **ATM** for any banking transactions in the past 12 months?
    a. Yes
    b. No

[IF Q10=A; NUMBER BOX; RANGE: 0-99]

11. In the past **month**, about how many times have you used an **ATM** for banking transactions? If none enter "0". ________times in the past month

[SP, IF Q1=A]

12. Which of the following best describes the location of the ATM that you typically use for banking transactions?
    a. I use an ATM close to my home, work, school or other place I go to frequently.
    b. I must go out of my way or travel for a while to access the ATM.
    c. I am not able to use an ATM for banking transactions because there is not an ATM in my area.
    d. I do not use an ATM.

[IF Q12=A OR B; NUMBER BOX; RANGE: 0-999]

13. About how long does it take you to travel to the ATM you typically visit (one way)?
_______minutes

[SP, IF Q1 = A]

14. **Telephone banking** is when you access your account by calling a phone number that your bank has provided. You interact with the system using either voice commands, your phone's numeric keypad, or speaking with a live customer service representative. It does not include accessing your bank using the internet or apps on your mobile phone.
Have you used telephone banking in the past 12 months, either with a land- line phone or your mobile phone?
    a. Yes

b. No

[IF Q14=A; NUMBER BOX; RANGE: 0-99]

15. In the past **month**, about how many times have you used **telephone banking** to access your account? If none enter "0". __times in the past month

[DISPLAY] [SAME AS S16674]

In this section we'll ask a few questions about your use of the Internet. Right now we are just interested in your use of the Internet **on a computer** (desktop, laptop) or **tablet**. Later on we will ask about use of the Internet on mobile phones.

[SP]

17. Do you currently have regular access to the internet, either at your home or outside your home (e.g., at school, work, public library, etc.) that is not provided by GfK, formerly Knowledge Networks?
    a. Yes
    b. No

[SP]

18. Which of the following best describes how easy it is for you to access the Internet on a desktop, laptop, or tablet (e.g., iPad)?
    a. Access is almost always available.
    b. Access is not always available, but is available at locations that are convenient for me (e.g., home, work, school).
    c. Access is available only at locations that require extra effort or planning to get to.

[SP, IF Q1=A]

19. **Online banking** involves checking your account balance and recent transactions, transferring money, paying bills, or conducting other related transactions with your bank or credit union using the Internet.
    Have you used online banking on a desktop, laptop, or tablet (e.g., iPad) computer in the past 12 months?
    a. Yes
    b. No

[IF Q19=A; NUMBER BOX; RANGE: 0-99]

20. In the past **month**, about how many times have you used online banking on a desktop, laptop, or tablet (e.g., iPad) computer? If none enter "0".
    _______times in the past month

Screener Question on Mobile Phone Usage

[DISPLAY][SHOW ON SAME SCREEN AS Q18]

In this section we would like to ask you about your use of mobile phones (cell phones).

[SP, PROMPT, TERMINATE IF SKIPPED]

21. Do you own or have regular access to a mobile phone (cell phone)?
    a. Yes → **[MOBILE = "YES"]**
    b. No → **[MOBILE = "NO"]**

DOV: MOBILE

1: "YES"
2: "NO"

[SP, IF MOBILE = "YES"]

22. A **smartphone** is a mobile phone with features that may enable it to access the web, send e-mails, download apps, and interact with computers. Smartphones include the iPhone, BlackBerry, as well as Android and Windows Mobile- powered devices.
    Is your mobile phone a smartphone?
    a. Yes
    b. No

[SP, IF Q22 = A]

23. Which type of smartphone do you have?
    a. Android
    b. BlackBberry
    c. iPhone
    d. Windows Mobile
    e. Amazon Fire
    f. Other
    g. Don't know

[SP, IF MOBILE = "YES"]

24. How confident are you in your ability to understand and navigate the technology and features of your mobile phone?
    a. Very confident
    b. Somewhat confident
    c. Not confident

[SP, IF Q22 = A]

25. Do you password protect your smartphone? Please count using a PIN, drawing a pattern, fingerprint or facial recognition, and other methods of securing your phone as password protection.
    a. Yes
    b. No

[SP, IF MOBILE= "YES"]

27. Which of the following best describes how easy it is for you to access the internet on your mobile phone through either WiFi or a wireless network (3G, 4G, LTE)?
    a. Access is almost always available.
    b. Access is not always available, but is available at locations that are convenient for me (e.g., home, work, school).
    c. Access is available only at locations that require extra effort or planning to get to.
    d. Access is not available.
    e. I do not need access to the Internet on my mobile phone.

Mobile Banking Users

[MOBILE = "YES" AND Q1 =A]

[DISPLAY; SHOW ON THE SAME SCREEN AS Q28 and Q29]

Mobile banking uses a mobile phone to access your bank or credit union account. This can be done either by accessing your bank or credit union's web page through the web browser on your mobile phone, via text messaging, or by using an app downloaded to your mobile phone.

[SP, MOBILE = "YES" AND Q1 =A; SHOW ON THE SAME SCREEN AS Q29]

28. Does your bank or credit union offer mobile banking?
    a. Yes
    b. No
    c. Don't know

[SP, MOBILE = "YES" AND Q1 =A; SHOW ON THE SAME SCREEN ASs Q28]

29. Have you used **mobile banking** in the past 12 months?
    a. Yes → **[MOBILEBANK = "YES"]**
    b. No → **[MOBILEBANK = "NO"]**

DOV: MOBILEBANK
1 "YES"
2 "NO"
[SP, IF MOBILE = "NO"]

30. Do you plan to use mobile banking in the next 12 months?
    a. Definitely will use
    b. Probably will use
    c. Probably will not use
    d. Definitely will not use

[MOBILE = "YES" and Q1=A; GRID; SP ACROSS]
[SHOW THIS TEXT INSTEAD OF DEFAULT INSTRUCTIONS: Please answer yes or no to each option]

32. Using your **mobile phone**, have you done each of the following in the past 12 months.

	1 Yes	0 No
a. Downloaded your bank's mobile banking app on your mobile phone		
b. Checked an account balance or checked recent transactions		
c. Made a bill payment using your bank's online banking website or banking app		
d. Received an alert (e.g., a text message, push notification, or e-mail) from your bank		
e. Transferred money between your bank accounts		
f. Transferred money from your bank account to another person		
g. Deposited a check to your account electronically using your mobile phone camera		
h. Located the closest in-network ATM for your bank		

[IF MOBILEBANK= "YES"; NUMBER BOX; RANGE: 0-999]

33. In the past **month**, how many times have you personally used mobile banking? If none, enter "0." _times in the last month.

[SP, IF MOBILEBANK= "YES"; SHOW ON SAME SCREEN AS Q33]

34. When did you start using mobile banking?
    a. In the last 6 months
    b. 6 to 12 months ago
    c. 1 to 2 years ago
    d. More than 2 years ago
    e. I don't remember

[SP, IF MOBILEBANK= "YES"]
35. What was the **main** reason why you started using mobile banking when you did?
    a. I got a smartphone
    b. My bank started offering the service
    c. There is no bank branch or ATM near my home or work

d. I became comfortable with the security of mobile banking
e. I liked the convenience of mobile banking
f. To receive fraud alerts or check my account for fraudulent transactions
g. Other (please specify):**[TXT]**_______

Mobile Payments Users

[MOBILE = "YES"]
[DISPLAY; SHOW ON SAME SCREEN AS Q36]

Mobile payments are purchases, bill payments, charitable donations, payments to another person, or any other payments made using a mobile phone. You can do this either by accessing a web page through the web browser on your mobile device, by sending a text message (SMS), or by using a downloadable app on your mobile device. The amount of the payment may be applied to your phone bill (for example, Red Cross text message donation), charged to your credit card, deducted from a prepaid card, or withdrawn directly from your bank account.

[SP, MOBILE = "YES"]

36. Have you made a mobile payment in the past 12 months?

a. Yes → **[MOBILEPAY = "YES"]**
b. No → **[MOBILEPAY = "NO"]**

DOV: MOBILEPAY
1 "YES"
2 "NO"
[SP, MOBILE = "YES"; GRID; SP ACROSS]
[SHOW THIS TEXT INSTEAD OF DEFAULT INSTRUCTIONS: Please answer yes or no to each option]

37. Using your **mobile phone**, have you done each of the following in the past 12 months?

PROGRAMMING NOTE: CODE "Yes" AS 1, "No" AS 0, AND REFUSED AS -1.

	1 Yes	**0 No**
a. Transferred money directly to another person's bank or other financial account within the United States (e.g., Paypal account) b. Send a remittance (used to send money to relatives or friends living outside the U.S through WesternUnion, USPS SureMoney, etc.) c. Received money from another person's bank or other financial account (e.g., Paypal account)		

	1 Yes	0 No
d. Paid for a product or service at a store (including at gas pumps and for restaurant meals) e. Paid for parking, a taxi, or public transit using an app f. Paid bills online through a mobile web browser or app g. Made a payment using a text message (including charitable donation by text message) h. Used an app to receive loyalty or reward points i. Made an online purchase or in-app purchase (e.g., from amazon.com or bestbuy.com)		

[IF MOBILEPAY = "YES"; NUMBER BOX; RANGE: 0-99]

38. In the past **month**, how many times have you used your mobile phone to make any type of mobile payment? If none, please enter "0." _______times in the last month.

[IF Q37d="YES"; GRID; SP ACROSS; SHOW ON SAME SCREEN AS Q40]
[SHOW THIS TEXT INSTEAD OF DEFAULT INSTRUCTIONS: Please answer yes or no to each option]

39. When you have used your mobile phone to pay for something **at a store in the past 12 months**, have you used your phone in each of these different ways?

PROGRAMMING NOTE: CODE "Yes" AS 1, "No" AS 0, AND REFUSED AS -1.

	1 Yes	0 No
a. Waved or tapped my mobile phone to pay at check out (e.g., Google Wallet or Apple Pay) b. Scanned a barcode or QR code using your mobile phone to make a mobile payment (e.g., Starbucks app) c. Used a mobile app that doesn't require tapping the phone to pay at check out or scanning a barcode to pay for a purchase (e.g., Square Wallet) d. Other (please specify): [txt]_______________		

[IF Q37d = "YES"; NUMBER BOX; RANGE: 0-99; SHOW ON SAME SCREEN AS Q39]

40. In the past **month**, about how many times have you used your mobile phone to pay for a product or service at a store? If none, please enter "0." _______times in the last month.

[MP, IF MOBILEPAY = "YES"]

41. When making mobile payments, which of the following payment methods do you use?
    a. Credit card
    b. Debit card
    c. Prepaid debit card

d. Bank account
e. Charge to your phone bill
f. Account at a non-financial institution (e.g., PayPal)
g. Other (please specify):**[TXT]**_______

[MP, IF MOBILEPAY = "YES" AND Q22= A]

42. Have you used any of the following mobile payment services in the past 12 months?
    a. Starbucks mobile payments
    b. Google Wallet
    c. Square Wallet
    d. Apple Pay
    e. Deluxe eCheck
    f. Amazon's Firefly
    g. CardNay
    h. PayPal
    i. LevelUp
    j. Dwolla
    k. Softcard
    l. Tabbedout

[SP, IF MOBILEPAY= "YES"; SHOW ON SAME SCREEN AS Q44]

43. When did you start using mobile payments?
    a. In the last 6 months
    b. 6 to 12 months ago
    c. 1 to 2 years ago
    d. More than 2 years ago
    e. I don't remember

[SP, IF MOBILEPAY= "YES"; SHOW ON SAME SCREEN AS Q43]

44. What was the **main** reason why you started using mobile payments when you did?
    a. I got a smartphone
    b. The ability to make mobile payments became available
    c. I became comfortable with the security of mobile payments
    d. I liked the convenience of mobile payments
    e. A store I visit started offering the service
    f. To take advantage of loyalty or rewards points and discounts
    g. Other (please specify):**[TXT]**_______

Non-Mobile Banking Users

[IF MOBILEBANK="NO" and Q28 = A]
[DISPLAY; SHOW ON SAME PAGE AS Q45]
We would like to ask you about some of your reasons for not using mobile banking.
[IF MOBILEBANK= "NO" AND MOBILE= "YES" AND Q28 = A]

[GRID; SP ACROSS; SHOW ON SAME PAGE AS DISPLAY]

[SHOW THIS TEXT INSTEAD OF DEFAULT INSTRUCTIONS: Please answer yes or no to each option]

45. Please tell us if each of the reasons below are why you do not use mobile banking.

PROGRAMMING NOTE: CODE "Yes" AS 1, "No" AS 0, AND REFUSED AS -1.

	1 Yes	**0 No**
a. I'm concerned about the security of mobile banking		
b. My banking needs are being met without mobile banking		
c. I don't see any reason to use mobile banking		
d. The mobile phone screen is too small		
e. I don't have a smartphone		
f. My bank charges a fee for using mobile banking		
g. I don't do the banking in my household		
h. I don't trust the technology		
i. It's too difficult to use mobile banking		

[SP, IF Q45a = "Yes"]

46. You mentioned that security was one of your top concerns with mobile banking; which one of the following security aspects are you **most** concerned with?
    a. My phone getting hacked
    b. Someone using my phone without permission to access my account
    c. Someone intercepting my data
    d. Losing my phone or having my phone stolen
    e. Malware or viruses being installed on my phone
    f. Companies misusing my personal information
    g. All of the above
    h. Other (please specify):**[TXT]_______**

[MP, IF MOBILEBANK= "NO" AND Q28=A]

47. Assuming that the concerns that you have about using mobile banking were addressed, would you be interested in doing any of the following activities with your mobile phone?
    a. Download your bank's mobile banking app
    b. Check an account balance or check recent transactions
    c. Make bill payments using your bank's online banking website or app
    d. Receive alerts (e.g., text message, push notification, or e-mail) from your bank
    e. Deposit a check electronically using your mobile phone camera f. Transfer money between your bank accounts
    g. Transfer money from your bank account to another person
    h. Locate the closest in-network ATM or branch for your bank
    i. None, I don't want to use mobile banking **[Exclusive]**

[MP, IF Q28=B OR Q28=C]

48. You mentioned that your bank does not offer mobile banking or you are not sure if you bank offers it. If your bank or credit union were to offer mobile banking, would you be interested in doing any of the following activities with your mobile phone?
    a. Download your bank's mobile banking app
    b. Check an account balance or check recent transactions
    c. Make bill payments using your bank's online banking website or app
    d. Receive alerts (e.g., text message, push notification, or e-mail) from your bank
    e. Deposit a check electronically using your mobile phone camera
    f. Transfer money between your bank accounts
    g. Transfer money from your bank account to another person
    h. Locate the closest in-network ATM or branch for your bank
    i. None, I don't want to use mobile banking **[Exclusive]**

Non-Mobile Payments Users

[IF MOBILEPAY = "NO"]
[**DISPLAY**; shown on the same page as Q49]

We would like to ask you about some of your reasons for not using mobile payments

[IF MOBILEPAY = "NO" AND MOBILE = "YES"]
[GRID; SP ACROSS]
[**SHOW THIS TEXT INSTEAD OF DEFAULT INSTRUCTIONS:** Please answer yes or no to each option]

49. Please tell us if any of the reasons below are why you do not use mobile payments.

PROGRAMMING NOTE: CODE "Yes" AS 1, "No" AS 0, AND REFUSED AS -1.

	1 Yes	**0 No**
a. I'm concerned about the security of mobile payments b. It's easier to pay with cash or a credit/debit card c. I don't see any benefit from using mobile payments d. The places I shop don't accept mobile payments e. I don't have the necessary feature on my phone f. I don't trust the technology		
	1 Yes	**0 No**
g. It's difficult or time consuming to set up or use mobile payments h. I don't need to make any payments or someone else pays the bills i. I don't really understand all the different mobile payment options		

[SP, IF Q49a = "YES"]

50. You mentioned that security was one of your top concerns with mobile payments; which **one** of these security aspects are you most concerned with?
    a. My phone getting hacked
    b. Someone intercepting my payment information or other data
    c. Losing my phone or having my phone stolen
    d. Malware or viruses being installed on my phone
    e. Companies misusing my personal information
    f. All of the above
    g. Other (please specify):**[txt]**_____________

[MP, IF MOBILEPAY = "NO"]

51. Assuming that the reason(s) why you do not currently use mobile payments was addressed, would you be interested in doing any of the following activities with your mobile phone?
    a. Making payments to another person (e.g., friend, relative, babysitter) within the United States
    b. Transferring money to someone in another country
    c. Using my mobile phone to pay for purchases at a store
    d. Paying for parking, a taxi, or public transit using an app
    e. Paying bills online through a mobile web browser or app
    f. Using your mobile phone as a "virtual wallet" to replace some cards in your wallet
    g. Making an online or in-app purchase (e.g., from amazon.com or bestbuy.com)
    h. Receiving money from another person's bank or other financial account (e.g., Paypal account)
    i. Receiving/using coupons and/or reward points on your phone
    j. None, I don't want to use mobile payments **[Exclusive]**

[SP, IF Q37d= "NO"]

52. You indicated that you have not made a mobile payment in a store in the last 12 months. Do you plan to use your mobile phone to make a payment in a store in the next 12 months?
    a. Definitely will use
    b. Probably will use
    c. Probably will not use
    d. Definitely will not use

Mobile Financial Services Security Questions

[MOBILE = "YES" FOR QUESTIONS 53 THROUGH 54]
[DISPLAY, SHOW IT ON THE SAME SCREEN WITH Q53 TO Q54]

Please rate your perception of the level of security for each of the following mobile financial services from Very Safe to Very Unsafe.

[SP, SHOW ON THE SAME SCREEN AS Q54]

53. How safe do you believe people's personal information is when they use mobile banking?
    a. Very safe
    b. Somewhat safe
    c. Somewhat unsafe
    d. Very unsafe
    e. Don't know

[SP, SHOW ON THE SAME SCREEN AS Q53]

54. How safe do you believe people's personal information is when they use a mobile phone to pay for a purchase at a store?
    a. Very safe
    b. Somewhat safe
    c. Somewhat unsafe
    d. Very unsafe
    e. Don't know

[SP, GRID; IF MOBILE = "YES"]

55. Would you like to or do you already use your mobile phone for any of the following purposes?

	1 **I already do**	**2** **I would like to**	**3** **I am unlikely to**
a. Track your finances, purchases, or expenses b. Organize, track and store gift cards, memberships, loyalty and reward points c. Compare prices when shopping d. Receive and manage discount offers and coupons e. Receive offers and promotions based on your location			

[SP, IF Q22=A]
[DISPLAY][SHOW ON THE SAME SCREEN AS Q56 AND Q57]

For the following two questions please rate how much you agree or disagree with the statement on a scale from strongly agree to strongly disagree.

[SP, IF Q22=A]
[SHOW ON THE SAME SCREEN AS Q57]

56. I am willing to allow my mobile phone to provide my location to companies I shop with regularly so that they can offer me discounts, promotions, or services based on where I am.
    a. Strongly agree
    b. Agree
    c. Disagree
    d. Strongly disagree

[SP, IF Q22=A]
[SHOW ON THE SAME SCREEN AS Q56]

57. I am willing to allow my mobile phone to provide personal information such as my sex, age, friends, and shopping history to companies I shop with regularly so that they can offer me targeted discounts, promotions, or services.
    a. Strongly agree
    b. Agree
    c. Disagree
    d. Strongly disagree

Shopping Behavior Questions

[IF MOBILE= "YES" AND Q22=A]
[DISPLAY][SHOW ON SAME SCREEN AS Q58]
In this section we would like to ask you about your shopping habits.

[SP, IF MOBILE= "YES" AND Q22=A][SHOW ON SAME SCREEN AS Q59]

58. Have you ever used your mobile phone to comparison shop over the Internet while at a retail store?
    a. Yes
    b. No

[SP, IF MOBILE= "YES" AND Q22=A][SHOW ON SAME SCREEN AS Q58]

59. Have you ever used a barcode scanning app on your mobile phone while shopping at a retail store to find the best price for an item?
    a. Yes
    b. No

[SP, IF Q58 = A OR Q59 = A]

61. Has using your mobile phone to compare prices while you were shopping at a retail store ever changed where you made your purchase?
    a. Yes
    b. No

[SP, IF MOBILE= "YES" AND Q22=A][SHOW ON SAME SCREEN AS Q62]

60. Have you ever scanned a QR code (similar to a barcode) in a retail store, newspaper, magazine, or billboard advertisement to obtain information about a product on your mobile phone?
    a. Yes
    b. No

[SP, IF MOBILE= "YES" AND Q22=A][SHOW ON SAME SCREEN AS Q60]

62. Have you ever used your mobile phone to browse product reviews or get product information while shopping at a retail store? This could be done by, for example, googling the product on your mobile browser or scanning a QR code.
    a. Yes
    b. No

[SP, IF Q62 = A]

63. Has reading product reviews on your mobile phone while shopping at a retail store ever changed which item you ended up purchasing?
    a. Yes
    b. No

[SP, IF MOBILEBANK = "YES" AND Q22 = A]

64. In the past 12 months, have you used your mobile phone to check your account balance or available credit before making a large purchase?
    a. Yes
    b. No

[SP, IF Q64 = A]

65. Thinking of the most recent time that you checked your account balance or available credit before making a large purchase, did you decide not to buy that particular item because of the amount of money left in your account or the amount of your available credit?
    a. Yes
    b. No

Financial Management (Saving, Budgeting) Questions

[MP, IF Q32 = D]

66. You previously mentioned that you receive text message, push notifications, or e-mail alerts from your financial institution. Do you receive each of the following kinds of alerts?
    a. Low balance
    b. Payment due
    c. Saving reminders
    d. Fraud
    e. Credit card balance
    f. Deposit or withdrawal
    g. Statement available notification
    h. Other (please specify):**[txt]__**

[MP, IF Q66= A]

67. Thinking of the most recent low-balance alert you received, which of the following actions did you take after receiving the alert?

    a. Transferred money into the account with the low balance from another account
    b. Deposited money into the account with the low balance c. Reduced my spending
    d. None of the above **[Exclusive]**

APPENDIX 3: CONSUMER RESPONSES TO SURVEY QUESTIONNAIRE

Table C.1. Do you or does your spouse/partner currently have some type of bank or credit union account such as a checking, savings, or money market account?

Percent, except as noted	
Q1	
Refused	0.3
Yes	87.0
No	12.7
Number of respondents	2,925

Table C.2. Have you or your spouse/partner ever had some type of bank or credit union account such as a checking, savings, or money market account?

Percent, except as noted	
Q2	
Refused	1.2
Yes	30.5
No	68.3
Number of respondents	**233**

Table C.3. Have you used a prepaid debit card in the past 12 months?

Q4a	
Refused	0.1
Yes	19.8
No	80.1
Number of respondents	**2,925**

Table C.4. Have you sent a remittance in the past 12 months?

Percent, except as noted	
Q5	
Refused	0.3
Yes	7.4
No	92.3
Number of respondents	**2,925**

Table C.5. In the past 12 months, have you used a money order, check cashing service, pawn shop loan, auto title loan, paycheck advance/deposit advance, or a payday loan?

Percent, except as noted	
Q5a	
Refused	0.3
Yes	16.7
No	83.0
Number of respondents	**2,925**

Table C.6. What are the three main ways you (or your spouse/partner) interact with your bank or credit union when you use your accounts? Use number 1 for most often, 2 for 2nd most often, 3 for 3rd most often used

Percent, except as noted			
Q16	1	2	3
Refused/no rank	0.8	6.8	16.9
ATM/cash machine	30.0	25.1	17.7
A teller in person at a branch	25.9	24.6	23.9
Mail	1.8	4.1	7.7
Phone – talking or using touchtone service	2.2	8.6	12.2
Over the Internet using a computer/tablet	30.0	20.6	12.0
Percent, except as noted			
Mobile phone app, mobile web browser, or SMS/text message	7.5	8.7	7.4
Family member, friend, or neighbor does the banking for me	1.5	1.4	2.0
Other	0.4	0.3	0.3
Number of respondents	**2,685**		

Table C.7. Have you visited a bank branch and spoken with a teller or a bank employee in the past 12 months?

Percent, except as noted	
Q6	
Refused	0.2
Yes	87.3
No	12.5
Number of respondents	**2,685**

Table C.8. In the past month, about how many times have you visited a branch and spoken with a teller or a bank employee? If none enter "0"

Q7	
Refused (percent)	0.3
Total respondents with zero uses (percent)	23.3
Mean number of uses (at least one use)	2.9
Median number of uses (at least one use)	2.0
Number of respondents	**2,389**

Table C.9. Which of the following best describes the location of your bank or credit union branch that you typically visit when you need to speak with a teller or bank employee?

Percent, except as noted	
Q8	
Refused	0.2
I visit a branch close to my home, work, school, or other place I go to frequently	85.0
I must go out of my way or travel for a while to visit a branch	7.0
I am not able to visit a branch because my bank does not have a branch in my area	2.3
I do not need to visit a branch	5.5
Number of respondents	**2,685**

Table C.10. About how long does it take you to travel to the branch you typically visit (one way)?

Q9	
Refused (percent)	0.2
Mean number of minutes	10.3
Median number of minutes	8.0
Number of respondents	**2,484**

Table C.11. Have you used an ATM for any banking transactions in the past 12 months?

Percent, except as noted	
Q10	
Refused	0.2
Yes	75.2
No	24.6
Number of respondents	**2,685**

Table C.12. In the past month, about how many times have you used an ATM for banking transactions? If none enter "0"

Q11	
Refused (percent)	0.6
Total respondents with zero uses (percent)	15.0
Mean number of uses (at least one use)	3.9
Median number of uses (at least one use)	3.0
Number of respondents	**1,977**

Table C.13. Which of the following best describes the location of the ATM that you typically use for banking transactions?

Percent, except as noted	
Q12	
Refused	0.4
I use an ATM close to my home, work, school, or other place I go to frequently	75.0
I must go out of my way or travel for a while to access the ATM	4.0
I am not able to use an ATM for banking transactions because there is not an ATM in my area	0.6
I do not use an ATM	20.0
Number of respondents	**2,685**

Table C.14. About how long does it take you to travel to the ATM you typically use (one way)?

Q13	
Refused (percent)	0.5
Mean number of minutes	8.4
Median number of minutes	5.0
Number of respondents	**2,073**

Table C.15. Have you used telephone banking in the past 12 months, either with a landline phone or your mobile phone?

Percent, except as noted	
Q14	
Refused	0.3
Yes	32.7
No	67.0
Number of respondents	**2,685**

Table C.16. In the past month, about how many times have you used telephone banking to access your account? If none enter "0"

Q15	
Refused (percent)	0.3
Total respondents with zero uses (percent)	27.1
Mean number of uses (at least one use)	3.8
Median number of uses (at least one use)	2.0
Number of respondents	**815**

Table C.17. Do you currently have regular access to the Internet, either at your home or outside your home (e.g., at school, work, public library, etc.) that is not provided by GfK, formerly Knowledge Networks?

Percent, except as noted	
Q17	
Refused	0.4
Yes	88.0
No	11.6
Number of respondents	**2,925**

Table C.18. Which of the following best describes how easy it is for you to access the Internet on a desktop, laptop, or tablet (e.g., iPad)?

Percent, except as noted	
Q18	
Refused	1.4
Access is almost always available	83.5
Access is not always available, but is available at locations that are convenient for me (e.g., home, work, school)	11.1
Access is available only at locations that require extra effort or planning to get to	4.0
Number of respondents	**2,925**

Table C.19. Have you used online banking on a desktop, laptop, or tablet (e.g., iPad) computer in the past 12 months?

Percent, except as noted	
Q19	
Refused	0.6
Yes	73.7
No	25.7
Number of respondents	**2,685**

Table C.20. In the past month, about how many times have you used online banking on a desktop, laptop, or tablet (e.g., iPad) computer? If none enter "0"

Q20	
Refused (percent)	0.1
Total respondents with zero uses (percent)	5.0
Mean number of uses (at least one use)	9.1
Median number of uses (at least one use)	5.0
Number of respondents	**2,026**

Table C.21. Do you own or have regular access to a mobile phone (cell phone)?

Percent, except as noted	
Q21	
Yes	86.8
No	13.2
Number of respondents	**2,925**

Table C.22. Is your mobile phone a smartphone?

Percent, except as noted	
Q22	
Refused	0.3
Yes	70.9
No	28.8
Number of respondents	**2,603**

Table C.23. Which type of smartphone do you have?

Percent, except as noted	
Q23	
Android	47.7
BlackBerry	1.1
iPhone	44.1
Windows Mobile	1.8
Amazon Fire	0.3*
Percent, except as noted	
Other	3.2
Don't know	1.9
Number of respondents	**1,775**

* Fewer than 10 responses were received for this option.

Table C.24. How confident are you in your ability to understand and navigate the technology and features of your mobile phone?

Percent, except as noted	
Q24	
Refused	0.5
Very confident	54.0
Somewhat confident	33.5
Not confident	12.0
Number of respondents	**2,603**

Table C.25. Do you password protect your smartphone?

Percent, except as noted	
Q25	
Refused	0.6
Yes	69.2
No	30.2
Number of respondents	**1,775**

Table C.26. Which of the following best describes how easy it is for you to access the Internet on your mobile phone through either WiFi or a wireless network (3G, 4G, LTE)?

Percent, except as noted	
Q27	
Refused	0.7
Access is almost always available	63.0
Access is not always available, but is available at locations that are convenient for mc (e.g., home, work, school)	9.1
Access is available only at locations that require extra effort or planning to get to	1.3
Access is not available	7.4
I do not need access to the Internet on my mobile phone	18.6
Number of respondents	**2,603**

Table C.27. Does your bank or credit union offer mobile banking?

Percent, except as noted	
Q28	
Refused	0.4
Yes	74.0
No	4.1
Don't know	21.5
Number of respondents	**2,437**

Table C.28. Have you used mobile banking in the past 12 months?

Percent, except as noted	
Q29	
Refused	1.2
Yes	38.7
No	60.1
Number of respondents	**2,437**

Table C.29. Do you plan to use mobile banking in the next 12 months?

Percent, except as noted	
Q30	
Definitely will use	1.2
Probably will use	9.8
Probably will not use	45.4
Definitely will not use	43.7
Number of respondents	**1,584**

Table C.30. Using your mobile phone, have you done each of the following in the past 12 months?

Percent, except as noted	
Q32	
No/refused to all	46.6
Downloaded your bank's mobile banking app on your mobile phone	30.2
Checked an account balance or checked recent transactions	44.9
Made a bill payment using your bank's online banking website or banking app	21.0
Received an alert (e.g., a text message, push notification, or e-mail) from your bank	28.5
Transferred money between your bank accounts	26.8
Transferred money from your bank account to another person	10.4
Deposited a check to your account electronically using your mobile phone camera	20.1
Located the closest in-network ATM or branch for your bank	20.2
Number of respondents	**2,437**

Note: This question was asked of those with a mobile phone and a bank account and includes those who did not identify themselves as having used mobile banking in the previous 12 months.

Table C.31. In the past month, about how many times have you personally used mobile banking?

Q33	
Refused (percent)	3.5
Total respondents with zero uses (percent)	6.4
Mean number of uses (at least one use)	10.0
Median number of uses (at least one use)	5.0
Number of respondents	**829**

Table C.32. When did you start using mobile banking?

Percent, except as noted	
Q34	
Refused	5.1
In the last 6 months	14.6
6 to 12 months ago	11.6
1 to 2 years ago	27.6
More than 2 years ago	36.3
I don't remember	4.7
Number of respondents	**829**

Table C.33. What was the main reason why you started using mobile banking when you did?

Percent, except as noted	
Q35	
Refused	0.1
I got a smartphone	32.5
My bank started offering the service	19.8
There is no bank branch or ATM near my home or work	3.5
I became comfortable with the security of mobile banking	5.7
I liked the convenience of mobile banking	34.6
To receive fraud alerts or check my account for fraudulent transactions	0.9*
Other (please specify):	3.1
Number of respondents	**829**

* Fewer than 10 responses were received for this option.

Table C.34. Have you made a mobile payment in the past 12 months?

Percent, except as noted	
Q36	
Refused	0.7
Yes	21.7
No	77.6
Number of respondents	**2,603**

Table C.35. Using your mobile phone, have you done each of the following in the past 12 months?

Percent, except as noted	
Q37	
No/refused to all	64.5
Transferred money directly to another person's bank or other financial account within the United States (e.g., Paypal account)	10.8
Send a remittance (used to send money to relatives or friends living outside the U.S through Western Union, USPS Sure Money, etc.)	2.2

Table C.35. (Continued)

Percent, except as noted	
Received money from another person's bank or other financial account (e.g.,Paypal account)	9.9
Paid for a product or service at a store (including at gas pumps and for restaurant meals)	12.9
Paid for parking, a taxi, or public transit using an app	4.8
Paid bills online through a mobile web browser or app	19.7
Made a payment using a text message (including charitable donation by text message)	2.8
Used an app to receive loyalty or reward points	12.0
Made an online or in-app purchase (e.g., from amazon.com or bestbuy.com)	20.9
Number of respondents	**2,603**

Note: This question was asked of those with a mobile phone and includes those who did not identify themselves as having used mobile payments in the previous 12 months.

Table C.36. In the past month, about how many times have you used your mobile phone to make any type of mobile payment? If none please enter "0"

Q38	
Refused (percent)	1.6
Total respondents with zero uses (percent)	26.6
Mean number of uses (at least one use)	4.9
Median number of uses (at least one use)	3.0
Number of respondents	**455**

Table C.37. When you have used your mobile phone to pay for something at a store in the past 12 months, have you used your phone in each of these different ways?

Percent, except as noted	
Q39	
No/refused to all	57.8
Waved or tapped my mobile phone to pay at check out (e.g., Google Wallet or Apple Pay)	11.6
Scanned a barcode or QR code using your mobile phone to make a mobile payment (e.g., Starbucks app)	28.6
Used a mobile app that doesn't require tapping the phone to pay at check out or scanning a barcode to pay for a purchase (e.g., Square Wallet)	18.6
Other	1.7
Number of respondents	**283**

Table C.38. In the past month, about how many times have you used your mobile phone to pay for a product or service at a store? If none please enter "0"

Q40	
Refused (percent)	12.0
Total respondents with zero uses (percent)	50.1
Mean number of uses (at least one use)	4.7
Median number of uses (at least one use)	3.0
Number of respondents	**283**

Table C.39. When making mobile payments, which of the following payment methods do you use?

Percent, except as noted	
Q41	
Refused	2.0
Credit card	51.2
Debit card	55.0
Prepaid debit card	7.6
Bank account	40.7
Charge to your phone bill	4.2
Account at a non-financial institution (e.g., PayPal)	15.4
Other	3.1
Number of respondents	**455**

Table C.40. Have you used any of the following mobile payment services in the past 12 months?

Percent, except as noted	
Q42	
Refused	42.3
Starbucks mobile payments	10.9
Google Wallet	9.0
Square Wallet	1.6*
Apple Pay	4.9
Deluxe eCheck	0.9*
Amazon Firefly	2.9*
CardNav	1.1*
PayPal	43.1
LevelUp	0.8*
Dwolla	0.0
Softcard	0.6*
Tabbedout	0.0
Number of respondents	**428**

* Fewer than 10 responses were received for this option.

Table C.41. When did you start using mobile payments?

Percent, except as noted	
Q43	
Refused	2.5
In the last 6 months	15.9
6 to 12 months ago	13.1
1 to 2 years ago	20.9
More than 2 years ago	25.6
I don't remember	21.9
Number of respondents	**455**

Table C.42. What was the main reason why you started using mobile payments when you did?

Percent, except as noted	
Q44	
Refused	4.5
I got a smartphone	33.7
The ability to make mobile payments became available	15.5
I became comfortable with the security of mobile payments	8.7
I liked the convenience of mobile payments	29.1
A store I visit started offering the service	2.3
To take advantage of loyalty or rewards points and discounts	2.6
Other (please specify):	3.5
Number of respondents	**455**

Table C.43. Please tell us if each of the reasons below are why you do not use mobile banking

Percent, except as noted	
Q45	
No/refused to all	4.8
I'm concerned about the security of mobile banking	62.1
My banking needs are being met without mobile banking	85.8
I don't see any reason to use mobile banking	73.0
The mobile phone screen is too small	39.4
I don't have a smartphone	32.3
My bank charges a fee for using mobile banking	6.5
I don't do the banking in my household	12.5
I don't trust the technology	34.3
It's too difficult to use mobile banking	19.9
Number of respondents	**945**

Table C.44. You mentioned that security was one of your top concerns with mobile banking; which one of the following security aspects are you most concerned with?

Percent, except as noted	
Q46	
Refused	0.5
My phone getting hacked	17.1
Someone using my phone without permission to access my account	4.1
Someone intercepting my data	22.3
Losing my phone or having my phone stolen	8.9
Malware or viruses being installed on my phone	1.8
Companies misusing my personal information	2.0*
All of the above	42.9
Other (please specify):	0.4*
Number of respondents	**600**

* Fewer than 10 responses were received for this option.

Table C.45. Assuming that the concerns that you have about using mobile banking were addressed, would you be interested in doing any of the following activities with your mobile phone?

Percent, except as noted	
Q47	
Refused	0.5
Download your bank's mobile banking app	21.3
Check an account balance or check recent transactions	32.2
Make bill payments using your bank's online banking website or app	14.9
Receive alerts (e.g., text message, push notification, or e-mail) from your bank	19.3
Deposit a check electronically using your mobile phone camera	17.4
Transfer money between your bank accounts	20.3
Transfer money from your bank account to another person	11.3
Locate the closest in-network ATM or branch for your bank	18.2
None, I don't want to use mobile banking	59.2
Number of respondents	**945**

Table C.46. You mentioned that your bank does not offer mobile banking or you are not sure if your bank offers it. If your bank or credit union were to offer mobile banking, would you be interested in doing any of the following activities with your mobile phone?

Percent, except as noted	
Q48	
Refused	0.3
Download your bank's mobile banking app	8.1
Check an account balance or check recent transactions	15.0
Make bill payments using your bank's online banking website or app	6.2

Table C.46. (Continued)

Percent, except as noted	
Q48	
Receive alerts (e.g., text message, push notification, or e-mail) from your bank	7.1
Deposit a check electronically using your mobile phone camera	6.7
Transfer money between your bank accounts	6.6
Transfer money from your bank account to another person	3.4
Locate the closest in-network ATM or branch for your bank	6.9
None, I don't want to use mobile banking	79.0
Number of respondents	**650**

Table C.47. Please tell us if any of the reasons below are why you do not use mobile payments

Percent, except as noted	
Q49	
No/refused to all	8.4
I'm concerned about the security of mobile payments	59.4
It's easier to pay with cash or a credit/debit card	75.3
I don't see any benefit from using mobile payments	59.4
The places I shop don't accept mobile payments	23.2
I don't have the necessary feature on my phone	37.0
I don't trust the technology	41.0
It's difficult or time consuming to set up or use mobile payments	31.0
I don't need to make any payments or someone else pays the bills	23.4
I don't really understand all the different mobile payment options	31.2
Number of respondents	**2,137**

Table C.48. You mentioned that security was one of your top concerns with mobile payments; which one of these security aspects are you most concerned with?

Percent, except as noted	
Q50	
Refused	0.2
My phone getting hacked	13.1
Someone intercepting my payment information or other data	20.7
Losing my phone or having my phone stolen	10.0
Malware or viruses being installed on my phone	1.7
Companies misusing my personal information	2.7
All of the above	51.0
Other (please specify):	0.6*
Number of respondents	**1,286**

* Fewer than 10 responses were received for this option.

Table C.49. Assuming that the reason(s) why you do not currently use mobile payments was addressed, would you be interested in doing any of the following activities with your mobile phone?

Percent, except as noted	
Q51	
Refused	1.0
Making payments to another person (e.g., friend, relative, babysitter) within the United States	11.2
Transferring money to someone in another country	4.3
Using my mobile phone to pay for purchases at a store	17.7
Paying for parking, a taxi, or public transit using an app	12.3
Paying bills online through a mobiel web browser or app	15.0
Using your mobile phone as a "virtual wallet" to replace some cards in your wallet	12.5
Making an online or in-app purchase (e.g., from amazon.com or bestbuy.com)	14.7
Receiving money from another person's bank or other financial account (e.g., Paypal account)	11.6
Receiving/using coupons and/or reward points on your phone	19.8
None, I don't want to use mobile payments	65.5
Number of respondents	**2,137**

Table C.50. You indicated that you have not made a mobile payment in a store in the last 12 months. Do you plan to use your mobile phone to make a payment in a store in the next 12 months?

Percent, except as noted	
Q52	
Refused	0.2
Definitely will use	3.6
Probably will use	11.2
Probably will not use	37.7
Definitely will not use	47.2
Number of respondents	**2,300**

Table C.51. How safe do you believe people's personal information is when they use mobile banking?

Percent, except as noted	
Q53	
Refused	0.9
Very safe	6.7
Somewhat safe	33.6
Somewhat unsafe	24.7
Very unsafe	19.0
Don't know	15.1
Number of respondents	**2,603**

Table C.52. How safe do you believe people's personal information is when they use a mobile phone to pay for a purchase at a store?

Percent, except as noted	
Q54	
Refused	0.9
Very safe	5.2
Somewhat safe	29.7
Somewhat unsafe	27.8
Very unsafe	21.0
Don't know	15.4
Number of respondents	**2,603**

Table C.53. Would you like to or do you already use your mobile phone for any of the following purposes?

Percent, except as noted				
Q55	**Refused**	**I already do**	**I would like to**	**I am unlikely to**
Track your finances, purchases or expenses	1.0	28.5	13.2	57.2
Organize, track and store gift cards, memberships, loyalty and reward points	1.2	13.3	19.3	66.3
Compare prices when shopping	1.2	29.7	24.3	44.8
Receive and manage discount offers and coupons	1.1	23.0	25.5	50.3
Receive offers and promotions based on your location	1.2	17.5	23.8	57.5
Number of respondents	**2,603**			

Table C.54. I am willing to allow my mobile phone to provide my location to companies I shop with regularly so that they can offer me discounts, promotions, or services based on where I am

Percent, except as noted	
Q56	
Refused	1.1
Strongly agree	6.2
Agree	33.5
Disagree	32.9
Strongly disagree	26.4
Number of respondents	**1,775**

Table C.55. I am willing to allow my mobile phone to provide personal information such as my sex, age, friends, and shopping history to companies I shop with regularly so that they can offer me targeted discounts, promotions, or services

Percent, except as noted	
Q57	
Refused	1.0
Strongly agree	3.4
Agree	19.4
Disagree	37.0
Strongly disagree	39.3
Number of respondents	**1,775**

Table C.56. Have you ever used your mobile phone to comparison shop over the Internet while at a retail store?

Percent, except as noted	
Q58	
Refused	0.9
Yes	46.5
No	52.6
Number of respondents	**1,775**

Table C.57. Have you ever used a barcode scanning app on your mobile phone while shopping at a retail store to find the best price for an item?

Percent, except as noted	
Q59	
Refused	0.8
Yes	32.8
No	66.4
Number of respondents	**1,775**

Table C.58. Has using your mobile phone to compare prices while you were shopping at a retail store ever changed where you made your purchase?

Percent, except as noted	
Q61	
Refused	0.4
Yes	68.6
No	31.0
Number of respondents	**894**

Table C.59. Have you ever scanned a QR code (similar to a barcode) in a retail store, newspaper, magazine, or billboard advertisement to obtain information about a product on your mobile phone?

Percent, except as noted	
Q60	
Refused	1.2
Yes	30.8
No	68.0
Number of respondents	**1,775**

Table C.60. Have you ever used your mobile phone to browse product reviews or get product information while shopping at a retail store? This could be done by, for example, googling the product on your mobile browser or scanning a QR code

Percent, except as noted	
Q62	
Refused	1.4
Yes	42.2
No	56.5
Number of respondents	**1,775**

Table C.61. Has reading product reviews on your mobile phone while shopping at a retail store ever changed which item you ended up purchasing?

Percent, except as noted	
Q63	
Refused	0.1
Yes	78.7
No	21.3
Number of respondents	**712**

Table C.62. In the past 12 months, have you used your mobile phone to check your account balance or available credit before making a large purchase?

Percent, except as noted	
Q64	
Refused	0.2
Yes	63.4
No	36.4
Number of respondents	**798**

Table C.63. Thinking of the most recent time that you checked your account balance or available credit before making a large purchase, did you decide not to buy that particular item because of the amount of money left in your account or the amount of your available credit?

Percent, except as noted	
Q65	
Refused	0.7
Yes	53.1
No	46.2
Number of respondents	**462**

Table C.64. You previously mentioned that you receive text message, push notification, or e-mail alerts from your financial institution. Do you receive each of the following kinds of alerts?

Percent, except as noted	
Q66	
Refused	1.9
Low balance	42.4
Payment due	32.8
Saving reminders	4.6
Fraud	32.2
Credit card balance	14.7
Deposit or withdrawal	36.7
Statement available notification	39.7
Other	7.1
Number of respondents	**629**

Table C.65. Thinking of the most recent low-balance alert you received, which of the following actions did you take after receiving the alert?

Percent, except as noted	
Q67	
Refused	0.2
Transferred money into the account with the low balance from another account	41.0
Deposited money into the account with the low balance	29.7
Reduced my spending	28.2
None of the above	20.2
Number of respondents	**256**

Summary Statistics for Demographics

Table C.66. Summary statistics for demographics: Full sample

	Weighted		Unweighted	
	Mean	Standard deviation	Mean	Standard deviation
Age	47.0650	17.2240	52.3371	16.9816
Male	0.4824	0.4998	0.5183	0.4998
Female	0.5176	0.4998	0.4817	0.4998
18–29	0.2140	0.4102	0.1323	0.3389
30–44	0.2532	0.4349	0.1993	0.3996
45–60	0.2684	0.4432	0.2882	0.4530
Ages over 60	0.2644	0.4411	0.3802	0.4855
Less than high school	0.1237	0.3293	0.0646	0.2459
High school degree	0.2963	0.4567	0.2745	0.4464
Some college	0.2874	0.4526	0.2868	0.4524
Bachelor's degree or higher	0.2925	0.4550	0.3740	0.4840
White, non-Hispanic	0.6552	0.4754	0.7665	0.4231
Black, non-Hispanic	0.1153	0.3195	0.0800	0.2713
Other, non-Hispanic	0.0777	0.2677	0.0687	0.2530
Hispanic	0.1518	0.3589	0.0848	0.2786
2 or more races, non-Hispanic	0.0128	0.1123	0.0294	0.1690
Less than $25,000	0.2164	0.4119	0.1590	0.3657
$25,000–$39,999	0.1543	0.3613	0.1398	0.3469
$40,000–$74,999	0.1651	0.3713	0.1689	0.3747
$75,000–$99,999	0.2306	0.4213	0.2537	0.4352
Greater than $100,000	0.2335	0.4231	0.2786	0.4484
Married	0.5105	0.5000	0.5959	0.4908
Not married	0.4895	0.5000	0.4041	0.4908
Metropolitan	0.8439	0.3630	0.8373	0.3692
Northeast	0.1821	0.3860	0.1867	0.3897
Midwest	0.2135	0.4098	0.2284	0.4199
South	0.3707	0.4831	0.3600	0.4801
West	0.2337	0.4233	0.2250	0.4176
Employed	0.5664	0.4957	0.5525	0.4973
Unemployed, in labor force	0.0850	0.2789	0.0547	0.2274
Not in labor force	0.3487	0.4766	0.3928	0.4885
Observations	2,925			

Table C.67. Summary statistics for demographics: All mobile phone users (feature and smartphone)

	Weighted		Unweighted	
	Mean	**Standard deviation**	**Mean**	**Standard deviation**
Age	46.1954	16.9504	51.6815	16.8657
Male	0.4818	0.4998	0.5167	0.4998
Female	0.5182	0.4998	0.4833	0.4998
18–29	0.2226	0.4161	0.1364	0.3433
30–44	0.2656	0.4417	0.2098	0.4072
45–60	0.2692	0.4436	0.2908	0.4542
Ages over 60	0.2426	0.4287	0.3630	0.4810
Less than high school	0.1059	0.3078	0.0553	0.2286
High school degree	0.2838	0.4509	0.2620	0.4398
Some college	0.2945	0.4559	0.2897	0.4537
Bachelor's degree or higher	0.3158	0.4649	0.3930	0.4885
White, non-Hispanic	0.6664	0.4716	0.7722	0.4195
Black, non-Hispanic	0.1096	0.3125	0.0772	0.2670
Other, non-Hispanic	0.0747	0.2630	0.0676	0.2511
Hispanic	0.1492	0.3563	0.0830	0.2759
2 or more races, non-Hispanic	0.0108	0.1033	0.0288	0.1673
Less than $25,000	0.1839	0.3875	0.1348	0.3416
$25,000—$39,999	0.1499	0.3570	0.1348	0.3416
$40,000–$74,999	0.1697	0.3754	0.1690	0.3749
$75,000–$99,999	0.2408	0.4277	0.2647	0.4413
Greater than $100,000	0.2556	0.4363	0.2966	0.4568
Married	0.5300	0.4992	0.6135	0.4870
Not married	0.4700	0.4992	0.3865	0.4870
Metropolitan	0.8530	0.3542	0.8444	0.3625
Northeast	0.1898	0.3922	0.1894	0.3919
Midwest	0.2034	0.4026	0.2197	0.4142
South	0.3731	0.4837	0.3665	0.4819
West	0.2337	0.4232	0.2244	0.4172
Employed	0.6114	0.4875	0.5843	0.4929
Unemployed, in labor force	0.0782	0.2685	0.0515	0.2210
Not in labor force	0.3105	0.4628	0.3642	0.4813
Observations	2,603			

Table C.68. Summary statistics for demographics: Smartphone users

	Weighted		Unweighted	
	Mean	Standard deviation	Mean	Standard deviation
Age	42.4617	15.4502	47.8068	16.0438
Male	0.4865	0.5000	0.5217	0.4997
Female	0.5135	0.5000	0.4783	0.4997
18–29	0.2652	0.4416	0.1707	0.3764
30–44	0.3223	0.4675	0.2642	0.4410
45–60	0.2531	0.4349	0.3020	0.4592
Ages over 60	0.1593	0.3661	0.2631	0.4404
Less than high school	0.0778	0.2679	0.0394	0.1947
High school degree	0.2611	0.4393	0.2287	0.4201
Some college	0.3023	0.4594	0.2946	0.4560
Bachelor's degree or higher	0.3588	0.4798	0.4372	0.4962
White, non-Hispanic	0.6403	0.4801	0.7487	0.4339
Black, non-Hispanic	0.1028	0.3037	0.0761	0.2652
Other, non-Hispanic	0.0847	0.2785	0.0744	0.2624
Hispanic	0.1723	0.3777	0.1008	0.3012
2 or more races, non-Hispanic	0.0098	0.0986	0.0270	0.1623
Less than $25,000	0.1376	0.3446	0.0969	0.2959
$25,000–$39,999	0.1347	0.3415	0.1149	0.3190
$40,000–$74,999	0.1739	0.3791	0.1645	0.3708
$75,000–$99,999	0.2489	0.4325	0.2659	0.4419
Greater than $100,000	0.3049	0.4605	0.3577	0.4795
Married	0.5431	0.4983	0.6248	0.4843
Not married	0.4569	0.4983	0.3752	0.4843
Metropolitan	0.8680	0.3386	0.8575	0.3497
Northeast	0.1836	0.3873	0.1803	0.3845
Midwest	0.1909	0.3931	0.2096	0.4071
South	0.3785	0.4851	0.3752	0.4843
West	0.2470	0.4314	0.2349	0.4241
Employed	0.6878	0.4635	0.6715	0.4698
Unemployed, in labor force	0.0803	0.2719	0.0552	0.2285
Not in labor force	0.2318	0.4221	0.2732	0.4457
Observations	1,775			

Table C.69. Summary statistics for demographics: Feature phone users

	Weighted		Unweighted	
	Mean	Standard deviation	Mean	Standard deviation
Age	55.4315	16.9421	60.0537	15.5039
Male	0.4695	0.4994	0.5049	0.5003
Female	0.5305	0.4994	0.4951	0.5003
18–29	0.1166	0.3211	0.0622	0.2417
30–44	0.1272	0.3333	0.0927	0.2902
45–60	0.3081	0.4620	0.2659	0.4421

	Weighted		Unweighted	
	Mean	Standard deviation	Mean	Standard deviation
Ages over 60	0.4482	0.4976	0.5793	0.4940
Less than high school	0.1762	0.3813	0.0902	0.2867
High school degree	0.3403	0.4741	0.3341	0.4720
Some college	0.2771	0.4478	0.2805	0.4495
Bachelor's degree or higher	0.2063	0.4049	0.2951	0.4564
White, non-Hispanic	0.7274	0.4455	0.8207	0.3838
Black, non-Hispanic	0.1276	0.3338	0.0805	0.2722
Other, non-Hispanic	0.0510	0.2202	0.0537	0.2255
Hispanic	0.0939	0.2919	0.0451	0.2077
2 or more races, non-Hispanic	0.0133	0.1145	0.0329	0.1786
Less than $25,000	0.2996	0.4584	0.2183	0.4133
$25,000–$39,999	0.1870	0.3901	0.1780	0.3828
$40,000–$74,999	0.1599	0.3667	0.1780	0.3828
$75,000–$99,999	0.2183	0.4133	0.2610	0.4394
Greater than $100,000	0.1352	0.3422	0.1646	0.3711
Married	0.4994	0.5003	0.5890	0.4923
Not married	0.5006	0.5003	0.4110	0.4923
Metropolitan	0.8147	0.3888	0.8146	0.3888
Northeast	0.2039	0.4031	0.2085	0.4065
Midwest	0.2345	0.4239	0.2415	0.4282
South	0.3596	0.4802	0.3476	0.4765
West	0.2021	0.4018	0.2024	0.4021
Employed	0.4212	0.4940	0.3951	0.4892
Unemployed, in labor force	0.0736	0.2612	0.0439	0.2050
Not in labor force	0.5052	0.5003	0.5610	0.4966
Observations	820			

Cross-Tabulations for Consumers' Use of Mobile Phones

Table C.70. Do you own or have regular access to a mobile phone?

Percent, except as noted					
Age categories	**No**	**Yes**	**Total**	**Number of respondents**	**Percentage of users in category**
18–29	9.7	90.3	100.0	387	22.3
30–44	8.9	91.1	100.0	583	26.6
45–59	12.9	87.1	100.0	843	26.9
60+	20.3	79.7	100.0	1,112	24.3
Number of respondents	**322**	**2,603**	**2,925**		**100.0**

Table C.71. Is your mobile phone a smartphone?

Percent, except as noted						
Age categories	**Refused**	**No**	**Yes**	**Total**	**Number of respondents**	**Percentage of users in category**
18–29	0.5	15.1	84.4	100.0	355	26.5
30–44	0.2	13.8	86.0	100.0	546	32.2
45–59	0.3	33.0	66.6	100.0	757	25.3
60+	0.2	53.3	46.5	100.0	945	15.9
Number of respondents	**8**	**820**	**1775**	**2,603**		**100.0**

Table C.72. Do you own or have regular access to a mobile phone?

Percent, except as noted					
Education	**No**	**Yes**	**Total**	**Number of respondents**	**Percentage of users in category**
Less than high school	25.6	74.4	100.0	189	10.6
High school	16.9	83.1	100.0	803	28.4
Some college	11.0	89.0	100.0	839	29.5
Bachelor's degree or higher	6.3	93.7	100.0	1,094	31.6
Number of respondents	**322**	**2,603**	**2,925**		**100.0**

Table C.73. Is your mobile phone a smartphone?

Percent, except as noted						
Education	**Refused**	**No**	**Yes**	**Total**	**Number of respondents**	**Percentage of users in category**
Less than high school	0.0	48.0	52.0	100.0	144	7.8
High school	0.2	34.6	65.2	100.0	682	26.1
Some college	0.1	27.1	72.8	100.0	754	30.2
Bachelor's degree or higher	0.6	18.8	80.5	100.0	1,023	35.9
Number of respondents	**8**	**820**	**1775**	**2,603**		**100.0**

Table C.74. Do you own or have regular access to a mobile phone?

Percent, except as noted					
Race/ethnicity	**No**	**Yes**	**Total**	**Number of respondents**	**Percentage of users in category**
White, non-Hispanic	11.7	88.3	100.0	2,242	66.6
Black, non-Hispanic	17.4	82.6	100.0	234	11.0
Other, non-Hispanic	14.4	85.6	100.0	115	6.4

Percent, except as noted					
Race/ethnicity	**No**	**Yes**	**Total**	**Number of respondents**	**Percentage of users in category**
Hispanic	14.7	85.3	100.0	248	14.9
2+ races, non-Hispanic	26.7	73.3	100.0	86	1.1
Number of respondents	**322**	**2,603**	**2,925**		**100.0**

Table C.75. Is your mobile phone a smartphone?

Percent, except as noted						
Race/ethnicity	**Refused**	**No**	**Yes**	**Total**	**Number of respondents**	**Percentage of users in category**
White, non-Hispanic	0.4	31.5	68.1	100.0	2,010	64.0
Black, non-Hispanic	0.0	33.6	66.4	100.0	201	10.3
Other, non-Hispanic	0.0	17.0	83.0	100.0	101	7.5
Hispanic	0.0	18.2	81.8	100.0	216	17.2
2+ races, non-Hispanic	0.0	35.5	64.5	100.0	75	1.0
Number of respondents	**8**	**820**	**1,775**	**2,603**		**100.0**

Table C.76. Do you own or have regular access to a mobile phone?

Percent, except as noted					
Income group	**No**	**Yes**	**Total**	**Number of respondents**	**Percentage of users in category**
Less than $25,000	26.2	73.8	100.0	465	18.4
$25,000–$39,999	15.6	84.4	100.0	409	15.0
$40,000–$74,999	10.7	89.3	100.0	494	17.0
$75,000–$99,999	9.3	90.7	100.0	742	24.1
Greater than $100,000	4.9	95.1	100.0	815	25.6
Number of respondents	**322**	**2,603**	**2,925**		**100.0**

Table C.77. Is your mobile phone a smartphone?

Percent, except as noted						
Income group	**Refused**	**No**	**Yes**	**Total**	**Number of respondents**	**Percentage of users in category**
Less than $25,000	0.0	47.0	53.0	100.0	351	13.8
$25,000–$39,999	0.3	36.0	63.7	100.0	351	13.5
$40,000–$74,999	0.2	27.2	72.6	100.0	440	17.4
$75,000–$99,999	0.6	26.1	73.3	100.0	689	24.9
Greater than $100,000	0.2	15.3	84.5	100.0	772	30.5
Number of respondents	**8**	**820**	**1775**	**2,603**		**100.0**

Cross-Tabulations for Consumers' Use of Mobile Banking and Mobile Payments

Table C.78.a. Cross-tabulations for consumers' use of mobile banking by age, race, gender, education, and income: Smartphone users

Percent, except as noted						
Use of mobile banking in past 12 months	**Refused**	**No**	**Yes**	**Total**	**Number of respondents**	**Percentage of users in category**
Age categories						
18–29	0.2	33.4	66.4	100.0	260	31.2
30–44	1.8	38.5	59.8	100.0	437	36.9
45–59	1.0	53.5	45.5	100.0	518	23.4
60+	1.1	73.1	25.7	100.0	457	8.5
Number of respondents	**15**	**859**	**798**	**1,672**		**100.0**
Race/ethnicity						
White, non-Hispanic	0.8	51.2	48.0	100.0	1,282	61.8
Black, non-Hispanic	0.8	43.3	55.8	100.0	117	10.1
Other, non-Hispanic	1.8	43.2	55.0	100.0	81	8.3
Hispanic	2.1	34.3	63.6	100.0	149	18.6
2+ races, non-Hispanic	0.0	38.8	61.2	100.0	43	1.1
Number of respondents	**15**	**859**	**798**	**1,672**		**100.0**
Gender						
Female	1.7	46.7	51.6	100.0	797	51.0
Male	0.4	47.6	52.0	100.0	875	49.0
Number of respondents	**15**	**859**	**798**	**1,672**		**100.0**
Education						
Less than high school	2.9	55.0	42.2	100.0	53	5.0
High school	0.1	56.3	43.6	100.0	367	20.9
Some college	1.5	42.5	56.0	100.0	492	33.3
Bachelor's degree or higher	1.1	43.8	55.2	100.0	760	40.9
Number of respondents	**15**	**859**	**798**	**1,672**		**100.0**
Income group						
Less than $25,000	1.3	40.9	57.8	100.0	138	12.2
$25,000–$39,999	0.5	52.2	47.3	100.0	188	12.1
$40,000–$74,999	0.7	42.0	57.3	100.0	279	20.1
$75,000–$99,999	1.1	47.6	51.3	100.0	453	25.4
Greater than $100,000	1.3	49.8	48.8	100.0	614	30.2
Number of respondents	**15**	**859**	**798**	**1,672**		**100.0**

C.78.b. Cross-tabulations for consumers' use of mobile payments by age, race, gender, education, and income: Smartphone users

Percent, except as noted						
Use of mobile payments in past 12 months	**Refused**	**No**	**Yes**	**Total**	**Number of respondents**	**Percentage of users in category**
Age categories						
18–29	0.6	61.8	37.6	100.0	303	35.1
30–44	1.4	64.0	34.6	100.0	469	39.3
45–59	0.4	78.8	20.8	100.0	536	18.5
60+	0.1	87.3	12.6	100.0	467	7.1
Number of respondents	**7**	**1,340**	**428**	**1,775**		**100.0**
Race/ethnicity						
White, non-Hispanic	0.2	75.9	23.9	100.0	1,329	53.8
Black, non-Hispanic	0.0	58.3	41.7	100.0	135	15.1
Other, non-Hispanic	2.0	73.5	24.6	100.0	84	6.5
Hispanic	2.5	58.8	38.6	100.0	179	23.4
2+ races, non-Hispanic	0.0	65.0	35.0	100.0	48	1.2
Number of respondents	**7**	**1,340**	**428**	**1,775**		**100.0**
Gender						
Female	0.8	68.9	30.3	100.0	849	54.8
Male	0.6	73.0	26.4	100.0	926	45.2
Number of respondents	**7**	**1,340**	**428**	**1,775**		**100.0**
Education						
Less than high school	2.6	72.7	24.7	100.0	70	6.8
High school	0.6	74.8	24.5	100.0	406	22.6
Some college	0.7	67.7	31.5	100.0	523	33.6
Bachelor's degree or higher	0.4	70.3	29.4	100.0	776	37.1
Number of respondents	**7**	**1,340**	**428**	**1,775**		**100.0**
Income group						
Less than $25,000	1.5	65.0	33.6	100.0	172	16.3
$25,000–$39,999	0.5	67.8	31.8	100.0	204	15.1
$40,000–$74,999	0.9	69.3	29.8	100.0	292	18.2
$75,000–$99,999	0.0	70.8	29.2	100.0	472	25.6
Greater than $100,000	0.9	75.9	23.2	100.0	635	24.9
Number of respondents	**7**	**1,340**	**428**	**1,775**		**100.0**

End Notes

[1] See the "Consumers and Mobile Financial Services" reports series for previous years' survey findings. Results of the 2011, 2012, and 2013 surveys (published in March 2012, 2013, and 2014, respectively) are available at www.federalreserve.gov/communitydev/mobile_finance_publications.htm.

[2] The 2014 survey also included an oversample of respondents from rural areas. For comparability with prior years of the survey, the oversample was not used in computing the results in the main body of this report; therefore, respondents from the over- sample are not included in table 1. However, selected statistics based on the oversample are included in box 1. Additional information on the sample is provided in appendix 1.

[3] Throughout this report, percentages are calculated as a share of all those who were asked a question, including those who did not respond. Results on phone ownership from the Board's 2013 survey are very similar to those from the Pew Research Center for that year. In the June 2013 Smartphone Ownership—2013 Update, the Pew Research Center reported that 91 percent of U.S. adults owned a mobile phone and 61 percent of adults with a mobile phone (or 56 percent of adults overall) had a smartphone. (See http:// pewinternet.org/ ~/ media//Files/Reports/2013/PIP_Smartphone_adoption_2013_PDF.pdf.) The 2013 Federal Deposit Insurance Corporation (FDIC) Survey of Unbanked and Underbanked Households provides measures of mobile and smartphone access at the household level. In 2013, its estimates showed that 83 percent of households owned or had regular access to a mobile phone and 67 percent of households with a mobile phone (or 56 percent of households overall) had a smartphone. (See www.fdic.gov/householdsurvey/2013report.pdf).

[4] In 2011 and 2012, the wording of the bank account question was "Do you or does your spouse/partner currently have a checking, savings, or money market account?" In 2013 and 2014, the wording of the bank account question changed slightly from the prior years to explicitly reference "bank or credit union" accounts: "Do you or does your spouse/partner currently have some type of bank or credit union account such as a checking, savings, or money market account?"

[5] Due to changes in the way this question was asked, the 2014 figures for underbanked households may not be comparable to results from earlier years. Most notably, relative to the 2013 report, "money order" was added to the list of alternative financial services used by underbanked households, and "payroll card" was removed.

[6] Here, the figures for mobile banking in the 2011 survey are expressed as percentages of mobile phone users with bank accounts. These figures differ slightly from those published in the 2011 report, which were calculated as a percent of all mobile phone users. Similarly, other estimates in the text may differ from the figures presented in appendix 3 or from estimates published in earlier reports because a subsample of the respondents was used for the calculation.

[7] At least one major mobile phone operating system has changed its default settings to require users to set a password unless they opt out. This change in default setting could also increase the incidence of password protection.

[8] The definition of online banking changed slightly between the 2012 and 2013 surveys. For the 2011 and 2012 surveys the definition was "Online banking involves checking your account balance and recent transactions, transferring money, paying bills, or conducting other related transactions with your bank or credit card company using the Internet." For the 2013 and 2014 surveys, the definition was "Online banking involves checking your account balance and recent transactions, transferring money, paying bills, or conducting other related transactions with your bank or credit union using the Internet."

[9] The relative prevalence of channel usage in the Board's Mobile Survey is similar to results from the 2013 FDIC Survey of Unbanked and Underbanked Households. Of the households with bank accounts that reported accessing their accounts in the previous 12 months, 79 percent used a bank teller; 70 percent used an ATM/kiosk; 55 percent used online banking; 26 percent used telephone banking; and 23 percent used mobile banking. Comparing these FDIC figures to the results from the 2013 Mobile Survey, the relative ranking of the channels is the same across the two surveys, but the incidence of use is higher in the Mobile Survey for all channels. The incidence of online banking and of households with Internet access are notably higher in the 2013 Mobile Survey than in the FDIC survey. This may be due to differences in the survey methodology. The FDIC survey is conducted by phone and in person. The Mobile Survey is conducted via an online panel.

[10] The definition of mobile banking in the 2011 and 2012 surveys differed slightly from the definition above. In the earlier surveys, mobile banking was defined as using "a mobile phone to access your bank account, credit card account, or other financial account. This can be done either by accessing your bank's web page through the web browser on your mobile phone, via text messaging, or by using an application downloaded to your mobile phone."

[11] This group represents 6 percent of panel respondents who were mobile phone users in both years.

[12] This group represents 4 percent of panel respondents who were mobile phone users in both years.

[13] For the purposes of this report, "high-intensity" users are identified as those respondents who have used mobile banking within the year prior to the 2014 survey and have used mobile banking more frequently than 75 percent of all mobile banking users, which corresponds to a frequency greater than 10 times in the month prior

to the 2014 survey. Based on this definition, high-intensity users represent 22 percent of mobile banking users in the 2014 survey.

[14] A Quick Response (QR) code is a type of barcode that quickly transfers information to a device when scanned. Some mobile payment applications use QR codes displayed on the user's smartphone screen to communicate the payment credentials to merchants when scanned at the POS.

Respondents who answered that, using their mobile phone, they had "Paid for a product or service at a store (including at gas pumps and for restaurant meals)" were asked a follow up question (question 39) asking about ways of paying in a store. The follow up question listed four ways of paying with a phone, including "Other (Please Specify)." However, 58 percent of those who were asked this follow up question refused the question or did not select any of these four options.

[15] The most commonly reported mobile payments services used in the last year were PayPal (43 percent), Starbucks (11 percent), Google Wallet (9 percent), and Apple Pay (5 percent). Forty- three percent of those who were asked the question about mobile payment services (question 42) refused to provide an answer. This question was asked of all those with smartphones who had made a mobile payment in the last year. Because the answer choices did not include options such as "Other" or "Do not know," refusing to answer would have been a likely response for those who have not used these services.

[16] For further details on how existing consumer regulations relate to the various methods for making mobile payments, see Stephanie Martin (2012), "Statement before the Committee on Financial Services Subcommittee on Financial Institutions and Consumer Credit U.S. House of Representatives" (Washington: Federal Reserve Board, June), www.federalreserve.gov/ newsevents/testimony/martin20120629a.pdf.

[17] For the purposes of this report, "high-intensity" mobile payments users are identified as those respondents who have used mobile payments within the year prior to the 2014 survey and have used mobile payments more frequently than 75 percent of all mobile payments users, which corresponds to a frequency greater than five times in the month prior to the 2014 survey.

[18] For further details on the KnowledgePanel® sampling methodology and comparisons between KnowledgePanel® and tele- phone surveys see www.knowledgenetworks.com/accuracy/ spring2010/disogra-spring10.html.

[19] Information on RUCA codes is available from the U.S. Department of Agriculture's Economic Research Service. (See www.ers.usda.gov/data-products/rural-urban-commuting-area- codes.aspx).

[20] David S. Yeager, Jon A. Krosnick, LinChiat Chang, Harold S. Javitz, Matthew S. Levendusky, Alberto Simpser, and Rui Wang (2011), "Comparing the Accuracy of RDD Telephone Surveys and Internet Surveys Conducted with Probability and Non- Probability Samples," Public Opinion Quarterly, vol. 75(4), pp. 709–47.

INDEX

A

B

C

D

E

I

L

M

N

O

P

R

S

T

U